CHINA'S MILLENNIUM TRANSFORMATION

The Belt and Road Initiative

T0413318

CHINA'S MILLENNIUM TRANSFORMATION

TRANSFORMATION

The Belt and Road Initiative

Da Hsuan Feng

World Scientific

NEW JERSEY · LONDON · SINGAPORE · BEIJING · SHANGHAI · HONG KONG · TAIPEI · CHENNAI · TOKYO

Published by

World Scientific Publishing Co. Pte. Ltd.

5 Toh Tuck Link, Singapore 596224

USA office: 27 Warren Street, Suite 401-402, Hackensack, NJ 07601

UK office: 57 Shelton Street, Covent Garden, London WC2H 9HE

Library of Congress Cataloging-in-Publication Data
Names: Feng, Da Hsuan, 1945–   author.
Title: China's millennium transformation : the Belt and Road Initiative / Da Hsuan Feng,
    China Silk Road iValley Research Institute, China.
Description: New Jersey, World Scientific, [2020]
Identifiers: LCCN 2019045128 | ISBN 9789811210914 (hardcover) | ISBN 9789811216909
    (paperback) | ISBN 9789811210921 (ebook) | ISBN 9789811210938 (ebook other)
Subjects: LCSH: China--Commercial policy. | China--Foreign economic relations. |
    Economic development--China. | Economic development--Developing countries.
Classification: LCC HF1604 .F4283 2020 | DDC 382/.30951--dc23
LC record available at https://lccn.loc.gov/2019045128

British Library Cataloguing-in-Publication Data
A catalogue record for this book is available from the British Library.

For any available supplementary material, please visit
https://www.worldscientific.com/worldscibooks/10.1142/11569#t=suppl

Desk Editor: Tan Boon Hui

Typeset by Stallion Press
Email: enquiries@stallionpress.com

This book is dedicated to my late father Paul Feng (whom I do not know well since he passed away when I was five years old). He interviewed Jawaharlal Nehru, India's first Prime Minister on January 20, 1946, and was one of the deep reasons for me writing this book!

About the Author

 **Feng Da Hsuan** (冯达旋) is currently the Honorary Dean of Hainan University Belt and Road Research Institute and the Chief Advisor of China Silk Road iValley Research Institute. He grew up in Singapore and received his physics PhD from the University of Minnesota (1972). He was the M Russell Wehr Chair Professor of Drexel University. He also served as the United States National Science Foundation Program Director in Theoretical Physics for two years. Since 2002, Feng has taken roles as the Vice President for Research and Economic Development at the University of Texas at Dallas, the Senior Vice President of National Cheng Kung University and National Tsing Hua University in Taiwan.

Feng is a Fellow of the American Physical Society. He was also the honorary professor of fifteen Chinese universities, including Peking Union Medical College, Fudan University, Jilin University, Huazhong University of Science and Technology, Institute of Applied Physics of the Chinese Academy of Sciences and more. Feng was also the 2009 Bian-Zhong laureate for individuals with outstanding contributions to Hubei Province (2009 年度湖北省编钟奖) and recipient of "The Light of Civilization, the 2017 Chinese Cultural Exchange Award" (文明之光·2017 中国文化交流年度人物).

Feng is the Chairman of the International Advisory Board of Hainan University, a member of the Board of Trustees of Nanjing

University, Shantou University (2006–2015), as well as a former member of the Academic Advisory Board of Universiti Teknologi Petronas of Malaysia and Binus University of Indonesia. Feng is also a frequent author and co-author of editorials of major newspaper in East Asia, in Chinese and English. This includes China's *China Daily, Global Times, UK's Financial Times (Chinese Edition)*, and *South China Morning Post* of Hong Kong, *Straits Times* and *Lianhe Zaobao* of Singapore. He is the author of two books, *Edu-Renaissance: Notes from a Globetrotting Higher Educator* and *Belt and Road Initiative: Chinese Version of "Marshall Plan"?*, both published by Singapore's World Scientific Publishing Company.

Acknowledgement

To be able to write an acknowledgement for the book is a joy because that means I am done with the writing. As in all efforts of writing a book, there are simply too many individuals to be thankful for. Fortunately, I think I have given enough words of acknowledgement to nearly everyone scattered throughout the book whom I feel have contributed in one way or another to the completion of the book.

However, I think there are at least three people in the professional world whom I must single out to give my heartfelt thanks.

The first is Dr. Low Hwee Boon, who told me at breakfast in Singapore in 2015, that my speech at Hsinchu in 2013 had something to do with the Belt and Road Initiative (BRI). His perception was truly profound, and without those few words I may never have begun this "new" phase of my life.

The second is Dr. Phua Kok Khoo, my lifetime friend, from elementary school to today, who took a chance on me to enable me to present a talk about the BRI in Singapore on July 5, 2016. It is hard to believe that such an invitation literally restructured my life.

Last but not least, I must thank Dr. Liang Haiming, my collaborator regarding the BRI, for the past three years. I have to admit that when I was about to depart from the University of Macau, I had made the decision, as the Chinese would say, to 退出江湖 (or in English, it means leaving the topsy turvy world of the professionals). Then just before doing so, I met Dr. Liang and, almost overnight, we began an intense collaboration regarding the BRI. In our first telephone conversation, I asked him an impertinent question: "How do you think the United States can play a role in the BRI?" His answer was quick and succinct. He said that: "China has kung fu and pandas, but it is the US that has *Kung Fu Panda*!" My collaboration with him is still going strong. Naturally, it makes leaving the professional world impossible.

Of course, beyond my professional association, I am deeply grateful to my life partner, Evelyn. It is her love that sustains me in all my professional activities, and this one is no exception.

Foreword

In 2013, the President of China, Xi Jinping spoke for the first time in public about a philosophy and ideas that would underpin what became known as the Belt and Road Initiative (BRI). As Feng Da Hsuan, the author of the current book explains, this thinking represented a significant departure from the way China had previously thought about itself, conducted its affairs and engaged with the world.

As he relates in the opening chapter, Da Hsuan did not particularly follow Xi Jinping's speeches on this topic in the early years and therefore did not appreciate the significance and implications of these new ideas and concepts. All of that changed in July 2016 when Da Hsuan was invited to give a speech on the BRI in Singapore. Following his custom, Da Hsuan, understanding how little he understood about the concept at that time, conducted extensive research on the topic and began to think about its significance and implications. Since that time, he has given innumerable presentations on BRI, all fashioned with his typical flair, at many prestigious institutions and universities. It is fair to say that BRI has dominated his thinking over the last several years. The initial chapter describes the genesis of his thinking and actions with respect to the BRI and where that led. The current book, *China's Millennium Transformation: The Belt and Road Initiative*, is a summary, distillation and presentation of Da Hsuan's deep thinking and reflections on the topic, how it may influence China's policics and geopolitical aspirations and its relationship with other countries in Asia and around the world.

His thinking is captured in three ideas that represent the major intellectual contributions of the book. These are the ideas that the BRI could lead to: i) a supercontinent that would bring Europe and Asia closer together, ii) neo-renaissance thinking that would unite the intellectual and cultural traditions of the East and the West, and iii) a change in how China communicates about itself and its culture to the rest of the world. Each of these ideas is explored in detail in three interesting chapters, one devoted to each of these themes. A recurring theme is why the BRI emerged in 2013 and not before. The reader will not be surprised to read that the spectacular economic growth and influence of China are seen as major contributors. The reader may be surprised to read Da Hsuan's assessment, though, of the predominance of the role of Xi Jinping in the development and implementation of BRI.

This exposition is followed by a set of fascinating and engaging case studies that capture Da Hsuan's life history and experiences throughout his illustrious career that influenced his thinking about the origins and implications of BRI. Case studies are unusual in a book like this, but they make for compelling reading. Each case is also brought back to the central themes of the book. Specifically, the implications of the BRI policy to the countries discussed and their future relationship to China. The discussion of the relationship between China and India, two Asian giants that have not enjoyed necessarily the most harmonious or aligned policies and cultures, is particularly fascinating. It is also deeply personal to the author given that India is his country of birth but China's special areas (Taiwan and Macao) are the places in which he has spent so many of his recent years. Personally, I also resonated strongly to two of his other case studies. One was his description and interpretation of the meaning of the Jewish community in Kaifeng China in the Song Dynasty nearly 1000 years ago. The other was his analysis of Canada, my home country, and the lessons that my country could derive from BRI and the current geopolitical thinking in China. The implications of BRI for other Asian countries, like Singapore and Vietnam are also discussed. Given the years he spent in universities as both an academic and administrator, Da Hsuan is also not hesitant to expound on the role of universities in society, the differences between Asian and Western universities, and how universities could promote and teach about China and the BRI. The book ends with a useful set of recommendations for China — how it might best promote and spread the BRI.

Those of us (and there are thousands) who have followed Da Hsuan's writings and talks throughout the years will not be surprised by the nature and style of the book. He has a flair for presentation, a mixture of story-telling supported by facts and figures. He uses personal anecdotes and his life history to elucidate and underscore important points. He thinks in broad sweeps. There are not many who attempt to link events and actions of hundreds or thousands of years ago and show how they are relevant to what is happening today. I do not know how many followers Da Hsuan has on Facebook or other social media, but I can tell you that there are thousands of us who follow his writing. Graphics and pictures of luminaries are used extensively in the book — they make the reading engaging and pleasurable. You may not agree with all of Da Hsuan's conclusions and opinions presented in the book, but you will not find them boring. Readers will learn a lot from this book, everything from history, science, politics, biographies of the famous and world events. Throughout his career, Da Hsuan has always been an educator. This book is a shining example of his continuing in this tradition.

Da Hsuan is perhaps the most eminently qualified individual I know to write this book. Born in India, raised in Singapore, educated in the United States and a working career in that country and Asia, few have had the life experiences, personal and professional, to address the broad range of issues and topics covered in the various chapters. It is no wonder that he is a much sought after lecturer on the BRI and, in general, on China and other countries' relationships to it.

Unlike Da Hsuan, I am neither a physicist nor rocket scientist, but it does not take a rocket scientist to predict that this book by Da Hsuan, written now, may be the most significant contribution he has made to intellectual thought. Even absent the American isolationist policies of Donald Trump, the economic growth and influence of China — which are so well detailed in the book — make China a world superpower that rivals, and may eclipse, the influence, economic and social aspects of the United States. If nothing else, the world's ability to handle its significant issues — like climate change, economic crises or pandemics — is going to depend upon cooperation and collaboration with China. As Da Hsuan so aptly describes in his book, Europe and the United States do not understand China well. This has to change, and this book by Da Hsuan is a significant and important primer for anyone who wishes to deepen their understanding of China and Asia. It was a pleasure to read. I learned a great deal. It was entertaining and informative. What more could a reader ask for?

Harvey P. Weingarten
President Emeritus, University of Calgary
Past President, Higher Education Quality Council of Ontario
April 27, 2020

Preface

Why I Wrote this Book

This book is my perspective of how China can be a transformative force for the world!

Not being an economist, a social scientist or a political scientist, and merely being a theoretical physicist and a university administrator, there could be a thousand reasons why I should not and could not write this book. However, there is only one reason why I should, and that is because my cultural heritage is Chinese. With that in my DNA, deflecting the Belt and Road Initiative (BRI) from my cognition is simply an impossibility.

As a young boy growing up and attending Chinese Schools (both elementary and secondary) in Singapore, I was aware of a historical figure of China, the great Han Dynasty's diplomat and explorer Zhang Qian (张骞). Yet it was not until I became interested in the BRI in 2013 that I began to learn more about him. In China's counterpart to Google, Baidu (百度), among the long description of Zhang Qian who lived between 164 BC and 114 BC, the following few words truly stunned me:

张骞被誉为伟大的外交家、探险家，是 "丝绸之路的开拓者"、
"第一个睁开眼睛看世界的中国人"[1]

---

[1] Zhang Qian (n.d.). In *Baidu*. Retrieved September 1, 2019, from https://baike.baidu.com/item/%E5%BC%A0%E9%AA%9E/660225?fr=aladdin.

Statue of Zhang Qian.

Source: Retrieved from https://baike.baidu.com/pic/%E5%BC%A0%E9%AA%9E/660225/
0/359b033b5bb5c9ea613ceb91d339b6003bf3b3f1?fr=lemma&ct=single#aid=0&pic=359b033
b5bb5c9ea613ceb91d339b6003bf3b3f1

The translation of this phrase is "Zhang Qian is known as a great diplomat and explorer. He is the pioneer of the Silk Road and the first Chinese to open his eyes to see the world."

When I first read this phrase sometime in the Spring of 2016 (the reason why I read it should become obvious as you read on), I was stunned. I was stunned not because he was a great diplomat and explorer, which he clearly was; I was not even stunned by the fact that he was credited as the pioneer of the Silk Road; I was stunned that Baidu would consider him as the *"first Chinese to open his eyes to see the world"*! Those were both surprising and shocking words for me. It made me suddenly realized why I was emotionally and intellectually attracted to the BRI. It made me realize that the BRI could and should be the first deep and broad global initiative taken by China, a nation with many millennia of profound history, a nation which essentially defined the meaning of "Eastern civilization," to persuade the 1.4 billion Chinese people in the 21st century to truly "open" their eyes and "see the world."

As a nation which is home to 25% of the world's population and endowed with a long and rich history spanning of nearly 5 millennia, China had to struggle, and in some sense is still struggling to "see the world." By the time Han dynasty rolled around, China already had several millennia of history under its belt. Yet despite the fact that it was endowed with such an incredibly long history, Zhang Qian was — according to Baidu — "the first Chinese" to open his eyes to see the world.

Of course, since Zhang Qian, China today also has seen several more millennia of history. I cannot help but ask myself, has China/the Chinese now opened its/their eyes to see the world? It is for this reason that I have come to the conclusion that if the BRI can achieve the monumental effort for China of "opening its eyes to see the world," it will not only be transformative for China, but also for humanity.

This book is my perspective of how China can be a transformative force for the world!

Like I said, until 2016, this was a book I never would have thought of writing, or believe that I could write — I did not had the propensity and desire to write it. Around that time, I had a career transformative experience. That experience made me aware of how modern China was, and still is in transition, because of the BRI. It is something I simply cannot separate myself from as it is a profound manifestation of the Chinese culture I inherited, a culture that could "do good" for humanity.

By now it is well known to everyone that in the fall of 2013, President Xi Jinping had delivered two significant speeches. One was in September at Kazakhstan's Nazarbayev University, with the title "Promote People-to-People Friendship and Create a Better Future",[2] and the other was in October to the Indonesian Parliament.[3] In those two speeches, President Xi proposed and outlined for the

---

[2]Xi, Jinping. "Promote Friendship Between Our People and Work Together to Build a Bright Future". *Ministry of Foreign Affairs of, the People's Republic of China*, Ministry of Foreign Affairs, the People's Republic of China, September, 8, 2013, https://www.fmprc.gov.cn/mfa_eng/wjdt_665385/zyjh_665391/t1078088.shtml.

[3]Wu, Jiao. (October 02, 2013). *President Xi gives speech to Indonesia's parliament.* Retrieved from http://www.chinadaily.com.cn/china/2013xiapec/2013-10/02/content_17007915_2.htm.

first time, the fundamental concept of an epoch transformative initiative, which eventually became known as the "Belt and Road Initiative."

In his Kazakhstan and Indonesia speeches, President Xi proposed to revitalize the ancient land-based and maritime Silk Roads, and with it search for a common future for humanity.

In September 2013 in Kazakhstan, according to the Website of the Chinese Ministry of Foreign Affairs[4]

"Xi expressed that more than 2,100 years ago, during China's Western Han Dynasty (206 BC-AD 24), imperial envoy Zhang Qian was sent to Central Asia twice to open the door to friendly contacts between China and Central Asian countries as well as the transcontinental Silk Road linking East and West, Asia and Europe. Kazakhstan, as a major stop along the ancient Silk Road, has made important contributions to the exchanges and cooperation between different nationalities and cultures. People in regional countries created the history of friendship along the ancient Silk Road through the ages.

Xi Jinping pointed out that the 2,000-plus-year history of exchanges had proved that countries with differences in race, belief and cultural background can absolutely share peace and development as long as they persist in unity and mutual trust, equality and mutual benefit, mutual tolerance and learning from each other, as well as cooperation and win-win outcomes."

In October 2013, according to China Daily,[5] President Xi said in his Indonesian speech that

---

[4]Ministry of Foreign Affairs, the People's Republic of China. (September, 07, 2013). *President Xi Jinping Delivers Important Speech and Proposes to Build a Silk Road Economic Belt with Central Asian Countries.* Retrieved September 1, 2019, from https://www.fmprc.gov.cn/mfa_eng/topics_665678/xjpfwzysiesgjtfhshzzfh_665686/t1076334.shtml.

[5]Wu Jiao. (October, 02, 2013). *President Xi gives speech to Indonesia's parliament.* Retrieved from http://www.chinadaily.com.cn/china/2013xiapec/2013-10/02/content_17007915_3.htm.

"Over the centuries, the vast oceans have served as the bond of friendship connecting the two peoples, not a barrier between them. Vessels full of goods and passengers travelled across the sea, exchanging products and fostering friendship. A Dream of Red Mansions (红楼梦), a Chinese classic novel, gives vivid accounts of rare treasures from Java. The National Museum of Indonesia, on the other hand, displays a large number of ancient Chinese porcelains. All these bear witness to the friendly exchanges between the two peoples. And they are convincing interpretation of the Chinese saying that "A bosom friend afar brings a distant land near.""

With these two speeches, President Xi unveiled for China and the world, the Belt and Road Initiative!

Nearly four years since President Xi gave those speeches, on May 14 and 15, 2017 in Beijing, a high-level forum entitled "Belt and Road Forum for International Cooperation" was held, with President Xi lending the bully-pulpit of his Presidency to organize it. At this forum, 29 heads-of-state and delegations from some 160 nations attended. Essentially none of the leaders of the Western nations attended.

Then again, from May 24 to 27, 2019, the second high-level forum was held. It took place in the same city, Beijing. This time, 37 heads-of-state attended the forum. More important, every head-of-state — including the glaringly absent Singapore Prime Minister Lee Hsien-Loong in the first forum — and the representatives of the 10 Association of Southeast Asia Nations (ASEAN) (Indonesia was represented by its Vice President Jusuf Kalla) were all in attendance. Also, leaders from Italy, Switzerland and Austria participated. I was fortunate to attend this forum and presented my talk (see Appendix A) there.

I have to admit that my relationship with China and everything Chinese is not linear but highly convoluted. Unlike my many Chinese friends from all corners of the globe, I never attended a single day of schooling in what I would refer to as "Greater China," which encompasses Mainland China, Taiwan, Hong Kong and Macau. While I did receive a Chinese-based education, certainly in

This is the photo taken when I was fortunate to deliver a speech with the title "Belt and Road Initiative (BRI): China's Mindset Millennium Transformation" at the Second Forum.

the elementary and partially in the secondary levels in Singapore, I am sure there is a great deal of room for improvement in my understanding of Chinese language, history and literature. Looking back, I learned most of the Chinese history from bits and pieces of reading, rather than from systematic schooling. Maybe because I spent many decades in the United States, especially in its Northeast during my four years as an undergraduate student in New Jersey, one of my best American friends who is a Southerner in the United States had "accused" me of being "more Yankee than a Yankee!"

Interestingly, I think I may very well be qualified as a candidate having the most citizenships in the Guinness Book of Records. I was born in India as a British subject, and an interesting fact was that my first so-called travel document had the unforgettable phrase "Bearer has no right to abode in the British Isles" on the cover. Interestingly, it was this phrase which defined the status of

Indians living in Uganda in 1972 that caused a massive international incident in 1972!

I departed from Singapore for the United States in 1964. It was the year when Singapore joined Malaysia as a state, in order to be independent from the British colonial rule. Thus, my passport then was a Malaysian passport. After a year in the United States, Singapore was literally kicked out of Malaysia. I thus lost my Malaysian citizenship.

Since 1983, after 19 years living in and building a professional career in the United States, I became a United States citizen. Since Singapore disallowed dual-citizenship, I had to, with some sadness and reluctance, relinquish my Singapore citizenship. I remember talking to a good friend who is Jewish who informed me that because Israel allows dual-citizenship, he holds both US and Israeli passports. I must say, when I heard that he could do so, I was a little jealous that Singapore could not be a bit more magnanimous so that I could maintain some connection to my "hometown"! My separation as Singapore's citizen in 1983 was the first time I understood the meaning of the word "geopolitics"!

The year China opened up to the outside world in 1977 with "reform and opening up" (改革开放) was unquestionably a watershed moment for me, academically and professionally. In April 1981, invited by the Institute of High Energy Physics of the Chinese Academy of Sciences (中国科学院高能物理研究所), I visited China for the first time since our family hurriedly left in 1949. Travelling around China in three weeks, I saw first-hand what China was like. I travelled extensively, from Beijing to Changchun (in Jilin Province) to Wuhan and finally to Shanghai. I was both depressed and exhilarated. I remember how excited I was when in Shanghai I could hear nearly everyone speaking the language I spoke at home, first with my mother, and later with my wife, and now with my UK-born daughter — Shanghainese! I was depressed to see the poor living conditions of my friends and relatives. Many lived in dilapidated housing known as Tongzilou (筒子楼). In those three weeks in 1981, I saw what a nation could be like if it were to shut itself from the outside world. Indeed, I saw a destitute China.

In four decades, while I have undertaken many hundreds of visits to East Asia, especially the Mainland, I never really lived on the Mainland *per se*. It was not until the month of April 2019, when I spent the entire month as the Chairman of the International Advisory Board and Honorary Dean of the Belt and Road Research Institute of Hainan University, whose campus is in Haikou of Hainan Province, that I began to have some deeper understanding of Chinese higher education system. Yet interestingly, I have never experienced what it truly would be like living within China and experiencing its ways and means.

A photo taken at Hainan University.

The closest I came to "living in China" would be my three years in Macau, which is a Chinese territory but under what is known as the "One Country, Two Systems" political structure. My apartment in Macau was only 50 feet "on this side of the wall" which separates

Macau from the Mainland, and each morning I could see just over the wall the rising of the "Five Star" Chinese red flag above the police station. Indeed, late at night, the only traffic sound I could hear from my apartment would be those from the Mainland.

A visit to Hao-Jiang High School in Macau. This is one of the most famous "red" high schools in Macau.

It is probably not an exaggeration to say that the people from Macau are "schizophrenic." They literally think that Macau is both China and not. Observing the chaos in Hong Kong, I jokingly told my Macau friends that

"In Hong Kong, you concentrate more on "two systems" and less on "one country." In Macau, it's the vice versa!"

There is another major difference between Hong Kong and Macau, *vis-à-vis* the Mainland. In Hong Kong, the majority of people live in Hong Kong Island and Kowloon. The border between Hong Kong and the Mainland is not in the vicinity and cannot be seen on a day-to-day basis. In Macau, as long as your eyes are open, you can see the Mainland, which makes the feeling palpable.

Still, even living in Macau, I can consciously observe China and interact with the Chinese in the Mainland as an outsider. But because my parents were Chinese, and I received Chinese education in Singapore throughout my formative years, Chinese culture was subconsciously deeply immersed in me. In hindsight, it is precisely this subconsciousness that forms another reason which rendered writing this book unavoidable.

As was mentioned, until about two and a half years ago, even the idea of writing such a book was farfetched for me. After all, for most of my career in the United States, I was a cocoon professor of theoretical physics. I was not an economist, and not even a political scientist. Subsequently, my career led me to become a higher education administrator in the United States followed by a few years working in industry. In the 10 years I spent in Asia as a senior higher education administrator, I was deeply involved in the development and running three educational institutions: National Cheng Kung University and National Tsing Hua University in Taiwan and the University of Macau. In every administrative position I held, my portfolios were to try my best to render the university a better institution in fulfilling its mission in education. Larger national and/or international events, unless they were connected with the vectors of the university development, I would either have no time or no interest in paying attention to them.

With that as my background, as far as BRI was concerned, in 2016, it was rather far from my cognizance and probably from my day-to-day life. Hence, it was not until I had to sit down and seriously learn about it in order to give a talk in Singapore, did I know that I would be interested or involved in it, let alone that it now appears to be a life-altering experience for me. Yet, once I heard about it and studied it, I could literally feel that something deep inside me was stirring me immeasurably.

As was mentioned, I was born in India in 1945, right after WWII. Soon after I was born, the family returned to China and was caught in four years of bloody and bitter civil war between the Communists and the Nationalists (also known as Kuomintang). Although I had no

A photo I took with both my bosses on June 16, 2017 in Taiwan: The former presidents of National Cheng Kung University Dr. Michael M. C. Lai (赖明诏) (middle) and National Tsing Hua University Dr. L. J. Chen (陈力俊). Both are doctorates from the University of California at Berkeley in molecular biology and physics, respectively, outstanding world-renowned scholars in their respective fields and rare leaders who truly understand the goals of higher education. To work with these two outstanding individuals was a sheer joy, and a privilege anyone would request for.

recollection of that short period of my life, I was told that the family moved around China quite a bit because of the civil war. Around 1950, the family finally left, or more like being driven out of the Mainland. Prior to my father Paul Feng accepting a position on the editorial board of the then English language newspaper in Singapore, *Tiger Standard*, and relocating from China to Singapore, we lived very briefly in Macau and Hong Kong.

The next 14 years in Singapore were my formative years. Singapore, a British colony for most of that period, was my home, and the city — as cliché as it may be — will always be my "hometown!" In Singapore, I attended Chinese schools, from elementary to secondary level. The elementary school which I attended, Yang Ching

According to Wikipedia, the Tiger Standard, which is also known as Singapore Standard or Singapore Tiger Standard, was founded by Mr. Aw Boon Haw. Mr. Aw was also the founder of the famed "Tiger Balm (虎标万金油)."

Source: Retrieved from https://en.wikipedia.org/wiki/Singapore_Tiger_Standard

Elementary School (养正小学), had a deep impression on me, much more so then other schools I attended after I graduated from it in Singapore.

Yang Ching Elementary School was established in 1905 by the Cantonese community in Singapore, which was way before China became a Republic in 1911. As is well known, except for the 3 years and 8 months during WWII, where Singapore was brutally occupied by the Japanese military, for nearly 144 years until 1963, Singapore was a British colony, the school was *de facto* one which the local Cantonese clan wanted their children to go to for studies as much as possible, to get a Chinese education with a Cantonese flavor. I still vividly remember in the main auditorium of the school there was a large Confucius plaque.

There is one aspect of Yang Ching Elementary School that deserves special mention here. A significant fraction of the faculty of the school at that time came from China after WWII. One of them, Ms. Gui Cheng-Ping (桂承平), who sadly passed away recently, was an elegant lady whom I remember spoke perfect and beautiful Beijing-accented Mandarin, something that was truly rare in Singapore. I found out later that Ms. Gui was quite a talented artist. I found this picture of her in the 1990s.

The lady in the photo is Ms. Gui Cheng-Ping.

Source: Retrieved from http://sgcls.hi2net.com/blog_read.asp?id=99&blogid=3310

Ms. Gui was an engaging and loving teacher. She used to tell us many of her experiences in China. One thing she told us on several occasions, which was etched into my memory, was when crossing the Yellow River, one would find the water very much muddied by the sand. The river really looked yellow she would say longingly! In hindsight, it was quite obvious that although she was living in Singapore, her heart was in China!

Ms. Gui mentioning about the Yellow river was why I had always found it serendipitous that the most well-known alumnus of the school was the world-famous composer Xian Xinghai (冼星海), who composed the "Yellow River Cantata 黄河大合唱" in Yan'am in early 1939 during the Sino-Japanese War.

Photo of Xian Xinghai.

Source: Retrieved from https://zh.wikipedia.org/wiki/%E5%86%BC%E6%98%9F%E6%B5%B7

In my six years of elementary school, I was basking in utter Chinese ambiance. These facts underlined clearly where the soul of the school was then, from which I was fortunate to inherit. I should also point out that quite serendipitously, before going to Singapore at the age of 6, Xian Xinghai lived in Macau. Despite the fact that he stayed only a very short period in Macau, there is a boulevard in the city named after him because his music is iconic in China!

The street sign of Xian Xinghai Boulevard in Macau.
Source. Retrieved from https://macaulifestyle.com/city-guide/cafe-little-tokyo/

So somehow, Xian's life and mine seem to have intertwined, albeit in a different space-time! Nowadays, I often joke with friends that Yang Ching Elementary School has at least one world-renowned alumnus, and unfortunately it is not me!

I should mention that there was another episode during my 14 years of school in Singapore which had a life-long impression on me. It happened during my first year of Senior High School (equivalent to the United States' 10th grade). The teacher of Chinese literature assigned the class to memorize the poem Pípa Xíng (琵琶行) by the famous Tang dynasty poet Bai Juyi (白居易) who lived between 772–846 AD.

Although assignments to memorize a piece of literature were rather common for this teacher (whom I obviously don't like since I cannot remember his name), I remember my classmates and I were particularly annoyed this time because Pípa Xíng was 700 words long and very complex. The memorization process was understandably grueling and time consuming. Hours upon hours, I had to pace back and forth in my home to drum the poem into every fiber of my memory.

But when I finally memorized it, I recall I was overcome with a sense of elation. Indeed, such an effort made me felt like I had

Photo of Bai Juyi.

Source: Retrieved from https://www.renminbao.com/rmb/articles/2017/4/12/65375.html

integrated the poem into my soul. Quite recently, after a break of nearly 50 years, I read the poem again. I was amazed that there were some unusual Chinese characters in it, such as 篦 (pronounced as *bi*) which, if it were to appear without any context today, I am confident that I would not be able to pronounce it. Yet, in reciting the poem, all the words, including this one (钿头银篦击节碎), simply emerged from my memory archive and rolled off my tongue effortlessly!

I remember vividly that I had an odd feeling immediately after the memorization that my elation was not simply because I had accomplished an arduous task of memorizing something so magnificently and graciously written more than a millennium ago. It was because I had the strange and palpable feeling that I had made a vital step towards recognizing that my Chinese heritage would be forever a part of me. Indeed, at that young age, I did not have the intellectual capacity to articulate such a fervent feeling. That came to me only when I began to understand the BRI, and what it meant to me in particular, some six decades later!

Looking back, as I had mentioned earlier, I have to admit that while the education in Chinese culture I received in Singapore both in depth and breadth were probably not as rigorous as those I could have received in Taiwan, Hong Kong, Macau and the Mainland, it did construct within me a sturdy scaffolding of the magnificent Chinese civilization so that I could gain an indelible appreciation of the Chinese ways and means and how I view myself as someone having Chinese culture as a form of my absolute being.

As far as my emotional and deep relationship with people of the Mainland are concerned, the two years I spent as a postdoctoral fellow at the Department of Theoretical Physics at the University of Manchester and a year as a Visiting Professor at the Niels Bohr Institute in Copenhagen were inerasable in my mind.

In my eight years (1964–1972) as a physics undergraduate and graduate student in the United States, the science scenario of China was never in my cognizance. Therefore I was so surprised when I arrived at the Department of Theoretical Physics of the University of Manchester to see the Physics Department Library had subscribed to the *Acta Physica Sinica* (物理学报). Until then, for all practical purposes, China was a black hole to me. In reading the journals, I was surprised and stunned to learn that there was serious physics research conducted in the Mainland.

As I am a theoretical physicist, I was attracted by a paper in one of the issues authored by He Zuo Xiu (何作庥). The subject matter was on something regarding quantum field theory. I recall even though my research area was quite far from the subject matter, and that reading physics text in Chinese was very difficult for me, but since he was the first theoretical physicist I encountered intellectually from the Mainland, I made a concerted effort to read it from beginning to end. In later years during my several visits to the Institute of Theoretical Physics of the Chinese Academy of Sciences, I did had the honor of meeting Professor He in person.

Perhaps what was most memorable about my Manchester experience was that I met, for the first time in my life, someone in person from Mainland China. That person was Dr. Wu Zuze (吴祖泽), a

A picture of a great memory. A picture of the members, faculty, postdocs, and students at the Department of Theoretical Physics of the University of Manchester, 1973–1974. The photo was taken right outside of Shuster Building, off Brunswick Street in Manchester. I am the second individual in the third row.

world-class hematologist and later the President of China's Academy of Military Medical Sciences. I recall since he is a Shanghainese and since both my wife and I speak this dialect fluently, we became instantly good friends. From Dr. Wu, I began to gain a superficial understanding of what it was like living in China in that era!

My knowledge of China made a significant quantum jump when in 1979, I went to the Niels Bohr Institute (NBI) in Copenhagen, Denmark, as a young visiting faculty member. NBI is a world-renowned theoretical physics center, which is responsible for the founding of quantum mechanics. As we all know, 1977–1978 was when China

Photo of Dr. Wu Zuze.

Source: Retrieved from https://baike.baidu.com/item/%E5%90%B4%E7%A5%96%E6%B3%BD/3502799?fr=aladdin

The Niels Bohr Institute. For two years, I lived in an office on the right of the photo.

Source: Retrieved from http://wotug.org/cpa2016/photos-copenhagen/NBI/niels-bohr-institutet-a.jpg

began a new era known as "reform and opening up," wherein scientists from China began to travel abroad. There I was truly fortunate to have met and collaborated with some of the most distinguished Chinese nuclear and particle physicists, such as Dr. Wu Cheng Li (吴成礼) from Jilin University, Dr. Yang Fujia (杨福家) from Fudan University, Dr. Xu Zhan (徐湛) from Tsinghua University, Dr. Chen Yongshou (陈永寿) from the Institute of Atomic Energy (which in China is known as 401 Institute) and the late Dr. Xian Dingchang (冼鼎昌) from the Institute of High Energy Physics.

Knowing these people from China, with such great intellectual capacities, and in flesh and blood, and who all became nationally and/or internationally known later on in their respective areas of expertise, China as a nation of human beings, with cultures, history, and ways and means, and idiosyncrasies, was no longer a black hole for me, both emotionally and professionally.

Photo taken in Copenhagen sometime in 1979. I am second from the left. Next to me is Wu Cheng Li. Standing next to the lady is Chen Yongshou. Sitting is Xu Zhan and the last is Xian Dingchang.

My seven years in Taiwan, from 2007 to 2014, allowed me to deepen my understanding of the Chinese society and its ways and means. There, I was first a Senior Executive Vice President of National Cheng Kung University (成功大学) in Tainan and later served as Senior Vice President of National Tsing Hua University (清华大学). These experiences gave me a thorough in-depth understanding regarding the mindset of a Chinese society. Those seven years was the first time in my life that I worked within the Chinese (even though it was Taiwan) system. It gave me a profound understanding of what it means to be living in a Chinese society.

Having lived in Taiwan with what Ma Ying-Jeou referred to as a "long stay" and having developed enormous number of extraordinarily close friends, such as the remarkable Chen Felice (陈嫦芬) and her husband Ku Leon (古台昭) and the many truly outstanding faculty members of the Chinese literature department of National Cheng Kung University, such as Professor Wang Wei Yung (王伟勇) and Professor Chen Yi-Yuan (陈益源), I became utterly convinced that the phrase that "Taiwan is more Chinese than China" could not be a more accurate description of the island.

Interestingly, Beijing Tsinghua University and Hsinchu Tsing Hua University (in Chinese both are 清华 or 清華) share the same school motto and the same school anthem. As for their respective logos (see the following photos), the one on top belongs to Beijing Tsinghua — they are essentially the same, with minute variations.

It is worth mentioning that the Hsinchu Tsing Hua's logo is the original, created when the university began in the early part of the 20th century in Beijing.

The deep connection between Tainan and Southern Fujian, in history, language and culture, and the historical lineage and academic closeness between National Tsing Hua University and Beijing's Tsinghua University also provided for me an unsurpassed intensity of my connection and my inalienable cultural heritage to China.

Seeing the transformation of China in the 21st century made me ask why China did not collapse in 1977 with the downfall of the "Gang of Four?" In the end, around 2000, I wrote an obituary for a

Logos of Beijing Tsinghua University and Hsinchu Tsing Hua University.

collaborator of mine, Professor Chen Jin-Quan (陈金全) of Nanjing University, where I gave my version as to why this is so.

I wrote

"My friend Professor Chen Jin-Quan, a world-renowned mathematical physicist, departed from this earth, sadly, in 1999. This scientific volume, contributed by many of his friends and colleagues, is published in his memory.

Professor Chen's life mirrors a generation of Chinese intellectuals. It was profoundly sad, yet exhilarating.

1976 was a defining year for modern China. Chairman Mao died on Sept. 9 that year, followed immediately by the spectacular

Book cover of *The Beauty of Mathematics in Science: The Intellectual Path of J Q Chen*.
Source: Retrieved from https://www.worldscientific.com/worldscibooks/10.1142/5163.

collapse of the so-called "Gang of Four," thus bringing closure to ten painful years of "Cultural Revolutions," and ushered China into a new era. Someday, historians will undoubtedly consider the new era as the "miracle of the world in the 20th century."

In 1976, after a decade of utter devastation, China was at the verge of a complete "meltdown", economically, technologically and intellectually. Having quarter humanity, and a land size spanning nearly half of Asia, such a meltdown would have horrifying global implications!

Yet, no meltdown occurred.

A fundamental reason why there was no meltdown was because of the Herculean contributions of the tens of millions of Chinese intellectuals. In their darkest hours during that era, enduring the hardest of hardships and suffering the deepest personal humiliations, they always maintained palpable hope for themselves, their family, their professions and their nation. Indeed, even without personal liberty, both physically and mentally, they remained important pillars of the nation, holding up its dignity. The successes of China of the 21st century are in no small part due to this group of individuals."

As I had mentioned, it is not by choice that I have four "nationalities." While I have deep and loyal feeling towards each, my Chinese cultural heritage is always the needle which threads them into my entire fabric and is lurking in my being! I am sure if in 2016 when Dr. Phua called me from Singapore, I did not have the experiences I mentioned here, in all likelihood, I would have turned down his invitation to speak about the BRI in Singapore.

For someone who was never been educated in the "Chinese" sense, I have always had a sense of uneasiness about "who am I?" Such an uneasiness was finally alleviated when I had a long conversation about my subliminal cultural heritage feeling with a good

A memorable photo taken when the President of Beijing Tsinghua University, Chen Jining (陈吉宁) and President of Taiwan's National Tsing Hua University, Li J. Chen (陈力俊) led their respective leadership team to pay tribute at the tomb in Hsin Chu's campus of the "eternal" president of both universities, Mei Yiqi (梅贻琦).

friend who happens to be a Jewish American. When I mentioned to him about my deep uneasiness and somewhat confusing feelings regarding the difference between my cultural heritage and my nationalities, it apparently resonated with him completely. In fact, he was able to answer without any hesitation that: "I can fully understand and appreciate that. Wherever Jews would hold nationalities of any country, I am confident that most of my fellow Jews would deeply feel that our Jewish heritage is eternally and deeply embedded in us!"

With the above as background, and without intentionally confronting it, it was my deep Chinese cultural heritage that made me first become fascinated and later deeply involved in trying to unravel the meaning of the Belt and Road Initiative for me, and hopefully for China and for humanity in general.

Hence this book.

Contents

About the Author   vii

Acknowledgement   ix

Foreword   xi

Preface   xv

Chapter 1   Introduction: Genesis of My BRI Fascination and Engagement   1

Chapter 2   Supercontinent: An Amalgamation of East and West   17

Chapter 3   Neo-Renaissance: Humanity's Possibility to "Think-Out-Of-The-Box" to Mitigate Existential Challenges   61

Chapter 4   Cultural Communication: An Ultimate Challenge of Chinese Culture   93

Chapter 5   Case Study 1 of "Cultural Communication": A Conversation With Lee Hong-Fah (李洪发), the Modern-Day Zhang Qian (张骞)   157

Chapter 6   Case Study 2 of "Cultural Communication": Search of Jewish Heritage in China   177

Chapter 7   Case Study 3 of "Cultural Communication":
             "Small Nations" Like Canada Need to
             Understand *Realpolitik*, Especially Now!   193

Chapter 8   Case Study 4 of "Cultural Communication":
             "Constructing" a True Supercontinent   235

Chapter 9   Case Study 5 of "Cultural Communication":
             Reflection on the "Re-Visit" to Millennium Hanoi   267

Chapter 10   Imminent Challenges of the Belt and Road
             Initiative   287

Chapter 11   Epilogue   303

Appendix A   *Belt and Road Initiative (BRI): China's*
               Mindset Millennium Transformation   309
Appendix B   *A Glimpse of Russian Scientific Prowess Through*
               the Late Vitaly Ginzburg, the 2003 Nobel Laureate 313

Chapter 1

Introduction: Genesis of My BRI Fascination and Engagement

Amid the geopolitical shifts, new concepts and platforms for regional cooperation have emerged, notably China's Belt and Road Initiative (BRI). Singapore supports the BRI. We see it as a constructive mechanism for China to be positively engaged with the region and beyond. That is why we are active participants. For example, we work with the World Bank to promote financial and infrastructure connectivity, and we provide supporting professional and legal services to BRI countries.[1]

The genesis of my interaction with BRI struck me like a lightning. Although Singapore was literally my "hometown," I left it right after my secondary and polytechnic education. It is indeed quite a surprise even for me that my connection with BRI came through it!

Around March 2016, out of the blue, my good friend and elementary school mate Dr. Phua Kok Khoo (潘国驹), founder of World Scientific Publishing Company, the largest international scientific publisher in the Asia-Pacific region and the

---

[1] In full: PM Lee Hsien Loong's speech at the 2019 Shangri-La Dialogue (May 31, 2019), *CNA*. Retrieved from https://www.channelnewsasia.com/news/singapore/lee-hsien-loong-speech-2019-shangri-la-dialogue-11585954.

Founding Director Emeritus of Nanyang Technological University's Institute of Advanced Studies, called me when I was in my office at the University of Macau. He said:

> There is quite a bit of murmuring in Singapore about this thing called the "One Belt One Road" which China initiated a few years ago. Since you are living in Macau, with its proximity to China's ways and means, can you come to Singapore to give a talk about this Chinese effort?

Dr. Phua Kok Khoo and I attending an ASEAN conference in Bangkok, Thailand.

That phone call struck me like a lightning. It was because until then, even though I was living in Macau, which was and still is politically part of China within the so-called "one country, two systems," I had only heard about this effort through the grapevine and did not give much thought to it. In fact, I had the perception — or in hindsight, a misperception — that this "Chinese endeavor" was entirely an economic and geopolitical initiative, and therefore, does not have much to do with me either personally or to the ecosystem, geopolitically and geoeconomically, that I was embedded in at the time. It was interesting to note that even for Macau, which is supposedly a part of China, BRI at that time was not commonly discussed in the society and its media.

For someone who loves acronyms, the only thing I had done with the little knowledge I possessed about this Chinese effort then was that I invented the acronym OBOR to denote "One Belt One Road." Unfortunately, this acronym did not last long. It should be noted that the current official English name is the "Belt and Road Initiative," or BRI.

I remember vividly that my knee-jerk reaction to Phua's invitation was: *"Don't you want to invite someone who is truly knowledgeable about One Belt One Road?"* Clearly, I was reluctant, and it was because I knew very little about BRI then. I thought that it would be very uncomfortable for me to discuss this issue in public as I would simply be regurgitating what I might have learned after digging through the literature. After all, Singaporeans could do that by themselves.

To my surprise, his answer to my reticence was quick and crisp,

> Since your return to Asia in the past decade, I have heard many outstanding talks delivered by you. Besides, we in Singapore, would really prefer to have someone who understands China sufficiently well and can discuss it, not as a participant and an insider, but a bystander, or even an outsider. As the old Chinese saying goes, "旁观者清" or a bystander can see it with a clear head!

Finally, Phua, whom I had known for over half a century (we went to the same elementary school where he was two years senior to me), said the following words that clinched the deal:

> Besides, I know you have never shied away from challenges. It was transparent that you could not resist the challenge of working in Cheng Kung University (成功大学) in Tainan, Taiwan, a university which you knew nothing about before going there to be its Vice President. I am equally certain that you knew very little about Taiwan, in general, before heading over. Therefore, how could you possibly resist this challenge to talk about such a bold initiative of

China, even though you know little about the effort at the moment, especially when it would be held in your hometown? What we would like to hear from you is: leveraging your global thinking, what can you say about the One Belt One Road effort?

With those words, and the knowledge that Phua had, for the past three to four decades, been one of the pioneers in bringing to Singaporeans the most relevant development in China, even though I had great trepidation, I was deeply honored. Hence, I surrendered my inhibitions and accepted the invitation.

Little did I know that by accepting Phua's invitation, I literally sealed my fate, altering the course of my life hitherto!

Ee Hoe Hean Club.

Source: Retrieved from https://en.wikipedia.org/wiki/Ee_Hoe_Hean_Club.

Phua then told me where the talk would be held. I was intrigued by the venue. It would be held in an elegant club known as Ee Hoe Hean (怡和轩), which was founded in 1895, way before China became a Republic in 1911. The club is right in the heart of

Singapore's old Chinatown (牛车水), and it has a glorious history *vis-à-vis* China. Visitors to the club since its founding include historical figures such as Sun Yat-Sen (孙中山), the Father of the Chinese Republic, and Jawaharlal Nehru, the first Prime Minister of India.

Mr. Tan Kah Kee.

Source: Retrieved from https://www.tkkfoundation.org.sg/biography.

Another frequent visitor worth underscoring here is the renowned Tan Kah Kee (陈嘉庚), a mega-successful entrepreneur who is also known to be a truly generous education philanthropist. Even when I was a young boy, I knew of his existence. Tan believed deeply in the importance of education and founded many educational institutions in Singapore, including the famous Hwa Chong High School (华侨中学), and the Xiamen University (厦门大学) in China. Legend has it that Tan spent nearly all his wealth building educational institutions, and hence left very little to his children. It is also interesting to note that while there are many foreign universities establishing campuses in China today, Xiamen University was the first, and thus far, the only Chinese university to have established a foreign campus in Kuala Lumpur, the capital of Malaysia.

A photo of Dr. Michael Szonyi, Director of Harvard University's Fairbank Institute of East Asia Studies and I, during the Centennial Celebration of Xiamen University.

I think the way Tan's name is spelled in English is worth a little elaboration. For Tan and the Club's Chinese names, if they were spelled in English by Pinyin, they should have been Chen Jia Geng and Yi He Xuan, respectively. The reason why they were not is because, more often than not, the romanization of Chinese names in Singapore (and in fact much of Malaysia as well) is based entirely on the Southern Fujian dialect, which is commonly known as Min-Nan (闽南). Min-Nan is exactly the Chinese dialect spoken by many Chinese in the southern part of Fujian Province and Taiwan. Of course, it is also spoken by a large proportion of Southeast Asian Chinese with southern Fujian Province ancestry. What is important to note here is that the way Chinese names, be it person or street, are spelled in English in Singapore is a profound reflection of how the deep Chinese roots are manifested. Indeed, when I was growing up, many of my classmates had the surnames Tan, and not Chen, for precisely the same reason. In fact, it was so much so that I had always assumed that this was the natural thing to do, until I came to the United States and learned differently.

A display room in Ee Hoe Hean.

Ee Hoe Hean Club was founded during the British colonial days by well-to-do Chinese businessmen. Members of the club today are also well-known Singapore Chinese business leaders. It is worth underscoring that, today, the Club has taken on a new importance in that it is not merely a venue for "high-level business leaders" to relax and interact with their peers, but since it often invite speakers to deliver open lectures about global social issues, especially those relevant to China, it has also become a venue for the public to learn about the social and political developments of Asia and China in the new century, often from the "horses' mouths"! To this end, as far as my first lecture on BRI is concerned, it is clearly the most appropriate venue. The following is the poster of my talk on July 5, 2016. I delivered my talk with the title "Belt and Road Initiative: Challenges of Asian Higher Education in the 21st century."

I was told to deliver my lecture in Chinese. Unfortunately, by doing so, it attracted an audience who could only understand Chinese. In Singapore, the Chinese of my generation would either go to Chinese schools (as I did) or schools that teach entirely in English. Such an education system naturally divided the population into two segments: those who could understand Chinese comfortably and those who could not. In interacting with many of the audiences, I could tell that except for those who came from Mainland China in the past several decades, the Singaporeans of my generation were all "Chinese educated," as one would say in Singapore.

E-poster of my speech.

Once I accepted Phua's challenge, I began to earnestly study what BRI was all about. To that end, I tried to get my hands on as much information as I could. I was immediately confronted by the fact that at least around 2016, there was essentially little or no discussion about BRI in the English language media. Furthermore, a significant part of the writings emerged primarily from China and, not surprisingly, nearly all were in Chinese.

With the above as background, the fact that I could proceed was attributed to the following two benefits.

First, I have always been fluent in spoken Chinese, in Mandarin, Cantonese (my father's mother-tongue) and Shanghainese (my mother's mother-tongue). However, if this invitation from Phua occured prior to my return to Asia in 2007, where at that point, my knowledge of written Chinese had became rather rusty due to lack of use, I certainly would have had great difficulty understanding the enormous volume of information about BRI that I found on the Internet, especially since they were all in the so-called simplified Chinese characters (简体字). My rustiness in Chinese would had hampered my plowing through the great number of Chinese articles in a short time with sufficient understanding of the subject. However, the invitation from Phua came in 2016, which was nine years after I returned to Asia. My Chinese, by then, was more than adequate to handle the BRI materials published in Chinese.

Second, after I landed a position at the University of Macau in 2014, I was surrounded by colleagues and friends who immediately told me about an amazing Chinese social media app known as WeChat. WeChat, which was developed by a high-tech company in Shenzhen named Tencent (腾讯), is a social media platform that is exceedingly easy to navigate. Wikipedia introduces it as follows:

WeChat is a Chinese multi-purpose messaging, social media and mobile payment app developed by Tencent. It was first released in 2011, and by 2018 it was one of the world's largest standalone mobile apps by monthly active users, with over 1 billion monthly active users (902 million daily active users). Described as one of the world's most powerful apps by Forbes, it is also known as

China's "app for everything" and a "super app" because of its wide range of functions and platforms…"

Once I became aware of WeChat, I made it a point to become a well-versed and frequent user. Armed with this new tool, I was able to immediately gain access to the flood of BRI writings in China and began my journey towards understanding this entirely Chinese-initiated global effort. I spent several months reading and digesting what I had read.

It goes without saying that, through interacting via WeChat with the vast number of netizens from the Chinese academic, industrial and general population, it gave me an opportunity to reach a deeper understanding of China, especially the minds of its people since the "reform and opening up" era (改革开放时代). Looking back, this understanding, no doubt, has an enduring impact on my intense interest in the BRI.

On the day of my speech, which was July 5, 2016, at 2:30 pm, Phua and a few friends and I had a simple lunch in a restaurant near Ee Hoe Hean. Afterwards, we walked the short distance to the lecture venue. As we got closer, I was surprised to notice a long line of people waiting at the elevator. Once I got into the elevator, I was immediately greeted by an elderly lady who apparently knew me from my picture in the newspaper advertisement for the event. I remember distinctly what she said to me:

Are you the speaker today? I am so excited to learn about this new initiative of China in which there is so little news reporting in Singapore about it.

Those words startled me!

By the time I got to the lecture hall on the third floor in the Club, I was flabbergasted by the very large number of people of all ages gathered there. The publicity of my talk must have been so wide-spread that I was amazed that among the audience was a high school classmate of mine whom I had not met for more than 4 decades. He told me later on that he saw the advertisement for my lecture and felt compelled to attend the lecture. Since the lecture hall could only accommodate about 150 people, and there were at least 300 people crammed in it, many were standing on the sides and at the back! I was concerned that we would see the fire marshal coming to the lecture hall and shutting down the event!

As I was giving my talk, I could tell people were all listening very attentively. After my talk, I was peppered by a large number of questions in all directions. Even after the conclusion of the Q&A section, I was surrounded by a large crowd who wanted to know more! The atmosphere was one of electrifying anticipation, which coupled with what the lady told me inside the elevator, gave me a profound appreciation that the BRI had already captured the deep interest, and maybe even a great deal of anxiety, by the Singapore's Chinese speaking community.

The lecture at Ee Hoe Hean opened up the floodgate for my lectures regarding the BRI in North America and Asia Pacific. The BRI lecture took me to many institutions which I never thought in my wildest dream I would visit, such as Harvard Law School. Following are some of the posters announcing my lectures.

In retrospect, there was no better venue to launch my BRI "career" than in Singapore's Ee Hoe Hean. To paraphrase a common Texan vernacular, "I was not born in Singapore, but I came as soon as I could!" After all, although I was not born in Singapore, it was there that I had the first cognition of my existence, a cognition which was deeply rooted in a primary school, as well as my first home in Singapore on Lim Teck Kim Road (林德金路), both of which are literally within walking distance from Ee Hoe Hean. That region of Singapore, known as Tanjong Pagar, which ironically is known as Chinatown, although is highly developed since the days I grew up, remains deeply a part of me. After all these decades since my youth, during which I had the opportunity to go around the world many times over, if there were no BRI which projected China as a nation so palpably to the world, I probably would not have felt so deeply connected to China as the origin of my cultural heritage.

The Global Implication and Impact of the
Belt and Road Initiative

Dr. Da Hsuan Feng

Senior Fellow, Institutue for Advanced Studies of Nanyang Technological University, Singapore

Thursday, March 1, 2018

3:00-4:00 PM

1221 Anderson Hall

- A small reception will follow -

The Belt and Road Initiative is a major cultural and economic project to connect Eurasia and the world. Professor Feng explores the implications of this multi-continent initiative: the creation of a Super Continent, a Neo-Renaissance, and unprecedented cultural communications between China and the outside world, which he argues would not be possible without the millennium mindset of China.

 Professor Da Hsuan Feng has accumulated three decades of academic and corporate experience in the United States, including the Vice President for Research at the University of Texas, Dallas and the M. Russell Wehr Chair Professor of Physics at Drexel University. He served as Vice President for Fortune 500 Science Applications International Corporation and has been a fellow of the American Physical Society since 1996. Professor Feng has lectured around the world and published extensively in East Asian newspapers on the Belt and Road Initiative.

TEMPLE
UNIVERSITY
Confucius Institute
天普大学孔子学院

Posters and advertisements of my lectures.

On May 31, 2019, the Prime Minister of Singapore, His Excellency Lee Hsien Loong, delivered a heartfelt keynote speech during the annual Shangri-La Dialogue in 2019 where he said:

> Amid the geopolitical shifts, new concepts and platforms for regional cooperation have emerged, notably China's Belt and Road Initiative (BRI). Singapore supports the BRI. We see it as a constructive mechanism for China to be positively engaged with the region and beyond. That is why we are active participants. For example, we work with the World Bank to promote financial and infrastructure connectivity, and we provide supporting professional and legal services to BRI countries.[2]

A comment from the Prime Minister of my hometown is certainly another strong boost to my confidence in writing this book.

Thus, this was how it all began.

---

[2]In full: PM Lee Hsien Loong's speech at the 2019 Shangri-La Dialogue (May 31, 2019), *CNA*. Retrieved from https://www.channelnewsasia.com/news/singapore/lee-hsien-loong-speech-2019-shangri-la-dialogue-11585954.

Chapter 2

Supercontinent: An Amalgamation of East and West

> How can BRI induce changes at a deep-seated level, such that it
> can affect, even transform, the Chinese mindset in this millennium
> so that the nation can play a fundamental role in the 21st and
> beyond to make significant positive contributions to humanity!

As was mentioned in Chapter 1, in the fall of 2013, President Xi Jinping delivered two significant speeches. One was to Kazakhstan's Nazarbayev University to "Promote People-to-People Friendship and Create a Better Future," and the other was at the Indonesian Parliament. In both of these speeches, President Xi outlined the fundamental concept of an epoch-transforming concept, which eventually became known as the "Belt and Road Initiative" or BRI. A high-level forum, the Belt and Road Forum for International Cooperation, was held on May 14 and 15, 2017, in Beijing. It was attended by 29 heads-of-state and some 160 nations' delegations. On April 24–27, 2019, a second forum with the same overarching goal and title was again held in Beijing. I was unable to attend the first forum but was fortunate enough to participate in it this time, and even delivered a speech (see Appendix A).

In this chapter, I will discuss one of the three major outcomes that I discovered the BRI can have upon its successful implementation. They are the formation of a *supercontinent* mindset (discussed in the current chapter), the creation of a *neo-renaissance* (explained in Chapter 3) and China proactively engaging in a hitherto unprecedented *cultural communications* phase with the outside world (discussed in Chapter 4). In my opinion, all three are the consequences of transforming the millennium mindset of China and Chinese. Without the BRI, this probably will not happen, which could be a tremendous loss to humanity.

Since the BRI could have very broad and deep implications, it has stimulated global intense interest and debates in a variety of disciplines, such as economics, geography, science and technology, transportation, geopolitics and healthcare. Indeed, as discussed extensively in the book *Belt and Road Economics* by Haiming Liang, as well as what Liang and I recently had proposed in the chapter "Omnipresent Economics," (Chapter 1 of *Belt and Road Initiative: Chinese Version of Marshall Plan?* published by World Scientific Publishing Company), the opportunities and the challenges of BRI are so wide ranging and deep that it is difficult for people outside of China, and sometimes even for the Chinese, to wrapping their arms around it.

Dr. Liang Haiming is the Chairman of China Silk Road iValley Research Institute (the third most influential think tank in China) and Dean of Hainan University's Belt and Road Research Institute.

Although it was not elucidated as such, a successful BRI is intended for and expected to be an enduring initiative for China in particular and the world in general. It is also expected to influence, to varying degrees, a plethora of different disciplines. When I began to seriously study the subject of BRI before my speech in Singapore in 2016, I asked myself the most tantalizing question — in the long run, how can BRI, with all the above-mentioned profound implications, as well as its much unintended consequences, transform China in particular and the world in general?

Conditions for the Belt and Road Initiative

For China to kick-start such an enormous effort with far-reaching implications, it is understood that various conditions must be absolutely perfect. Indeed, it is interesting to ask why it was initiated in 2013 and not, say, 1997? This is an especially intriguing question because on July 1, 1997, a globally profound event took place in greater China. On that day, the British Union Jack was lowered in Hong Kong and replaced by the Five-Star Red flag of the People's Republic of China. The sovereignty of Hong Kong was reverted to China, signaling not just the end of the British colonial rule in Hong Kong, but also the end of centuries of British colonial rule in the Asia-Pacific region. Would it not be truly beneficial to China if the closure of the British Empire was coupled with such a profound undertaking as the BRI?

Photo taken during the change of soverignty ceremony in Hong Kong in 1997.

Source: Retrieved from https://tr.wikipedia.org/wiki/Hong_Kong_devir_teslim_t%C3%B6reni.

While the 1997 event had enormous geopolitical and symbolic importance, in terms of the profound and real impact in the long run for China as a nation, it was still relatively meager compared to what came later, i.e. the Belt and Road Initiative.

The following diagram could help clarify what I mean by the above statement.

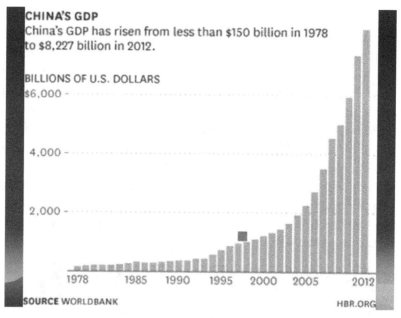

CHINA'S GDP

China's GDP has risen from less than $150 billion in 1978 to $8,227 billion in 2012.

BILLIONS OF U.S. DOLLARS

SOURCE WORLDBANK   HBR.ORG

China's GDP from 1978 to 2012. The red dot is the year Hong Kong reverse in sovereignty.

Source: Retrieved from Worldbank data, https://data.worldbank.org/country/china

I have been told by knowledgeable economists, that the "Gross Domestic Product (GDP)," which is the total value of everything produced by all the people and companies in the country, should not be considered as a panacea of economic indication. Nonetheless, it is an indicator and it does portray, to a certain extent, the overall national economic strength.

Chairman Mao passed away in 1977. Soon after that, China entered the era of "reform and opening up (改革开放)." In 1977, China's GDP was US$150 billion. By comparison, for the same year, the US GDP was \$2.086 trillion. By the time 1997 rolled around, China's GDP was US\$961 billion — an increase of 640% from 1977. In 2017, however, China's GDP was US\$12.24 trillion, — a whopping increase of 12.7 times or 1270% compared to that of 1997.

For me, there are a few personal ways in which I can understand the growth of China's economy, from 1977 to 1997 and to 2017.

The first was what China was like when I visited it for the first time since my family left the country in 1949. That year was 1981, when I was very honored to receive an invitation from the Institute of High-Energy Physics of the Chinese Academy of Sciences for a three-week scientific visit to the country. While I was truly exhilarated by the visit, I also saw a China that bore absolutely no resemblance to the world I was used to, even compared to Singapore in 1964, when I left for the United States. When my United Airline Boeing 747 was descending into Shanghai's Hongqiao Airport late in the evening, I was startled because as I looked out the window, all I saw was pitch darkness — and this was supposed to be a city of more than 10 million people! The utter darkness provided me a way to vividly remember what China was like in my own diminutive manner at that moment.

Starting from 1981, the number of my visits to Mainland China in the following four decades increased rapidly. Since then, and to this day, every year I visit the country at least once or twice, and sometimes more. In the 1980s, and certainly the 1990s, with every visit, whenever I departed from China, I would stop at Tokyo on my way back to the United States. My reasons for doing so could have been professional, touristic or simply layovers, or all the above. I remember vividly that in the 1980s, and even around the time that Hong Kong was returned to China in 1997, as soon as I reached Tokyo's Narita airport, an uncontrollable feeling took over me, a feeling of "*I am reentering to the world I am more familiar with.*"

Indeed, after 10 years of the devastation caused by the Cultural Revolution, China was an impoverished nation in nearly every sense of the word. During that first visit to China in 1981, over the course of my three weeks of travel, although I was warmly welcomed by my various hosts, from Beijing to Jilin Province to Hubei Province, Lanzhou and Shanghai, what I saw were conditions of dilapidation. Fast forward 10 years — to the beginning of the 1990s — and I had the chance to visit one of the western provinces. I was heartbroken to see shattered windowpanes of a well-known national university. Such a feeling persisted for several decades, and only began to fade around the turn of the 21st century.

The reason for me having such a feeling was because of the overwhelmingly stark contrast in economic conditions between China and Japan. Looking at Chinese GDP between 1977 and 1997, a period of 20 years, there was only a modest increase of 6 times was observed, whereas in the 20 years between 1997 and 2017, it grew a whopping 12 times! More importantly, the baseline in 1977 was a low number of US$150 billion, while in 1997 it was already close to a trillion US dollars.

Having the largest population in the world, China's growth in the economic dimension unquestionably did and will have deep and profound global implications. For example, another area that can be corroborated with the Chinese GDP growth is the increasing number of Chinese students studying in the United States. During the 2006/07 academic year, only 67,000 students came to the US to study; 10 years later, in the 2016/17 academic year, it jumped to 350,000, an increase of more than 5 times. It is no accident that the growth in the number of Chinese students coming to the US coincided with the growth in GDP. It simply means that more and more Chinese families now have sufficient disposable income to pay for their children's education in the United States, even if it were paying the exorbitant out-of-state tuition in state universities!

Contrast this with what an aspiring United States presidential candidate, Senator Bernie Sanders, said in an Op-Ed in 2017[1] where he proposed that all public higher education institutions be tuition-free. Senator Sanders made such a drastic comment because "more than 44 million Americans have taken out student loans to pay for school, with their debt totaling $1.4 trillion."

If and when the dream of Senator Sanders becomes a reality, having more Chinese students pursue their education in US higher education institutions will become a "Plan B" for many universities,

---

[1] Sanders, Bernie. (October 9, 2017). *Bernie Sanders: We Must Make Public Colleges and Universities Tuition Free*. Retrieved from https://www.vice.com/en_us/article/9k3j87/bernie-sanders-we-must-make-public-colleges-and-universities-tuition-free.

both public and private, to meet their financial challenges. During this period of growth in China, because more and more Chinese students are pursuing their education, having a large number of Chinese students studying in a given university may be beneficial on the one hand, but could, on the other hand, drastically distort the financial planning of higher education institutions.

As the old saying goes, "vision without funding is merely a hallucination!" If China had, in 1997 (a mere 20-some years ago), despite global economic development implications, ambitiously announced a "whatever named" initiative to add to Hong Kong's sovereign return celebration, it could have ended up ignored at best or a laughing stock at worst. At that time, as I have argued, China neither had the ways nor the means to carry out such a bold move. However, when the BRI was announced in 2013, China was already economically the second most powerful nation in the world; thus, the condition certainly had altered fundamentally, and so the responsibility it must bear for humanity also becomes more acute.

Indeed, with all the above premises, with China engaging with the world rapidly and having a deeper and more profound global impact, once I got to know about the BRI, I could not resist asking myself one critical question constantly: How can the BRI induce changes at the deep-seated level, such that it can affect, or even transform the millennium Chinese mindset so that the nation can play a fundamental role in the 21st and beyond centuries and make significant positive contributions to humanity?

The Genesis of My Thinking: A Speech Entitled "Supercontinent and Neo-Renaissance," I Delivered in Taiwan's National Tsing Hua University in December 2013

In more ways than one, I was a "late comer" to the BRI effort by nearly three years. This was partially due to the fact that when President Xi made the announcement in September and October of 2013, I was serving as the Senior Vice-President of National Tsing Hua University (NTHU) in Taiwan. If my memory serves me accurately, in Taiwan there was, at best, little mentioning of the BRI, but no drumroll or excitement. I am not certain whether this was because media reports from the Mainland were usually not on the front burner in Taiwan, or whether the reports were primarily focused on local news. It could also be that as a senior university administrator, I was concentrating more on the development of the university I was responsible for. In any case, my utter lack of awareness of the BRI was also one of the reasons why I was a bit rattled by the phone call from Dr. Phua from Singapore in 2016, asking me to give a talk there about BRI.

It was not until about March 2015, when I had already been holding down my position at the University of Macau for nearly half a year, and when news about the Mainland was certainly more prevalent, that the BRI gradually seeped into my cognizance. During that time, there was one personal event which took place when I was attending a conference in Singapore that became a watershed moment for me.

One morning at breakfast, as my friend and fellow physicist Dr. Low Boon Hwee of the Institute of Advanced Studies of Singapore's Nanyang Technological University and I were enjoying the famous Singapore delicacy Bak Kut Teh, or Pork Rib Tea (排骨茶), he suddenly looked at me and made an off-the-cuff comment

Your speech at Tsing Hua University had much of the essence of the BRI!

Immediately I asked him what speech was he was referring to? Also, since I barely knew what BRI was, how could whatever speech I had delivered be related to BRI, even remotely? Dr. Low in his slow and methodical manner of speech replied to me:

You sent me the PowerPoint of your December 2013 speech in Hsinchu. I had gone through it carefully. I also thought about some implications of the Belt and Road Initiative, and I came to the conclusion that what you had said in December of 2013 had much of the essence of BRI from China!

To me, those few words from Dr. Low were truly provocative! As for the speech he had mentioned, it was one I had delivered to the university presidents' forum, held on December 8, 2013, at Hsinchu's National Tsing Hua University (NTHU). At that time, I was the Senior Vice President of that university. Quite by accident, that forum was held merely two and three months, respectively, after President Xi delivered his two speeches in Kazakhstan and Indonesia. It was an important and historical forum involving academic leaders from Europe, belonging to the League of European Research Universities (LERU)[2] and Asia, belonging to the Association of East Asia Research Universities (AEARU).[3]

To unravel what Dr. Low was talking about, please allow me to start from the beginning. AEARU is a consortium formed in 1996 by a number of presidents from the top research universities in East Asia, which included the Founding President of Hong Kong University of Science and Technology, Dr. Chia-Wai Woo and the President at the time of China's Fudan University, Academician Fujia Yang. According to its website, the mission of this consortium is that[4]

.... on the basis of common academic and cultural backgrounds among the member universities, (AEARU) will contribute not only to the development of higher education and research but also to the opening up of a new era leading to cultural, economic and social progress in the East Asian region.

When AEARU was officially started, 17 top-notch universities from Japan (Tokyo University, University of Kyoto, Tohoku University, University of Tsukuba, Osaka University and Tokyo Institute of Technology), South Korea (Seoul National University, Korea Advanced Institute of Science and Technology and Pohang University of Science and Technology), Mainland China (Peking University, Tsinghua University, Fudan University, Nanjing University and China University of Science and Technology), Taiwan (National Taiwan University and

---

[2]https://www.leru.org/about-leru

[3]http://www.aearu.org/

[4]About AEARU (n.d.). Retrieved from http://www.aearu.org/about.html

National Tsing Hua University) and Hong Kong (Hong Kong University of Science and Technology) became members.

Every two years, a subgroup of AEARU presidents would serve as its steering committee members, and one of them would serve as the Chair. The steering committee is responsible for organizing the Annual Conference. In 2013, NTHU's president, Dr. Lih J. Chen (陈力俊) was the Chairman of the steering committee. Hence, not surprisingly, in 2013, the venue for the annual forum was chosen to be Hsinchu — the home of NTHU.

From the beginning of 2013, Dr. Chen mobilized the university to organize the AEARU Annual Forum as well as possible. As I was the Senior Vice-President and had Global Strategy, Planning and Evaluation as part of my portfolio, this organizational task naturally became my responsibility.

Very early on during our organization, a colleague from NTHU's Institute for Law of Science and Technology (NTHU does not have a law school, so this is its closest to one) Professor Anton Ming-Zhi Gao (高銘志) somehow heard about this news and the effort required and came to discuss with me about a suggestion he had regarding the forum. He mentioned to me that his doctoral thesis advisor from the Institute of Environmental and Energy Law of Katholieke Universiteit (KU) Leuven in Belgium — Professor Kurt Deketelaere — was (and still is) the General Secretary of an organization known as the League of European Research Universities (LERU).[5] Professor Gao said that before coming to talk to me, he had conducted some research about both organizations and concluded that AEARU could be considered as the counterpart of LERU.

Once he told me what LERU was, I agreed wholeheartedly with Professor Gao's idea. Similar to AEARU, the LERU — which was founded in 2002 — had members who were at that time the 21 top-ranked university presidents from Sweden (University of Lund), Germany (Ludwig-Maximilians-Universität München, Universität Heidelberg and University of Freiberg), France (University of

---

[5]Members (n.d.). Retrieved from https://www.leru.org/members

Strasbourg, Université Paris Sud and Sorbonne University), Italy (University of Milan), Belgium (KU Leuven), United Kingdom (Imperial College London, University College London, Oxford University, Cambridge University and Edinburgh University), Spain (University of Barcelona), Switzerland (Université de Genève, University of Zurich), Holland (Utrecht University, Universiteit Leiden and University of Amsterdam) and Finland (University of Helsinki). In 2017, two additional universities, one from Ireland (Trinity College of Dublin) and one from Denmark (University of Copenhagen), joined the league.

According to LERU's website, the organization's mission is stated as follows[6]:

> LERU is a well-established network of research-intensive universities. We develop and disseminate our views on research, innovation and higher education through policy papers, statements, meetings and events helping to shape policy at the EU level. The League is a valued interlocutor for the European institutions and other policy stakeholders. It acts as a strong, outspoken voice of European research-intensive universities on a wide range of topics related to EU policies and initiatives.

Such a mission statement is essentially the same with AEARU.

Professor Gao asked me whether it would be prudent to invite some of the LERU presidents to participate in the AEARU annual meeting in Hsinchu, thus making it a joint LERU–AEARU Forum. He made a point that, in his opinion, this could be a great first opportunity to bring about a closer relationship between the higher education institutions of these two geographically, culturally and historically separated top university institutions. Also, Professor Gao said if NTHU was interested in pursuing this further, he would be more than happy to offer his help and request the assistance of Professor Deketelaere in his capacity as the Director General of LERU to explore the opportunity.

---

[6] About LERU (n.d.). Retrieved from https://www.leru.org/about-leru

I met one of the important members of LERU, the Universiteit Utrecht Rector Magnificus G. J. (Bert) van der Zwann, in Macau on May 7, 2015.

I firmly believe that in today's precarious world, there is an urgent need to globalize higher education. Therefore, I was excited to learn from Professor Gao about AEARU's counterpart LERU and was on board with his suggestion. Almost instantly, I was imagining the scenario of a joint AEARU–LERU Forum where top educators from both Europe and Asia could sit together under the same roof to explore educational directions for the betterment of humanity, since it was and still is so important in the chaotic 21st century world. I was also convinced that if this meeting were to happen, it would be unprecedented and historical. Hence, I immediately accepted Dr. Gao's gracious offer and agreed to do all I could to make this a reality.

That same day, Professor Gao and I went to seek the permission from President L. J. Chen to explore such an incredible opportunity. President Chen, who was unquestionably one of the most visionary and decisive higher education leaders in Asia then, without the slightest hesitation and without any serious calculations about the changes in budget needed to hold such a forum (as financial requirements would certainly go far above the normal threshold for AEARU annual meetings) instantly gave us the green light to pursue it.

Following the green light from President Chen, Dr. Gao and I immediately contacted Professor Deketelaere. Leveraging on the warm teacher–student relationship between him and Dr. Gao, I was able to strike up a meaningful conversation with Professor Deketelaere, and he was also enthusiastic about turning such a novel idea into reality.

As the old saying goes, "the devil is in the details," and so this effort spanned months of arduous organization. I must confess that there was no doubt that without Professor Deketelaere's hands-on commitment to this grand concept, our eventual success could have been stopped by numerous stumbling blocks. Since Dr. Deketelaere, Dr. Gao and myself all were convinced that something truly magnificent could emerge from such a forum, we never gave up on the idea even when it seemed hopeless. We pursued it with all the tenacity we could muster. Our effort was rewarded when the leaders of AEARU and LERU finally agreed to hold the joint forum in December 2013.

The forum happened on December 8, 2013 — a beautiful sunny day. Several days before, we dispatched many student assistants to go to the International Airport in Taoyuan to receive a large number of participants and escort them to the campus. The participants were leaders (presidents or senior vice presidents) from some of the 40 top universities in East Asia and Europe. It was indeed an exciting and unusual moment. After all, this was the first time in the almanac of higher education when top academic leaders from Asia and Europe could together galvanize their thoughts and wisdom to contemplate and plan for the future of higher education with a global perspective in mind.

Group photo of the AEARU–LERU Presidents forum.

During the months when we were in the process of organizing the joint AEARU–LERU Forum, something happened on a particular day which, in hindsight, was a major turning point of my life. On that day President Lih J. Chen invited me to meet with him in his office. With a serious demeanor, he said:

> This forthcoming forum is truly historical and could be an unprecedented highlight for NTHU. Since we are the organizer, and the forum is held in our university, I want to make sure that the keynote speech could reflect the unexplored importance of higher education in the 21st century, especially the role plays by Europe and Asia.

He then went on to say something that astounded me:

> As you were the one who brought this idea to me, and ever since I have known you, I have noticed that your thoughts regarding higher education have always allowed globalization to be in the forefront, I am now asking you to represent NTHU to give the keynote speech!

Coming from Dr. Chen, to say the least, this was a tall order. Actually, knowing Dr. Chen quite well by now, I understood that he was not making a request: it was an order for which declination was simply not an option. While I was stunned at that moment, I also felt deeply honored by his confidence in me.

From that moment onwards, I had to think long and hard as to how I could carry out this solemn duty for such an auspicious occasion. What was swirling in my head was, what could I possibly say that may or could have a long-term impact on such an august group in such a historically unprecedented forum?

I have to admit that ever since I came to Asia in 2007 in the capacity as a senior higher education administrator, I had represented my university at numerous higher education forums. To be perfectly honest, I found most of them either very boring or felt that they did not give rise to anything significant, and I include my own presentations in this statement. My joke is that every president's presentation has the same PowerPoint slides, just with different data representing his/her institution. I had the feeling of horror that all the attendees would remember nothing that was being transmitted the moment they stepped out of the lecture venue.

However, the AEARU–LERU Forum should and must be different. I certainly would hate it if in such a historical forum nothing important or memorable could be bestowed to the future generation or generations of education leaders. In the months leading up to the forum, I spent many hours thinking about what I could possibly say to such an august group. Indeed, there were moments when I was overcome with enormous reticent, so much so I almost wanted to pull out from the opportunity to speak. In the end, after I convinced myself that some real impact could be felt not just by the audience, but the higher education community in general, I moved forward.

Once I made the decision, I began to think about what I could say so that perhaps the audience may remember some of the things I could profess. I finally decided that having leading educators from Europe and Asia in the audience, the title of my talk would be

Supercontinent and Neo-Renaissance!

I did not reach this title or the accompanying content lightly. Needless to say, I should mention that as the content of the talk was rather novel, at least for me, I was filled with trepidation.

Supercontinent

Now back to my December 2013 speech at the AEARU–LERU Joint forum. How I formed the essence of my talk was as follows.

Believe it or not, the genesis of my Hsinchu talk could be traced to my lifelong fascination with maps. For as far back as I could remember, there was one thing that had truly bewildered me. I remember as a very young boy that I was in possession of a very small model of the globe. It was one of my favorite companions. I was fond of staring at it, especially at night, before I went to sleep.

I was living in Singapore at that time. For most of my life there, Singapore was either a British colony, or a state within Malaysia. The country occupied a grand total of 220 square miles in area then (it is slightly larger now because of reclaimed land!). I had wondered how small Singapore was (and still is,) compared to all other countries in the world, and how minute I must be. My fondness of the model globe was perhaps a subconscious way for me to feel that I could at least mentally imagine traveling around the world even when I physically could not.

In staring at my little globe, I had often thought to myself: It is obvious that for whatever reasons, when the world was geologically formed, the dynamics behind it was such that the land masses of North America, South America, Africa and Australasia were made to look amazingly like continents. To me it was truly a miracle that from the map, North and South America appear as though they could be cut open with a pair of scissors at the narrowest point of 50 kilometers in the country of Panama. Indeed, it was President Theodore Roosevelt of the United States who saw this opportunity and pushed for the construction of the Panama Canal!

The question I had in my head was "why are Europe and Asia that both lie on one enormous landmass considered as two continents?"

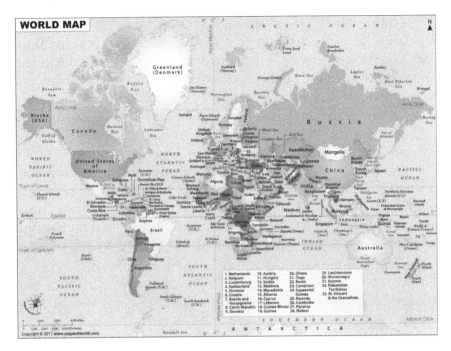

Map of the world.

Source: Retrieved from https://www.mapsofworld.com/world-map-image. html.

My mother who wanted us to know more than just textbook knowledge bought the entire Encyclopedia for the family. I remember going through it to find the answer to that puzzle. Unfortunately, no convincing answer was available.

In later life, I had given myself what I thought was a reasonable but non-scientific explanation for the separation of Europe and Asia. It had to do with how the population was distributed in this vast European–Asian landmass. For example, as we know, there are six central landlocked Asian nations, each occupying an enormous landmass and each with a name ending with "stan." They are Kazakhstan, Uzbekistan, Kyrgyzstan, Tajikistan, Turkmenistan and Afghanistan. Except for Afghanistan, in recent history, all were part of the Soviet Union and became independent nations only after its dissolution in 1989.

As far as population is concerned, even to this day, the combined population of these six countries is 75 million. To have an idea as to what 75 million means, it is instructive to compare this with the population of today of China's southernmost Province, Guangdong Province, and India's state of Chennai. These two administrative divisions of China and India are home to around 104 million and 70 million, respectively. This is already much higher or nearly the same as the combined population of the six Central Asian nations.

Although in population these six nations are small, their respective landmasses are the opposite. Since I now am living in the State of Texas in the United States, it is common for Texans to boast that "Texas is an enormous State!" And it is. The distance from where I live in Dallas to the western end of the State, El Paso, is half the distance from Dallas to San Diego in the State of California! Yet, if one were to compare it with Kazakhstan, Texas in landmass is only one-quarter the size of that country! Finally, the combined landmass of all six central Asian nations is around 40% and 120% of China and India, whose populations are 1.4 billion and 1.2 billion, respectively. I think it is not difficult to imagine just how underpopulated central Asia was, and still must be! It is then a fact that throughout the millennia of history, the population of this area of central Asia must have been even less than what it is today.

This is a photo of the border between Kyrgyzstan and Kazakhstan. It was taken by my friend Lee Hong-Fah of Malaysia when he and his entourage were driving from Singapore to London.

Ever since humanity existed, so did the desolate nature of central Asia. This fact tells us that through millennia, the enormous distance between the population centers in the extreme West, what we now refer to as Europe, and the extreme East and South of this large Euro-Asian landmass, may very well be the fundamental reason for the mindset of people in considering themselves either as Europeans or Asians. Such a vast and deep separation could also give rise throughout the course of human history to anthropological, appearance, cultural and many other differences. While the wide separation of population centers in space and time may not be the sole reason, it must surely be a reasonable explanation for Europeans and Asians mentally considering themselves as belonging to two different continents. Indeed, however this mindset was germinated, it is today a profoundly deep-seated one.

Despite the fact that Europe and Asia stand on one giant landmass, the mindset of separation of the "Europeans" from the "Asians" did not prevent human beings, either for economic, cultural, and especially military reasons, to want to "tie" the two ends together. Two of the best-known examples are of course the brutal military excursions by Alexander the Great (356 BC–323 BC) and Genghis Khan (1162 AD–1227 AD).

The following two maps give a very clear view as to how these two historical giants, separated almost by more than a thousand years, built empires and attempted to link Europe and Asia and bring them under their control.

Map showing the extent of the empire of Alexander the Great.
Source: Retrieved from https://commons.wikimedia.org/w/index.php?curid=656066.

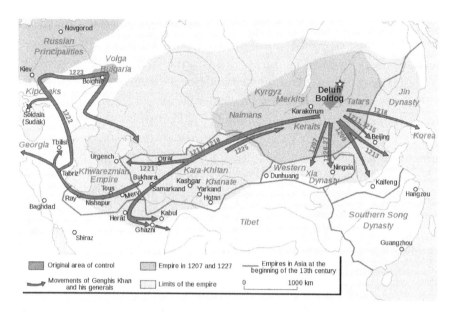

Significant conquests and movements of Genghis Khan and his generals.

Source: Retrieved from https://en.wikipedia.org/wiki/Genghis_Khan#/media/File:Genghis_Khan_empire-en.svg.

It is interesting that while the empires of Alexander the Great and Genghis Khan spanned many thousands of kilometers from East to West, they lasted only as long as these two individuals were alive. Soon after their death, their vast empires seemed to evaporate. This might be due to the fact that the empires needed to exert tight control of enormously large areas, and thus only extremely tough leaders like Alexander the Great and Genghis Khan, who must have possessed deep inner brutal strength, could hold on to their kingdoms. What is also nevertheless true is that except for some historical relics, the remnants of these empires are few and far between. Furthermore, and perhaps what is most important, is that despite the fact that they were militarily all-powerful, their presence on earth played no role in changing the mindset of people living in their empires to think of "Europe" and "Asia" as a single continent.

In today's world, there is only one country on earth whose territory encompasses both "Europe" and "Asia." That country is Russia. While in terms of landmass, the Asian part of Russia occupies nearly 77% of the total landmass; in population it is the opposite — only 23% of the population resides on the Asian part of Russia. Perhaps because the major part of the population has always been in "Europe," and a significant part of Russia's rich history shows that it interacts far deeper with European nations than Asian ones, for most Russians it is a mental slippery slope to think of themselves as Europeans. I made an extensive trip to Russia in 2006 where I mentioned how "European Russians" played a fundamental role in science. In this book, I briefly mentioned it in Appendix B. It is not surprising that even to this day, there is an ongoing debate as to whether Russians are Asians or Europeans.[7]

There is a fascinating and defining book on this topic titled *The Myths of Continents: A critique of metageography*, coauthored by Martin W. Lewis and Kären Wigen, published by the University of California Press. The book is what seems to be an authoritative source on this subject. In this book, there is an in-depth discussion about the many myths of how and why we have "continents"! The term "metageography" is used by the two authors to mean "the set of spatial structures through which people order their knowledge of the world."

In a review of the book,[8] it was poignantly pointed out that:

> The Myth of Continents sheds new light on how our metageographical assumptions grew out of cultural concepts: how the first continental divisions developed from classical times; how the Urals became the division between the so-called continents of Europe and Asia; how countries like Pakistan and Afghanistan recently shifted macroregions in the general consciousness.

In Chapter 1 of the book, Martin W. Lewis and Kären Wigen wrote:

> According to Arnold Toynbee, the original continental distinction was devised by ancient Greek mariners, who gave the names Europe and Asia to the lands on either side of the complex interior waterway

---

[7] Oleg Yegorov. (January 19, 2018). Is Russian European or Asian? *Russia Beyond.* Retrieved from https://www.rbth.com/arts/327309-is-russia-europe-or-asia.

[8] Martin W. Lewis and Kären Wigen. (1997). *The Myths of Continents: A Critique of Metageography.* Berkeley: University of California Press, pp. 21–46.

running from the Aegean Sea through the Dardanelles, the Sea of Marmara, the Bosporus, the Black Sea, and the Kerch Strait before reaching the Sea of Azov. This water passage became the core of a continental system when the earliest Greek philosophers, the Ionians of Miletus, designated it as the boundary between the two great landmasses of their world. Somewhat later, Libya (or Africa) was added to form a three continent scheme. Not surprisingly, the Aegean Sea lay at the heart of the Greek conception of the globe; Asia essentially denoted those lands to its east, Europe those lands to its west and north, and Libya those lands to the south.

It is clear from reading this passage that even though, as Toynbee had claimed, it was the "ancient Greek mariners, who gave the names Europe and Asia," the demarcation between the two continents in the minds of the Greeks was based on much of the disconnected waterways like Dardanelles. Such bodies of water, as we would refer to them now, are more like gigantic lakes. Indeed, it is at best what we now probably know as a small waterway, especially when we compare them to oceans like the Pacific Ocean, Atlantic Ocean or Indian Ocean. The same is true with the Sea of Azov. In fact, beyond Azov, there are no more significant bodies of waters. One simply cannot find such geographical entities to separate the two continents.

Clearly, based on the Greeks' knowledge of the geography, which was the height of knowledge of Western civilization at the time, they had gone as far as they could in comprehending the separation of the "continents." Yet by today's understanding, one would have to say that such a manner of thinking was at best inaccurate.

I cannot dispute Tonybee's claim that even in the ancient times of the Greeks, the names Europe and Asia had already arisen. However, judging on what bodies of water they based their separation of the continents on, it is at best amorphous by today's standard. Reading as much as I could about the continents of Asia and Europe, it made me ponder more deeply on the question:

When do Asians, like me, refer to themselves as Asians; and when do Europeans, like many of my Caucasians friends, refer to themselves as Europeans?

In many of the lectures on this subject I delivered globally, I had repeatedly posed it as a question to the audience. In searching the literature, I was unable to pinpoint a particular time or an era where these two names, Asians and Europeans, were used to describe people from more or less two ends of the same vast landmass.

Compared to all beings, humans have the most advanced intellectual capacity and it is not a surprise that they will and have developed complex cultures. Therefore, it is an interesting and significant fact that the two basic human cultures, what we now refer to as the Western and Eastern civilizations, essentially arose from Europe and Asia. Since the populations of Europe and Asia are so far apart from one another, it was possible almost from the start of human history for these two civilizations to evolve virtually in parallel but on non-overlapping tracks. Each civilization in its own manner has created its deep-seated "cultural habits" in assisting the humanistic evolution of the people it is designed to serve. Yet, to this day, never could the two civilizations be merged to create a new civilization for the betterment of humanity. Although starting in the 19th and 20th centuries, there has been increasingly more East–West movements, it nevertheless is true that the separation of the civilizations still remains obvious.

Many years ago, I took an English literature course during my undergraduate days at Drew University, Madison, New Jersey. I had an opportunity to read what the great English poet Rudyard Kipling wrote, as recently as in 1889, in his "Ballad of East and West" where he states:

Oh, East is East, and West is West, and never the twain shall meet,
Till Earth and Sky stand presently at God's great Judgment seat;
But there is neither East nor West, Border, nor Breed, nor Birth,
When two strong men stand face to face, though they come from
the ends of the earth!

At the time when I first read the poem, I was probably too young and too naïve to comprehend the profound implications. For several decades, on numerous occasions I noticed people would quote the first line of the poem to depict how far the East and the West were separated from one another culturally. In fact, the next three lines were, except for experts in English literature, almost forgotten by the general public. Looking at the poem now, I was quite exhilarated, especially the last line where Kipling may be predicting that the East and West become equal in strength: "*When two strong men stand face to face.*" How much such a meeting could impact humanity! With hindsight, I truly felt that these were elegant words that I wish I could have mastered the English language to express my feelings of substantial depth when I first encountered them.

For many years, this query of mine about why Europe and Asia are two continents and not one, and what it would mean if the two were to be considered as one, and how that could impact not just East and West, but humanity in general, has remained dormant in my mind. Indeed, as my life went in different directions, as a scientist, as corporate Vice-President and Senior Vice-President of different universities, this question was always lodged in the back of my mind. It was not until I started to learn about BRI that it again came to the forefront of my thoughts.

Transportation in the 21st Century

There is an ancient Chinese saying "要想富, 先造路," or "*the path to wealth is to first construct roads.*" The reason for this wisdom is transparently obvious. As long as there are human activities, there will be economic activities. Furthermore, as long as there were/are economic activities, humans must be transplanted from point A to point B. The more humans travel, as quickly as possible, the more economic development there will be.

In fact, such wisdom was not a prerogative of the Chinese. More than two centuries before Christ, the Romans had already mastered the skill of constructing roads. According to C. N. Trueman,[9]

Rome made a great deal of money from trade in Europe. Some of this trade involved transport by sea. More frequently, the Romans

---

[9] Trueman, C. N. (December 6, 2019). *Roman Roads.* Retrieved from https://www.historylearningsite.co.uk/ancient-rome/roman-roads/

used roads. Also, with so much of Western Europe conquered by the Romans, the Romans needed roads to move their troops around quickly. Poorly built roads would not help this.

By and large, as a species, humans are very slow-moving animals. Utilizing human's power to *walk* on the roads is a very slow process. After all, even the fastest runner in the world, Usain Bolt, can run at a maximum output of the energy from his body only a very short distance of 100 meters at a speed of 27.8 miles per hour. Normal people obviously can run at speeds that are significantly slower. Therefore, very early on, humans realized that they could travel much longer distances, only if they were to utilize the strengths of animals such as horses, who could on average gallop faster than humans over longer distances, such as 15 miles or so, without having human's intellect to comprehend the meaning of being "tired"!

An enormous transformation took place when humanity began to understand the principle of thermodynamics in the 19th century and leveraged it to invent mechanical devices, such as steam engines, to help humans move faster and longer distance. Very soon, trains powered by steam, and later on by coal, were invented, and humans and goods were able to cover longer distances. A defining moment for the United States was the construction of the "Trans-Continental Railroad" in the middle of the 19th century. It is obvious that this Railroad had a profound impact on the comprehensive development, economics or otherwise, of the United States in that century.

As a Chinese-American, it is certainly an ethnically proud moment for me to realize that Chinese migrant workers had made yeoman contributions to the "Trans-Continental Railroad." In an article entitled *Geography of Chinese Workers Building the Transcontinental Railroad: A virtual reconstruction of the key historic sites,* written by Gordon H. Chang, Shelley Fisher Fishkin and Hilton Obenzinger, it states that[10]

---

[10] Chang, G. H., Fishkin, S. F. and Obenzinger, H. (2019, August 15). Geography of Chinese Workers Building the Transcontinental Railroad A virtual reconstruction of the key historic sites. Retrieved from: https://web.stanford.edu/group/chinese-railroad/cgi-bin/website/virtual/.

Chinese were involved in building railroads in California long before 1863, when construction of the western portion of the transcontinental railroad, the Central Pacific Railroad (CPRR), began. In 1858 the Sacramento Union reported that 50 Chinese were hired for the construction of the California Central Railroad, and later Chinese worked on the railroad that linked San Francisco and San Jose. In 1864 Chinese began to work for the CPRR. In early 1865, when only a few white men answered the call for workers, large numbers of Chinese from communities in California began working on the CPRR. Soon shiploads of workers recruited from Guangdong province in China began to arrive. The Chinese worked until the CPRR was linked to the Union Pacific Railroad (UPRR) on May 10, 1869, and many continued to work on the CPRR and UPRR, as well as other railroads from California to New York.

Chinese migrant workers at the Trans-Continental Railroad construction site.

Source: Retrieved from http://web.stanford.edu/group/chineserailroad/cgi-bin/website/virtual/.

Two inventions from the beginning of the 20th century fundamentally thwarted the development of the rail network in the United States.

The first was the invention of automobiles. The name Henry Ford is certainly well known to nearly everyone on earth, and the story of how Ford almost singlehandedly built the company that would put fast-moving objects known as automobiles on the roads to transport goods and humans, was one such obstacle.

A moment when Ross Perot and I were chatting about something that amused us!

In 2006, I had a conversation with the former United States presidential candidate, Ross Perot. A very successful Texan entrepreneur, Mr. Perot's office was literally no more than a mile from my office at the University of Texas at Dallas. He told me that he knew the Ford family well and knew an interesting anecdote regarding Henry Ford and his good friend Thomas Edison. Perot told me that:

> Henry Ford was very proud of his assembly line concept of manufacturing cars. Although it should be pointed out that the first line was one in which the workers moved and the automobiles stood still. One day, Henry invited Edison to watch his proud creation. Edison watched it carefully, then asked "Henry, have you thought about moving the automobiles and not the workers?

I was absolutely flabbergasted by this story. It tells me never to take anything as "set in stone."

Something remarkable happened right after World War II. Recognizing the importance of land-based military personnel transportation, President Dwight D. Eisenhower made the proposal of the so-called "Interstate-Highway System"! Just like human blood vessels, the Interstate Highways are *de facto* the blood vessels of the nation, and the cars or trucks are the blood! Since automobiles can be and usually are privately owned, especially after WWII when more and more American families had significant disposable incomes, the rail transportation system, which cannot compete with the convenience of automobile transportation, was naturally outcompeted and diminished rapidly. Rail transportation in the United States essentially was relegated to only goods transportation.

A completed interstate (I-495) on Long Island, New York, in the late 1950s. (30-N-60-101).

Source: Retrieved from https://www.archives.gov/publications/prologue/2006/summer/interstates.html.

The second obstacle to rail transport came in 1903, just three years after the new century began. Two brothers, Orville Wright and Wilbur Wright, from Youngstown, Ohio, USA, invented a mechanical device which could (sort of) fly. This prompted Massachusetts Institute of Technology (MIT), which did not even know whether such a device was simply a science project or had real long-term business opportunities, to initiate a full aeronautical engineering program, from Bachelors to Master degrees, in 1909. An interesting fact about the MIT aeronautical engineering program, which few people are aware of, even at MIT today, is that it had a significant Chinese connection.

Remarkably, for some unknown reasons, many of MIT's first Master degree graduates were Chinese. This is poignant for the present discussion. This was because this group of Chinese, until their arrival to the United States to study, lived in the last and dilapidated years of the Qing Dynasty. Worldly sophistication could not have been part of their life experience. Yet, without the knowledge of whether aeronautical engineering could bring them a secure future or not, they pursued this discipline with full gusto!

Wong Tsoo when he was with Boeing in 1916.

Among them was Wong Tsoo (王助), who was sent by the Qing Government nearly in its last year, to study mechanical engineering in United Kingdom's Durham University. After graduation, Wong entered MIT's Aeronautical Engineering program to pursue a Master Degree.

It was remarkable that in 1916, Wong Tsoo, upon graduation from MIT, was immediately recruited by the "technologically ignorant" businessman Bill Boeing to be the Chief Technical Engineer for the company, to manufacture more flying machines. Later on, Wong Tsoo returned to China and played a significant role in developing the then fledgling Chinese aeronautical program.

A precious photo of Wong Tsoo (right) and Qian Xue-Sen (钱学森). The photo, a gift from Wong Tsoo's adopted son to me, was taken in 1947 in Shanghai Long-Hua (龙华) airport.

Throughout the 20th century, the flying device created by the Wright brothers in 1903 evolved into jumbo jets such as the Boeing 787 or the European Airbus A380 which unfortunately due to business reasons will be discontinued soon.

A giant poster in the International Airport of Seattle, Washington.

A truly memorable photo when I led the University of Texas at Dallas delegation to visit the Airbus headquarters in Toulouse, France, in 2004. Behind us is a model of the A380. A few years later, the A380 became commercially available.

More importantly, air transportation became one of the most important modes of long-distance travel, especially when it involved travel across vast oceans. In many ways, air transportation had essentially replaced rail transportation.

In the middle of the 20th century, there was a watershed moment for rail transportation. From October 10 to 24, 1964, the Olympics would be held in Tokyo, Japan. For a country that merely 19 years ago was one of the three which initiated World War II, one of the bloodiest human conflicts and towards the end of the war experienced massive and ubiquitous destruction, such a grand international event which could capture the world's attention was a great opportunity to showcase in a spectacular manner, that Japan had recovered and was reentering to the civilized world.

Surely it was no accident that because of the XVIII Olympics being held in Tokyo, the world's first so-called "bullet train," known as Shinkansen, made its debut on October 1, 1964, travelling from Tokyo to Osaka at a speed of 210 kilometers/hour (or 130 miles/hour). Although compared to the current fastest high-speed rail, which runs at around 400 kilometers/hour (or 250 miles/hour), the first Shinkansen may seem like a "slow coach," it was in fact the first sleek looking "high-speed rail" humanity had invented. It certainly created "oohs and ahhs" around the world and ushered into the world a new paradigm of rail transportation.

In the second half of the 20th century, "bullet trains," more commonly now known as "high-speed rail," grew rapidly in Japan, South Korea and Western European countries, such as France and Spain. In fact, the high-speed rail of France known as *Train à Grande Vitesse* (TGV) made worldwide news when it claimed for a while to be the fastest train clocking a speed of 574.8 km/h (357.2 mph).

Curiously, it should be noted that in the 20th century, none of the countries with enormous landmasses, such as United States, Canada, Soviet Union, China, India, Russia, and Australia, each with their own population size and distributions, financial and/or political reasons, showed any real movement in developing the high-speed rail. Indeed, at the beginning of the 21st century when I was the Vice-President for

This spectacular photo of the Shinkansen zipping by with Mount Fuji in the background is one of the best icons of high-speed rail.

Source: Retrieved from https://www.japanstation.com/shinkansen-high-speed-train-network-in-japan/.

Research and Economic Development at the University of Texas, Dallas, I noticed there was quite a bit of interest from various people in Texas who were enthusiastic in pushing for the creation of a high-speed rail network for the Dallas–Houston–San Antonio triangle. Thus far, as we are about to enter the third decade of the 21st century, there is still no sign that construction will begin anytime soon!

China's High-Speed Rail System

China began to study the feasibility of having a national high-speed rail system in the 1990s and started to build such a system in the 21st century. However, the initial construction, as can be expected, with financial and administrative challeges, was very slow. For example, in 2008, when the nation was hosting the Olympics in Beijing, some 44 years after the Tokyo Olympics, the country had only two high-speed rail lines. The first, which is essentially an engineering project, is the 30.5-kilometer magnetic levitating train the Chinese government had purchased from Germany. It runs from Shanghai Pudong Airport to downtown Pudong. The second is the "normal" high-speed rail that runs with a speed of 330 kilometers/hour covering the 117 kilometers between Beijing and Tianjin. This train was initiated on August 1, 2008. Of course, it is worth noting that Beijing hosted the Olympics between August 8 and August 24 the same year. Surely that was not a coincidence!

In 2004, I had my first and only experience on the Pudong Maglev Train.

From 2008 onwards, Chinese high-speed rail development simply exploded. During the next 10 years, what one observed in China was an ever-expanding and ubiquitous national high-speed rail system, with over 30,000 kilometers of the rail system constructed (see diagram.)

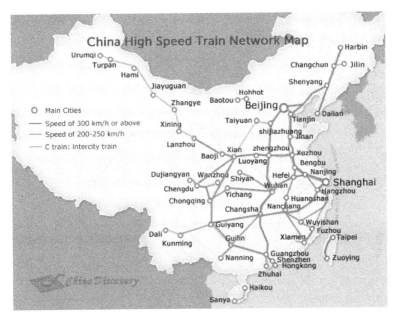

China High Speed Train Network Map (updated on December, 2019).

Source: Retrieved from https://www.chinadiscovery.com/china-maps/high-speed-railway-map.html.

One could certainly make numerous arguments as to why China, a nation with massive landmass and extremely high population density and with great aspiration, wants to develop the world's most advanced transportation system. However, unlike Japan, South Korea and Taiwan, all with very small landmasses and high populations, as long as there were political wills and financial means, they could build the high-speed rail systems, and they did. But China is different. For China to create a massive and nationally ubiquitous high-speed rail system, there must be something spectacular to cause it to so aggressively move forward in this direction.

In 2008, an absolutely disastrous global event took place, first in the United States. Soon afterwards, it spread to the world at large. On the surface, this seemed to have nothing to do with China's high-speed rail development. However, upon careful examination, it had everything to do with it. The following is what I learned from discussing about this issue with one of China's leading new-generation of economists, Dr. Liang Haiming. Dr. Liang is the Director of China's Silk Road Research Institute, the third largest think-tank of China.

On September 15, 2008, roughly two months before the U.S. Presidential election, Lehman Brothers Holdings Incorporated, a global financial services firm which began in 1850, and which had at that moment US$639 billion in assets and was US$619 billion in debt, declared bankruptcy. Such an action became the first salvo that caused what is now known as the 2008 global financial meltdown.

To meet the challenge of the financial meltdown, the United States government instituted the so-called "Quantitative Easing QE" policy. QE is an "expansionary monetary policy whereby a central bank buys predetermined amounts of large-scale assets."[11] For the laymen, this could simply be the government printing an excessive amount of money! From 2008 to 2014, the Federal Reserve Bank (The Fed) implemented a total of three QEs and one OT (reversal operation). Eventually, on October 29, 2014, when the US QE program was completely terminated, the Fed had purchased a total of US$4.5 trillion worth of assets.

Roughly during the same period, Europe subsequently experienced a massive debt crisis. The crisis began with Greece, and soon spread to Portugal, Spain and Italy, and each had to face its own respective sovereign debt crises. Confronted by this challenge, the European Central Bank also initiated an unprecedented QE. By the same token, in the Asia-Pacific region, Japan had also carried out a large-scale QE, printing a significant amount of Yens in order to purchase bonds. For the first time in history, the amount of currency "printed" by most countries in the world during that period far exceeded the historical average.

Against this unprecedented and virtually global campaign of money printing, the depreciation of national currencies was obviously very conducive to these countries' exports. Furthermore, the

---

[11] Quantitative easing. (n.d.). In *Wikipedia*. Retrieved September 1, 2019, from https://en.wikipedia.org/wiki/Quantitative_easing.

economic crisis experienced by Europe and the United States led to their economic downturn, and the consequences of this was significant reduction of their respective imports.

Therefore, due to the global financial crisis in the second half of 2008, in countries such as the United States, people obviously needed much less goods. This had the immediate impact of a severe reduction in imports. As a result, China's exports would and had experienced a very sharp downturn as well. China saw its export growth, which at the beginning of 2008 was in double digits, rapidly decline to negative growth at the end of the year. Indeed, in the first quarter of 2009, Chinese export was hit with a double-digit negative growth. Coupled with the export downturn, industrial production naturally fell sharply as well, and power generation showed no increase at all. In fact, a large number of small and medium-sized export enterprises were simply forced to shut down, thus causing many coastal areas of China to experience a massive wave of unemployment.

Facing an economic calamity, the Chinese government had to do something drastic in order to hedge such a dire challenge. To this end, the Chinese government began to print a vast amount of Renminbi. Indeed, in 2009, China, following the US QE policy, also decided to inject 4 trillion RMB to stimulate the Chinese economy. However, it should be noted that this action by the Chinese government was technically not a QE policy. The reason for this is very simple: the extra money injected into the market was not used to buy assets. From the Chinese perspective, the economic challenge it had at that time was large-scale unemployment. Therefore, it would be best if the extra money could be used to create jobs. So, China faced a new and interesting challenge: what to do with the printed "new money." Having an enormous amount of money sitting in financial institutions like banks certainly made no economic sense and could definitely not create jobs.

It is well known that any massive project requiring technically and logistically sophisticated and vast engineering input can, on average, stimulate fifty additional and different businesses downstream. This idea was deployed in 1935 when the United States was facing massive unemployment as a result of the "Great Depression." To overcome this challenge, President Roosevelt initiated the "Works Progress Administration" and got the US Congress to appropriate US$4.8 billion (nearly US$90 billion in 2018 dollars or RMB0.6 trillion) to build roads and miscellaneous public works. An enormous number of jobs was indeed created as a result. With that as a preamble, having to spend a massive amount of 4 trillion RMB, it seemed that constructing a nationwide "high-speed rail" system was obviously what " the doctor had precisely ordered."

On the one hand, to construct high-speed rail is a very expensive high-technology endeavor. This is especially so because China had to start the business from scratch. Not only did China needs to manufacture the trains, lay down the rails, construct tunnels and bridges and so on, it also needed to somehow obtain the sophisticated technology to run the system. Unlike Taiwan, which simply purchased lock stock and barrel and then transferred the technology from Western countries, China could not do so. Indeed, if China were to purchase high-speed rail technology from advanced nations like Japan and Germany, it would forever be dependent on the whims of the foreign countries for a transportation system which not only has civil benefits but military ones as well.

Thus, starting from 2009, with the trillions of Renminbi printed, China poured a significant proportion of these funds to initiate aggressive "money-burning" projects. One of them was to create a high-speed rail system nationwide. The project literally began with research and development in the field of high-speed rail technology, and then the tracks were laid down. Since the Chinese high-speed rail system is expected to be massive, many new technological advancements, previously thought unnecessary, were required. This and other projects were one of the many reasons stimulating China's economy, propelling it forward to surpass Japan in 2010 to become the 2nd largest economy in the world.

It is very ironical that if not for the 2008 financial crises, there would have been no incentive for China to create a nationwide high-speed rail system.

So, from 2008 when the global financial tsunami began until today, China has built a magnificent national high-speed rail system!

What Global Implication Does China's High-Speed Rail Have for the World

Until the 20th century rolled around, transcontinental transportation was mainly the responsibility of the large liners (remember the Titanic?) for ocean travel and automobiles or trains on highways and railways for continental travel, respectively. As far as hauling passengers was concerned, superhighways known as the "(President) Dwight D. Eisenhower National System of Interstate and Defense Highways," commonly known as the "Interstate Highway System," began to emerge in North American after WWII. Soon after, this trend was followed by United Kingdom and European nations. The West German Autobahn probably became world famous because it had no speed limit. I remember one time I had to drive from Frankfurt to Munich, and what I saw as merely a dot on the rearview mirror would become a car in no time at all!

Once the superhighway became ubiquitous, at least in North America, rail transportation was essentially relegated to a minor role, if it indeed had any at all!

As I have mentioned, the two historical large-scale intercontinental efforts were military (à la Alexander-the-Great and Genghis Khan) in their missions. In the 21st century, while there exist many regional military campaigns, such as those in Afghanistan and the Middle East, there is no obvious military intension or propensity to link Europe and Asia as in the ancient days. But it appears that the desire to "link-up" for economic, cultural, geopolitical and other reasons is no less intense today.

In the mid-1960s, Japan was the first country in the world to begin building a nationwide high-speed rail system known as Shinkansen. The definition of a "high-speed rail" is a train system that must achieve a speed of at least 250 kilometers/hour. For such a rail system to become prevalent, economic, technological development and political will must independently and simultaneously reach a certain threshold level. Japan was the first country in the world to "bite the bullet" to move into this rail new era. As time went on, nations in East Asia and Western Europe in the 21st century met this threshold, and now such rail systems can be found in many East Asian and Western European nations. Currently, Japan has a very extensive nationwide high-speed rail system.

Indeed, by the first decade of the 21st century, other countries such as South Korea and many European nations also built their own comprehensive high-speed rail systems. In fact, in this game, China is a "Johnny-come-lately" player. This is because China's nationwide high-speed rail network did not really begin until the global financial crises of 2008, by which time the other countries already reached a robust system. Of course, for whatever reason China constructed a high-speed rail system (see above discussion) it was a gangbuster effort. Within a decade, China, in its 9.5 million square kilometers landmass, built a full-fledged high-speed rail system spanning over 30,000 kilometers.

There is something fundamentally different between the high-speed rail systems of Japan, South Korea and European nations and China. Unlike China, all the other high-speed rail systems were created for countries with relatively small landmasses. China is the first country with an enormous landmass to construct such a system. To this day, other nations with massive landmasses such as Russia, United States, Canada, Brazil, India and Australia either do not have such a system or, at best, a very small and inconsequential — economically and socially — system. For example, Russia with a landmass 1.8 times larger than China has just completed a 770-kilometer high-speed rail between Moscow and Kazan in Central Asia.

From day one of humanity's existence, travel has been an insatiable and necessary part of human existence. This was why humans first walked, then leveraged animals' strength to travel further and faster, and ultimately knowing some of the fundamental principles of science, such as thermodynamics, hydrodynamics and electrodynamics, thus creating mechanical devices such as trains, automobiles, airplanes, and now possibly rockets, to assist transportation.

During the latter part of the 20th century, and certainly in the 21st century, extremely long-distance travel, especially intercontinental travel, was essentially the realm occupied by airplanes. For example, modern-day travel between Europe and Asia had entirely fallen on air travel. While there is a functional Trans-Siberian Railroad, no one in his/her right mind would want to use such a slow and probably very uncomfortable mode of transportation to go from one end of Asia to the other end of Europe, and vice versa.

In 1979, when I spent a year during my sabbatical at the Niels Bohr Institute in Copenhagen, I met many Chinese scientists visiting the Institute after China's "reform and opening up" transformation. I noticed that taking the trans-Siberian train to and from China was the cheapest transportation mode.

It is fair to say that flying from Shanghai to London is fast. However, unless you can fly first or business class where most people would not and cannot, a 12–14-hour flight cooped up in a narrow chair is extremely uncomfortable. Furthermore, all the land, nations, cultures, politics, and most important, people spread between Shanghai and London, for all intensive purposes, would be irrelevant and invisible to the traveler. Such irrelevance and invisibility have immediate and unintended consequences: the travelers cannot gain any appreciation and understanding of the histories, cultures, political systems, foods and ways and means of the people they travel over on their way to the destination.

In the 21st century, for whatever economical, sociological or political reason or reasons, except for the most remote and geographically challenging regions of the country, such as Tibet, China has nearly completed construction of high-speed rail system for a vast landmass.

What China has accomplished, in my mind, is that it has transformed the mindset of the 1.4 billion Chinese regarding how they would travel over fairly long distance. In fact, whether they know it or not, they have or could also transform the mindset of humanity on the subject of transportation. In the 21st century, this ancient wisdom needs to be modified to *"the path to wealth is to first construct high-speed rail"*! The 30,000 kilometers of the high-speed rail system, which is still expanding as we are writing this book, is making China's transportation leap modernized land transportation, and China's development from now on will no longer be deterred by a backward transportation system.

As China and other Asian and European nations discovered while developing a national high-speed rail system, it was met with technological, economic, social, legal and political challenges. One can imagine that developing an international high-speed rail system could be far more complex. Issues such as geopolitics and geo-legalities, for example, could be downright arduous. However, the fact that China in the past 10 years has developed a sophisticated high-speed rail system across a vast land with utterly different terrains, when no other country had done so, gives the anticipation that the world could take these accumulated knowledges and jump on this bandwagon to tackle the international challenges. Once again, BRI could be and is such an effort to take this on.

It is also worth underscoring that land and air travel are fundamentally different. In the latter, the passengers can only experience airports at both ends, while in the former they can actually come into contact with and experience everything in between, be it cities, villages and their associated respective cultures, histories, human behaviors, political changes and sensitivities, even cuisine, and so on. For an international high-speed rail system, from Asia to Europe, for example, this could greatly enhance people's understanding of each other and strengthen interactions, and these results could induce a broad and deep economic, cultural and even political impact and transformation.

In the current era, for the millions upon millions of travelers between Asia and Europe the journey is usually via air travel from one destination (such as Beijing, Hong Kong, Singapore or Mumbai) to the other (such as Frankfurt, Amsterdam or London). Great nations in between, such as the massive and resource-abundant Russia, the central Asian nations we mentioned before, the Eastern European nations and the Middle East are all "invisible" to the travelers. If, and when travelers could travel via the international high-speed rail system linking Europe and Asia, then on such a platform it is conceivable that the "cultural communication" (see Chapter 4) which is sorely lacking in the millions of travelers, can now be developed in a robust manner with hitherto unknown rapidity.

With the above reasoning, I have come to the conclusion that if there could be an Asia-Europe highspeed rail system, it could induce a profound millennium mindset transformation. A new mindset where "Europeans" and "Asians" think of themselves as people from the "Supercontinent." It was precisely for this reason in my talk in December 2013 in Taiwan's National Tsing Hua University that I felt that it was time to introduce the concept of "Supercontinent" to the audience.

I have to admit that being ignorant of the BRI introduced by President Xi Jinping just a few months before my talk in Hsinchu, Taiwan in December 2013, I had to approach the topic with a great deal of trepidation. In hindsight, had I known as I do now about the BRI, I would not have been as timid as I was throughout my talk. In fact, I would be shouting it out loud from the rooftops instead! It is also for this reason why I have confidence that by introducing BRI, which is "precisely what the doctor prescribed," it can and will in time induce a millennium mindset transformation of "Supercontinent."

Chapter 3

Neo-Renaissance: Humanity's Possibility to "Think-Out-Of-The-Box" to Mitigate Existential Challenges

> The creation of this culture will come from minds criss-crossing, admixing and colliding in the Supercontinent. It will be a culture which is neither East nor West. It is a way of thinking which is out of the "East" box and the "West" box!

In the last chapter, I discussed extensively the possibility of the creation of a Supercontinent mindset through BRI. The central theme is that even though from the beginning of earth's history, Europe and Asia have sat on a single enormous piece of landmass, they are now, in the mindset of humanity, "two continents." This distinguishable feature is unlike North America, South America, Africa and Australasia, where one can define them as continents simply by their geological structures.

One of the most remarkable outcomes of the conceptual and geographical separation of Europe and Asia as two continents is that two of the most important and dominating civilizations of humanity — the Eastern and Western civilizations — were initiated and flourished there, respectively. In fact, these two civilizations not only form the basic core of humanity's thinking in these respective continents, they are also the fundamental driving forces of the behavior, and indeed the ways and means of people from the East and the West. Due to the overreaching influences of the civilizations of the East and West, people from nearly all corners of the world, even when they are far from Europe and Asia, such as Africans and South Americans.

During the past 200 years, when people from the East and West interact, as is happening more than ever before, the separation has also become one of the fundamental sources of the misunderstandings and even conflicts between them. In this chapter, we will explore what could happen when people from Europe and Asia truly come together in the new Supercontinent mindset, and also what impact this could have on humanity.

East and West Merged into a New Civilization to Deal With Humanity's Challenges of Today?

Photo of Rudyard Kipling.

Source: Retrieved from https://commons.wikimedia.org/w/index.php?curid=44696911.

Rudyard Kipling (1865 AD–1936 AD) in his famous poem of 1889 "The Ballard of East and West" began with the stanza:

OH, East is East, and West is West, and never the twain shall meet.

Undoubtedly, this stanza profoundly outlines Westerners' inherent view about the two civilizations. Indeed, for many millenia, the twain, as mentioned by Kipling, developed their civilizations and ways and means in utterly different and non-overlapping manner. Although it is not transparent in what he wrote, for Kipling to put these words together at that moment in time surely displays his deep sense of superiority. It would have been very difficult, if not impossible, in Kipling's era, to even detect the minutest Eastern flavor in Western civilization. The reverse is equally and profoundly true.

It is worth underscoring that the sentiment of Kipling is also vividly reflected in the byline written by the Nobel Committee for the very first Asian Nobel Prize winner, Rabindranath Tagore from India, in 1913. This Nobel Prize in literature was awarded to an Asian just 13 years after the Prize was unveiled and 24 years after Kipling, who was also a laureate, wrote his poem. The byline describing why Tagore was awarded the prize is as follows:

> because of his profoundly sensitive, fresh and beautiful verse, by which, with consummate skill, he has made his poetic thought, expressed in his own English words, a part of the literature of the West.[1]

A remarkable photo of Tagore in China. Standing on Tagore's right was the brilliant and multidimensional, talented lady Ms. Lin Huiyin (林徽因) and on his left was the famous poet Xu Zhimo (徐志摩). This photo was supposedly taken on April 23, 1924 when Tagore visited China, with Ms. Lin and Mr. Xu serving as his translators.
Source: Retrieved from https://www.sohu.com/a/32222951_241433.

---

[1] Nobel Media AB 2019. (30 Dec 2019). *The Nobel Prize in Literature 1913*. Retrieved from the Nobel website https://www.nobelprize.org/prizes/literature/1913/summary.

As a reader of this byline in the 21st century, I was instantly struck by the last few words, which is "expressed in his own English words, a part of the literature of the West." Indeed, for the Nobel committee in 1913 to consider someone as intellectually powerful as Tagore to be worthy of a Nobel Prize in literature, one cannot help but to deeply feel that he received this highest accolade bestowed by the Western world only because his profound accomplishments were a part of the Western civilization! Viewing this through today's lenses, it is a marked sense of superiority.

By comparison, 100 years later in 2012, another Asian, Mo Yan of China, was also bestowed the Nobel Prize in literature. This time, the Nobel byline read as follows:

> who with hallucinatory realism merges folk tales, history and the contemporary.

Unlike the byline of Tagore, which not only discussed his work, but also portrayed his work within the context of Western civilization, this byline for Mo Yan simply zeroes in on the essence of his work without any discussion on how the work stands on any platform of civilization. Clearly, the superior tone of the Western civilization, which was so obvious in Tagore's byline, is now tempered down. Comparing the two bylines separated by a century, one can perceive there is a new realism of how West should view the East!

However, all is not well "on the Western front"! In May 2019, Hong Kong's *South China Morning Post* reported a speech by the US State Department Director of Policy Planning, Ms. Kiron Skinner. Ms. Skinner, a former student of the U.S. Secretary of State Condoleezza Rice, is a member of the brain trust within the State Department. In the SCMP report, it said that:

> Speaking about the challenge that the US perceives from China today — a challenge that is, broadly, appreciated across both major political parties — Skinner traversed dangerous ground. The fight with China, she said, was "a fight with a really different civilization and a different ideology and the US hasn't had that before."

I had the great fortune of meeting and discussing with Mo Yan the novel that won him the Nobel Prize at his office in Beijing Normal University in 2013.

...She added, most controversially, that China posed a particularly unique challenge as it represented "the first time that we will have a great power competitor that is not Caucasian."

While there is in the literature murmuring that Kipling could be a racist[2] and that his famous poem was merely a facade for his deep racial superiority mindset, a senior official in the U.S. State Department, Ms. Kiron Skinner, could so unabashedly cast the US–China conflict, which is an East–West conflict, in the rawest civilization terms. It is especially ironic that Skinner is *de facto* saying that in the 21st century, the United States, which encapsulates the Western civilization, is in her mind equivalent to the "white" Caucasian civilization.

Likewise, with China emerging now as a major economic power and encapsulating the Eastern civilization, it is one that belongs to

---

[2]Panda Ankit. (May 18, 2019). *'Declining' US Should Reject Race-Based Thinking and Embrace Innovation to Compete With China.* Retrieved from https://www.bbc.com/news/uk-england-manchester-44884913.

US State Department Director of Policy Planning Kiron Skinner trod dangerous ground when she spoke about the challenge the US perceives from China, Ankit Panda writes.

Source: https://www.scmp.com/news/china/diplomacy/article/3010577/declining-us-should-reject-race-based-thinking-and-embrace.

people of a different skin color. In this regard, all manifestations of East–West competition, be it a "trade-war," "financial competition (namely World Bank[3] vs. Asia Infrastructure Investment Bank[4])" or "military conflict" such as those brewing in the South China Sea, are simply reflections of something far deeper. The common denominator regarding all such conflicts is none other than the "clash of two civilizations," the civilizations that arose from the two ends of the supercontinent since human history began! This is the ultimate conflict confronting humanity today.

Graham Allison of Harvard University, looking at the East–West conflict purely through the Western lens said that[5]:

> When a rapidly rising power rivals an established ruling power, trouble ensues. In 11 of 15 cases in which this has occurred in the past 500 years, the result was war. The great Greek historian

---

[3] https://www.worldbank.org/

[4] https://www.aiib.org/en/index.html

[5] Top 15 Quotes by Graham T. Allison. (n.d.). Retrieved from https://www.azquotes.com/author/80216-Graham_T_Allison

Thucydides identified these structural stresses as the primary cause of the war between Athens and Sparta in ancient Greece. In his oft-quoted insight, "It was the rise of Athens and the fear that this inspired in Sparta that made war inevitable."

While the point of views expounded by Allison and Skinner could be open to debate, especially when contrasting it with the Eastern view point, it nevertheless is clearly and deeply embedded in the Western mindset. This minacious view of Allison was pointed out succinctly by Martin Jacques, a well-known British journalist, as follows[6]:

> Globalisation has obliterated distance, not just physically but also, most dangerously, mentally. It creates the illusion of intimacy when, in fact, the mental distances have changed little. It has concertinaed the world without engendering the necessary respect, recognition and tolerance that must accompany it.

Such an eventuality, as predicted by Allison and Skinner, could be catastrophic for humanity if it were allowed to run its course.

A photo that I took with Martin Jacques at the Second Belt and Road International Cooperation Forum in Beijing on April 27, 2019.

---

[6]Jacques, Martin. (April 27, 2019). *Martin Jacques Quotes.* Retrieved from https://www.brainyquote.com/quotes/martin_jacques_630669.

Therefore, the ultimate question confronting all of humankind, East or West or beyond, is whether there is a way to mitigate such a catastrophic eventuality. Perhaps what is needed now, more than ever, is for human beings to "break out" from its "Western mindset" or "Eastern mindset," and form a new mindset that has never existed in human history.

The Renaissance as the Best Human Lesson of Leveraging "Think-Out-Of-The-Box" Mentality to Solve the World's Challenges Existing at That Time

It is indisputable that one of the greatest human intellectual creative eras, if not the greatest, that profoundly impacted humanity in science, technology, arts, music, languages, even politics and every other conceivable social and cultural ways and means, not just then but also impacting us to the present day, is the Renaissance. This great era, which lasted from the 14th to the 17th century, was a prodigious manifestation of human vigor and vitality. Viewed from the lens of the 21st century, one could in fact categorically say without any hesitation that before and after the Renaissance, there were two unrecognizable worlds. The fact that the Renaissance happened entirely in Europe allowed Western nations, first in Europe and later including North America, especially the United States, to leverage the knowledge gained from it to dominate the world in nearly every possible dimension. For the first time since humanity existed, Western civilization's supremacy was able to impact Eastern civilization in a one-way manner for many centuries.

With the above preamble in mind, I will explore what, in my opinion, are some fundamental lessons humanity has learned from the Renaissance that have not been explored already. Furthermore, if, and when the mindset of a Supercontinent were to become commonplace, in which one could seamlessly fuse the Western and Eastern mindsets into a new Supercontinent mindset, how then will such an eventuality impact humanity?

The Renaissance allowed and still allows humanity to explore and understand nature and oneself with scientific methodologies.

In fact, the entire scientific scaffolding of today is erected on the foundations of the discoveries of the Renaissance. It created new and absolutely powerful intellectual tools, such as calculus in the field of mathematics, for the purpose of enabling progress and deepening our understanding of nature. It is known that the most startling impact the Renaissance had and still has is that with unprecedented ways of thinking about humanity's surroundings and oneself, it literally lifted humanity out of its enormous cocoon of ignorance and allowed it to overcome many challenges of the time. Ultimately, it also allowed a human being to have a deeper understanding of himself or herself. One can safely say that since the Renaissance, which began some 700 years ago, the Western civilization standing on this underpinning certainly has and continues to alter humanity's future path.

I believe that if it is successful, the BRI will be the driving force of the creation of a Supercontinent mindset. It may induce a similar but even mightier era. In the 21st century, with all the daunting and existential global challenges hitherto unmet by humanity, a new transformation is clearly needed, now more than ever. This is why I became enthusiastic about the neo-Renaissance, a new era which I am confident that the BRI could bring about.

My interest in this field occurred quite serendipitously. As I mentioned in the last chapter, the genesis of the idea was the LERU–AEARU meeting in December of 2013, at Taiwan's National Tsing Hua University. Among the participants attending the meeting were leaders of universities from Europe and East Asia. There is one stark characteristic difference between these two groups of universities: The European universities are all "old," namely they were founded either before, during or slightly after the Renaissance. For example, the oldest university is Oxford University, which was founded at the end of the ninth century, 1096 AD to be precise. Even though the East Asian universities, in terms of cultures they stood on are as "old," if not "older" than the European counterparts, they are all "new" universities. Among them, the oldest is Tokyo University, which was founded in 1886, more than 800 years after the founding of Oxford University!

Tokyo University (Founded in 1886 AD).

A photo that I took with the former President of Tokyo University, Professor Akito Arima.

Yet, despite the vast differences in their founding dates and possessing understandable yet deep cultural differences, in their approaches to academic ambiance with vitality, they are all institutions of higher learning that are seriously searching for the most efficient and appropriate manner in the present day to educate the youth to prepare them to be responsible and useful citizens of the 21st century.

Clair College, Cambridge University (founded in 1209 AD).

Source: Retrieved from http://www.universitytimes.ie/2018/05/cambridge-to-introduce-trinity-inspired-access-programme/.

One cannot help but be impressed that, in this respect, it is truly remarkable that even after nearly a millennium, weathering the enormous ups and downs of social changes and political turmoils, sometimes quite violent, of the British Empire, Oxford University and Cambridge University, which were founded in 1096 AD and 1231 AD, respectively, are able to firmly holding on to their deep and broad inherent intellectual strengths. Throughout nearly a millennium of existence, they have produced faculty and students whose lifetime achievements were able to alter the vectors of

Keble College, Oxford University (Founded in 1096 AD).
Source: Retrieved from https://en.wikipedia.org/wiki/Keble_College,_Oxford.

humanity's existence. For these reasons, the intellectual ambience of Cambridge and Oxford were and still are capturing the imagination of people around the world, even in the 21st century.

It is with the above background that in designing the agendas for the LERU–AEARU conference, I felt that for the first time ever, it was a unique setting of top-ranking universities' leaders and from two disparate regions of the world responsible for the creation of the East and West civilizations coming into direct contact, I felt that there were two pressing issues that should receive the attention of those in attendance.

The first is: what is the fundamental purpose of universities. While this may be an obvious question, it is one which I felt that currently — where universities are literally dotted in every country, from the most powerful to the least — rarely is this question raised. Failing to do so, I felt sometimes educators have missed the opportunity to truly and actively seek solutions to assist humanity to conquer some of its current and unprecedented challenges.

The second issue is what and how European and Asian universities that were endowed with the two major world civilizations could find common ground so that together they could shoulder some of the universal responsibilities and create innovative ideas and change mindsets to push the boundary of knowledge as well as to proactively meet humanity's 21st century challenges.

With these two issues in my mind, I began to wonder if indeed Europe and Asia were to become — in the mindset of people — an amalgamated Supercontinent, a subject which I had discussed extensively in the previous chapter. If so, what roles could these leading universities, represented by those in LERU and AEARU, play in this new paradigm?

During the Renaissance, even with just the most cursory examination, one could discover that universities were the fundamental venues for the proliferation of new and correct ideas. Thus, with this as the lesson, can universities in the Supercontinent be like those in the Renaissance era, be nurtured and grow from strength to strength? Could they play a similar pivotal role in systematically creating and transferring knowledge from one generation to the next and let each generation make its own respective fundamental contributions to humanity? Finally, would it be possible that "neo-Renaissance" universities seek out-of-the-box solutions to the challenges of today's world?

There is one fundamental difference between the Western "old" universities and the Eastern "new" universities. The Western universities are led by individuals who are all educated "locally," and therefore continue to bask in their Western civilization, essentially showing no propensity or desire to introduce Eastern civilization in a fundamental manner into their universities. The Eastern ones, however, are led by individuals, many of whom have had significant Western immersed education, and thus have followed the natural tendency to introduce Western civilization into their universities.

Having all the leaders of LERU's "old" universities that not only have deeply inherited the Western civilizations but also the Renaissance ways and means in totality, and all the leaders of AEARU's "new" universities who have deeply inherited the Eastern civilizations, are existing in one of the most vibrant regions of the world in the 21st century and are in the process of absorbing and sometimes extending the Western civilizations, I thought this would be a rare opportunity of historical significance to have the combined "old" and "new" institutional leaders engage in a serious dialogue on the meaning of universities and perhaps design an innovative road-map for higher education in today's global landscape.

This is especially exciting because the participants could utilize the Renaissance as a case study, in order to project some under-standing of what the present-day challenges of universities are. I also wanted to leverage this opportunity to plant the seed in the minds of those attending the forum what that would mean as we move for-ward in the 21st century. For me, this is because the modern form of universities was essentially created during the Renaissance, and this would be one of the rare occasions where contemporary leaders from East and West, especially when the Western universities' lead-ers lacking interest in the Eastern civilization, were all under the same conference roof and would be conducive to have a serious and extended conversation together about higher education.

Unquestionably, the Renaissance is one of the historical crown jew-els that fundamentally transformed the existence of humanity. Throughout my academic career, I have noticed that whenever there was a conversation regarding the Renaissance, it would inevitably and often exclusively be about the great maestros of that era, where early Renaissance names such as Leonardo da Vinci and Michelangelo and many of their contemporaries who pioneered arts, engineering, medi-cine and science, would be discussed. A central theme of their contributions is how they successfully amalgamated the various disci-plines together in a seamless manner, what we in modern-day lingo term as "interdisciplinary." If pressed further, names of geniuses of later generations, such as Galileo Galilei, René Descartes, Nicolaus Copernicus and Francis Bacon, to name just a few, would be expounded upon.

  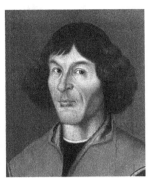

Portraits of Galileo Galilei, Descartes and Nicolaus Copernicus.

Source: Retrieved from https://en.wikipedia.org/wiki/Galileo_Galilei, https://en.wikipedia. org/wiki/Ren%C3%A9_Descartes, and https://en.wikipedia.org/wiki/Nicolaus_Copernicus.

Finally, those post-Renaissance geniuses such as Isaac Newton and James Clark Maxwell in the sciences, and even Charles Darwin, would be mentioned with great propensity. It is probably not an exaggeration that the 21st century economic powers of the world, such as China and the United States, would not exist if humanity did not understand nature through the works of Newton and Maxwell.

It is well known that great ideas do not come about in isolation. Indeed, how knowledge was accumulated, distilled and systematically distributed are also often cited as one of the reasons for the greatness of the Renaissance era. This was best summarized by Isaac Newton, who in 1675 AD said that:

If I have seen further it is by standing on the shoulders of Giants.

In hindsight, it is difficult to accept that Charles Darwin, great as he was, if he did not stand on the shoulders of all the great minds who created and accumulated knowledge from the Renaissance and the Post-Renaissance eras, would a Darwinian era have been possible? Also, if we did not fully comprehend Newtonian mechanics, Maxwellian electromagnetism and the quantum mechanics of Schrödinger, Bonn, Heisenberg and Bohr in the 20th century, would we have the global economics dominating semiconducting industries in the 21st century?

Of course, no one would or should argue that the accomplishments of the maestros are not everlasting. An intriguing question one could ask at this point is "what would be their commonality?" Since their accomplishments existed in disparate and fundamental areas of knowledge, their commonality cannot be their contributions in their respective disciplines.

In fact, a commonality of the maestros from the Renaissance and Post-Renaissance eras is that they were all intimately in one way or another associated with the universities of the era. While it was true that da Vinci and Michelangelo did not receive formal university education, their work surely became an inalienable component of the university curriculum during the Renaissance and Post-Renaissance eras — and some would say even to this day!

Since the maestros were so powerful in creating thoughts in the minds of humanity, one must inquire: "Are these giants and their profound contributions to all forms of knowledge the sole essence of the Renaissance?" While this question may be intriguing, the answer, for me, is "definitely not"!

Universities in the Renaissance Era

For me, the Renaissance era must be regarded as one which created one of the greatest, if not the greatest, social movements of human history. That social movement is the creation and proliferation of the modern form of universities. The consequence of such a creation which spans over many centuries is that a massive number of young minds coming from all economic backgrounds were given correct and systematic knowledge to collectively alter the course of human history. Indeed, there are numerous other social movements throughout human history which had risen and fallen, but the social movement of creating universities during the Renaissance appears to be sustainable.

As far as universities are long-lasting and sustainable, the best examples I can cite are Britain's Oxford University and Cambridge University. Despite the human darkness coming from many dimensions, despite the tremendous and profoundly deep ignorance about nature and human understanding of self during their nearly a millennium of existence, and despite their existence at a time where the lack of accurate scientific knowledge was the norm, these two universities were created for the purpose of bringing in thousands upon thousands young minds to effectively and systematically educate them by the best faculty one could find in order to make human beings acquire a more accurate understanding of nature and themselves. Ultimately, these students and faculty were able to collectively lift the masses of Europe, and eventually humanity, out of ignorance as much as possible.

As with all universities, past and present, there is a well-known but seldom mentioned fact, and that is sitting in the classes with the likes of *Copernicus, Bacon* and *Newton,* were many of their classmates. These classmates were also, presumably just like the maestros, admitted to the respective universities because they were the *crème de la crème.* In the years they were together as students, they would receive identical education and probably spent significant amounts of time engaging in discussions, and maybe even heated debates. It is well known that no matter how much inherent intelligence nature had bestowed the maestros, such debates would surely have had indelible impact not just on the classmates but on the maestros as well.

As I have emphasized, it is universally true that creation of new knowledge is always a cumulative and collaborative effort, directly or subliminally. It is certainly not beyond the realm of possibilities that the discoveries of the maestros may simply just be the end of a very long and arduous research process: It is "the straw that broke the camel's back," so to speak. Judging from my many years of university teaching, this was indeed the norm and not the exception. For this reason, and as human behaviors are quite predictable, I therefore am fully convinced that such must have been the case during the Renaissance. For most, if not all, of the thousands upon thousands of students who received the same and large volume of knowledge during the Renaissance, they may not have possessed the natural deep abilities of the maestros to create eternally and equally important masterpieces. But they too, I am sure, have contributed significantly in their own diminutive ways to the magnificent and enormous scaffolding of knowledge, even if it were simply just a piece of nail towards the growth of new knowledge at that time. Looking from this perspective, it is unquestionable that the core and fundamental contribution of universities is simply to bring forth a cadre of individuals to mold the future of humanity.

Therefore, these are the reasons why the universities must exist. It was true during the Renaissance era; it is no less true today.

There is another fundamental importance of how Renaissance could be beneficial to humanity, and that is how its scientific methodologies were instrumental in changing the course of human history. The best example is how the Renaissance led to a correct understanding of a natural phenomenon is the monumental work of the Polish mathematician and astronomer, Nicolaus Copernicus, who lived between 1473 AD and 1543 AD.

A statue of Copernicus.

Source: Retrieved from https://www.trekearth.com/gallery/Europe/Poland/West/Kujawsko-Pomorskie/Torun/photo1257314.htm.

Copernicus' work, which is given the glorious name "The Copernicus Revolution," was the utilization of mathematical and scientific methodology to overturn the long-held principle of "geo-centrism," which for several millennia erroneously places the earth at the center of the solar system, and replaced it with the principle of "heliocentrism," which places the sun at the center.

In the many centuries of the history of science, there were numerous well-known writings depicting the details of this monumental work of Copernicus. For this reason, I will not repeat them here. Suffice to

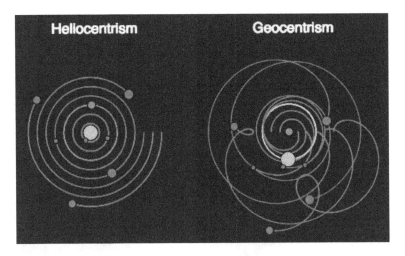

Comparison of Heliocentrism and Geocentrism.

Source: Retrieved from https://www.youtube.com/watch?v=waexG16WZrE.

say that from the above depiction, it is obvious that in order to have the model to fit the observation, geocentrism would require an enormous amount of twists and turns (and still not be successful) while heliocentrism is simple and direct. Einstein has a famous quotation, which is german in this regard — make many things as simple as possible, not simpler.

However, there is one important point that I have not seen discussed explicitly but which is of fundamental importance in our discussion of the Belt and Road Initiative. Thus, I would like to discuss it here.

Obviously, since the 19th century, when scientists proposed a revolutionary idea based on sound scientific arguments, he/she did not need to fear severe social repercussions. This was true with Maxwell writing down the famous Maxwell equations for electromagnetism in the mid-19th century and even for Einstein introducing special and general relativity in 1905 and 1915, respectively. Other breakthrough scientific discoveries that significantly altered the course of humanity were when Heisenberg, Schrodinger and Bonn agreed on their respective forms of quantum mechanics during the 5th Solvay Conference in 1927; when Watson and Crick proposed the Deoxyribonucleic acid or DNA model in 1953 at Cambridge University; and when Darwin came up with his theory of evolution (which did get some pushbacks from the religious-right.)

Photo of the 1927 Solvay Conference, a conference which gave birth to quantum mechanics. Fifth from the right in the front row is Albert Einstein.

Source: Retrieved from https://rarehistoricalphotos.com/solvay-conference-probably-intelligent-picture-ever-taken-1927/.

Unfortunately for Copernicus, and later Galileo, for example, they did not have the same "easy time" as their colleagues in the 19th and 20th centuries. The following paragraph is quoted from the preface of an article written by Maurice A. Finnachiaro[7]:

> In February–March 1616, the Catholic Church issued a prohibition against the Copernican theory of the earth's motion. This led

---

[7]Finocchiaro, M. A. (February, 2016). *400 Years Ago the Catholic Church Prohibited Copernicanism*. Retrieved from http://origins.osu.edu/milestones/february-2016-400-years-ago-catholic-church-prohibited-copernicanism.

later (1633) to the Inquisition trial and condemnation of Galileo Galilei (1564–1642) as a suspected heretic, which generated a controversy that continues to our day. Do these Church actions prove the incompatibility between science and religion? What lessons can be learned from the thought and actions of Galileo, who became the "Father of Modern Science"?

As can be seen from the above paragraph, it is clear that as great as the intellectual capacities of Copernicus and Galileo were, they existed in an era where humanity was deeply shrouded in profound ignorance. For this reason, in my mind, there is something even more important than there was a Copernicus revolution. If indeed these maestros were mentally not sufficiently resilient and succumbed to the pressure arising from the Roman Catholic church and did not "correct" the erroneous "geocentrism," and conducted their research based on the underpinning of the conventional Catholic doctrines, they would surely have met with utter failure.

This example signals that there are moments in human history where a "think-out-of-the-box" mindset is not just critical but absolutely necessary in seeking solutions to formidable challenges. With that understanding under our belt, we cannot stress enough here that the lesson we have learned from the above-mentioned Copernicus example is that besides the great works emerging from the Renaissance, it was the Renaissance which brought to the world an entirely new mindset which allow revolutionary ideas for humanity to think about its surrounding.

Fast forward to today, even the most casual observer will realize that humanity in the 21st century is facing a multitude of existential challenges.

Modern-Day Challenges

One could say that while the challenges to humanity such as profound ignorance during the Renaissance were severe, it is no comparison to the challenges of modern day. This is because in the modern day, the challenges are existential. Let us consider the challenges during the Renaissance era. Of course, it was deeply satisfying that Copernicus was able to make us understand with scientific precision that the earth is not at the center of the solar system. Yet if humanity were to prolong such ignorance, it would not have caused the earth as a planet in the solar system to endure irreparable harm to the point of causing the living creatures cease to exist.

Compared to the Renaissance era, the modern-day existential challenges are entirely of a different magnitude. One of them is population explosion. The following diagram clearly depicts the challenge in a most vivid manner.

HUMAN POPULATION GROWTH

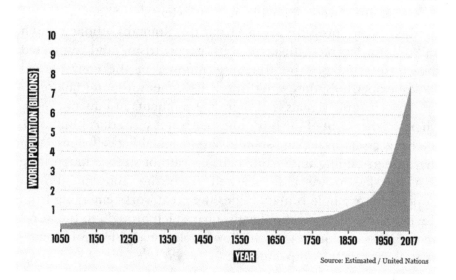

This graph clearly shows the explosive nature of human population.

Source: Retrieved from https://populationmatters.org/the-facts/the-numbers?gclid=Cj0KC QiAtvPjBRDPARIsAJfZz0pkPa3rOBjK8xhs6aFzNOw4PCOWyZiRynP2uPUKIgmMPq1W_ q2ZbyYaAkhdEALw_wcB.

From the above chart, it is obvious that the world population throughout the Renaissance era remained essentially at a plateau of around half of billion people. During the 20th and 21st centuries, the growth is exponential, rising from 1.5 billion to over 7 billion. This growth is a result of many factors, such as the abundance of food supply as well as improvement of healthcare. Facing such an explosive growth, which will bring about many collateral challenges, such as food and water shortage, humanity must now seek out-of-the-box mitigations.

Let me also discuss the example of global warming.

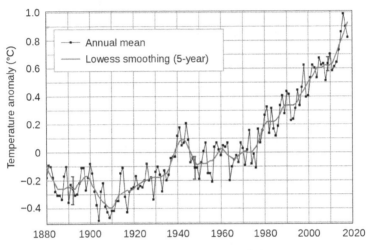

Global Land-ocean Temperature Index.

Source: Retrieved from https://en.wikipedia.org/wiki/Global_temperature_record#/media/File:Global_Temperature_Anomaly.svg.

Just as with population growth, before the 20th century, the earth's temperature remained fairly constant. There is an obvious acceleration in the growth of the earth's temperature in the 20th century, especially after 1980.

In a recent editorial with the title "How China and Asia can lead the fight against global warming along the belt and road" that Dr. Michael Celia, Theodora Shelton Pitney Professor of Environmental Studies, of Princeton University and I published in Hong Kong's *South China Morning Post*, we wrote that[8]:

---

[8] Celia, M. and Feng, D. H. (September 8, 2017). *How China and Asia can lead the fight against global warming along the belt and road*. Retrieved from https://www.scmp.com/comment/insight-opinion/article/2110296/how-china-and-asia-can-lead-fight-against-global-warming.

This photo was taken when Dr. Michael Celia visited the University of Macau.

The average global temperature for 2016 was already more than one degree above pre-industrial levels. Furthermore, the increases are not uniform globally. For example, there are much larger temperature changes in the high northern latitudes, as evidenced by rapidly melting Arctic sea ice and Greenland ice sheets. In addition, warming oceans and melting ice sheets contribute to accelerated sea level rise.

These observed temperature changes, and their associated impacts, are consistent with long standing scientific predictions. The current temperature increases show that we are approaching the 1.5-degree mark for the global average and are well on our way to the 2-degree limit set out in the Paris accords.

As the earth's temperature continues to rise, there will be many regions on earth where the temperature would be unsuitable for human existence. One of the obvious outcomes, even in the absence of wars, would be massive migration of the population.

Such migrations would have unimaginable political and social devastations. If climate change continues to progress unchecked, and the window of mitigating is rapidly closing, the survival of Earth in the 22nd century will be in question. Despite many pushbacks, even by some leaders of Western nations, the evidence that global warming is not a natural but rather a human-made phenomenon is scientifically irrefutable. Since it is human-made, then human as a species must find ways to overcome it.

The challenges facing humanity today go well beyond ignorance. They are impacting each living being in an existential manner. Obviously, to mitigate them, one would require a significantly new mindset. It is interesting to note that for the last millennium, as I have discussed, the Renaissance made the Western civilization dominant in all aspects of human interactions. It is therefore natural that whenever challenges arise today, the tendency is to find ways to mitigate it with the Western mindset.

In his 2018 MIT Compton Lecture,[9] Thomas Friedman, the world-renowned author mentioned the acceleration of climate change. His most stunning statement was that:

As far as climate change is concerned, "later" is officially over!

In other words, with acceleration of climate change, not mitigating it immediately and waiting until "later" is no longer a luxury but a must. However, it goes without saying that even those individuals as broad-minded and intellectually deep as Thomas Freidman can only think of mitigation that is based entirely on Western ways and means.

As a senior higher education administrator for nearly two decades, I had the pleasure and the honor to meet many of my counterparts from all corners of the world. I recall at every meeting, we had discussions on multiple of issues. One would inevitably be how universities should and could assume the responsibility of

---

[9]MIT Institute Events. (October 1, 2018). MIT Compton Lecture: Thomas L. Friedman, 2018. [Video]. YouTube. Retrieved from https://youtu.be/9WmWnIdhbq4.

shouldering this imminent challenge of humanity. It is interesting that in every conversation I had on this issue, my counterpart from the West would inform me how his/her university is carrying out excellent research in climate change. As politeness was an absolute necessity in such a discussion, I remember I could only tell myself in silence that "don't you know that despite your university's excellent work in this research area, the globe is still warming?"

It is obvious that these challenges such as climate change, despite many vigorous intellectual, social and geopolitical efforts to date (such as the "Paris Climate Agreement")[10] to find ways to mitigate it, one could only conclude that at present — just as what Professor Michael Celia and I have concluded — there is no sign of abatement.

Of course, one could argue that this may be because such efforts to date, however vigorous, are inadequate. For example, just recently, a group of scientists from Australia's Royal Melbourne Institute of Technology made the claim that they have developed an entirely innovative technique that in principle can efficiently convert CO_2 from gas form into solid form.[11]

As is well known in all technological developments, whether such "scientific bench efforts" could be scaled up is, of course, the arduous challenge. As Dr. Michael Celia, the Director of Princeton University's Institute of Environmental Studies said so succinctly:

> Perhaps at some point in the future, one of these technologies will scale up to the gigatonne scale and help to solve the climate problem

---

[10]Krifka, K. (April 23,2018). *Biodiversity and Meeting our Climate Goals Go Hand In Hand.* Retrieved from https://climatetrust.org/biodiversity-and-meeting-our-paris-climate-goals-go-hand-in-hand/?gclid=CjwKCAjw583nBRBwEiwA7MKvoLUdLX huHC67GhRMHG%20h7Kw5TLGskZXH14jL27MXrFhBvrWQ_QQhoiRoC07 EQAvD_BwE

[11]Kaszubska, G. (February 27, 2019). *Climate Rewind: Scientists Turn Carbon Dioxide Back Into Coal.* Retrieved from https://www.rmit.edu.au/news/all-news/2019/feb/carbon-dioxide-coal.

Such efforts, in the past, exciting as they may be, were not able to fulfil this requirement.

Another interesting example is the search for the cure of cancer. For Western medicine, when faced with enormous challenge of the complex disease of cancer, it could only introduce "fire power," namely, gaining a deeper understanding of human's biochemistry, developing more sophisticated and technologically advanced detection tools, introducing invasive operations and sophisticated chemotherapy to literally destroy the cancer cells. In 1971, President Richard Nixon proposed a "grand challenge" known as "War on Cancer." According to the report given in Wikipedia[12],

> The War on Cancer refers to the effort to find a cure for cancer by increased research to improve the understanding of cancer biology and the development of more effective cancer treatments, such as targeted drug therapies. The aim of such efforts is to eradicate cancer as a major cause of death. The signing of the National Cancer Act of 1971 by United States president Richard Nixon is generally viewed as the beginning of this effort, though it was not described as a "war" in the legislation itself.

It is worth noting that after half a century since President Nixon's declaration, there is no sign that humanity has won the war.

In the 21st century, there are increasing medical murmurs that cancer may require not just "targeted solutions," *à la* Western medicine, but a combination along with "holistic solution," *à la* Eastern medicine.[13] Yet, Western and Eastern medicines, respectively, are based entirely on Western and Eastern civilization platforms, and as

---

[12]War on Cancer. (n.d.). In *Wikipedia*. Retrieved September 1, 2019, from https://en.wikipedia.org/wiki/War_on_cancer.

[13]Wang, E. A. (n.d.) *East Meets West: How Integrative Medicine is Changing Health Care*. Retrieved from https://exploreim.ucla.edu/health-care/east-meets-west-how-integrative-medicine-is-changing-health-care/.

Kipling said, "and never the twain shall meet." At the moment, there indeed are some concerted efforts in Western medicine to inculcate Eastern medical practices, and the reverse is true as well. But, to date, such efforts have not created an entirely new medicinal culture that takes in the good and remove the bad of both.

From the above discussions, the solution to the challenges facing humanity today is a real necessity for "the twain to meet." After all, many of the major challenges are unlikely to be mitigated by the current mindset, East or West. In a sense, since the East and West mindsets still remain far apart, such a "meeting" has never been seriously tried before.

On March 28, 2019, at the 73rd Session of the High-Level Meeting on Climate and Sustainable Development, the General Assembly of the United Nations, Maria Fernanda Espinosa Garcés (Ecuador) warned that:

> We are the last generation that can prevent irreparable damage to our planet" in her opening remarks. She stressed that "11 years are all that remain to avert catastrophe".

Highlighting the meeting's theme, Ms. Espinosa called for an intergenerational approach to climate change. "Climate justice is intergenerational justice." she said, calling on countries around the globe to act collectively and responsibly.[14]

Confronted by these serious challenges, while it is still critically important, what is needed is no longer simply just scientific or human knowledge breakthroughs, which until today was what took place throughout and since the Renaissance era. After all, as with the example of climate change, despite the significant scientific and technological progresses, "the earth is still warming"! What this warming is signaling to us is that the current methodology — scientific, technological and political — humans have utilized to mitigate

---

[14]United Nations. (March 28, 2019). *Only 11 Years Left to Prevent Irreversible Damage from Climate Change, Speakers Warn During General Assembly High-Level Meeting.* Retrieved from https://www.un.org/press/en/2019/ga12131.doc.htm.

climate change, which is fundamentally via purely Western ways and means, may simply be inadequate to mitigate these imminent and existential disasters!

The fact that humanity is currently failing badly in mitigating the existential challenges surely means that one needs to try something that hitherto had not been explored. We need to be reminded that from 14th to 17th centuries, the Renaissance introduced a form of thinking which was entirely "out-of-the-box." In the 21st century and beyond, one way to also "think-out-of-the-box" is to combine the efforts of people from different civilizations, different ways and means, different public policies and so on so that one could come up with an entirely new mindset, one which is neither tied to Eastern nor Western civilizations but both.

While humanity has developed various civilizations, the Eastern and Western civilizations are obviously the most dominating ones. Yet, to date, they are still so far apart in nearly all dimensions. Hence, if there were a way to amalgamate them into one that carries the flavor of both but is significantly neither, humanity with this new paradigm may have the opportunity to be able to jump out from the Eastern and Western "sandboxes." In this new platform, humanity may just find some truly innovative ways to mitigate existential challenges. The question is how one could reach such a lofty goal?

Neo-Renaissance Induced by the Belt and Road Initiative

As I have mentioned, one of the fundamental missions of BRI is to create a new mode of transportation across the globe so that human beings as well as goods can be transported quickly and easily across vast distances. Such an unprecedented initiative could in the short run, and certainly in the long run, be economically, socially and even politically transformative.

What has not been discussed extensively, and maybe not at all, is the creation of a "supercontinent," which will literally force the amalgamation of the East and West civilizations leading to engagement in something truly unthinkable. This can, for the first time in human history, rebuff the dictum of Rudyard Kipling that "never the twain shall meet." Just as Renaissance had grown and flourished on the European Continent, by human nature, we could assume that a "Neo-Renaissance," by letting Eastern and Western civilizations truly come into deep contact, would flourish in the Supercontinent. The creation of this culture will come from minds crisscrossing, admixing and colliding. It will be a culture which is neither East nor West.

It is certainly conceivable that in the Supercontinent, there will be generation after generation of new intellectuals absorbing and creating an entirely new ways and means. In such a new civilization, challenges of humanity will be met with mitigations that hitherto have never been considered. Indeed, at the apex of such a neo-Renaissance intellectual pyramid, there will definitely be neo-Galileos, neo-Copernicusus, neo-Descartes, neo-Bacons, neo-Newtons and neo-Maxwells. These neo-maestros, together with their classmates would give rise to a new sense of "inherent self-confidence," which they will leverage to overcome the modern-day global challenges.

I developed my keynote speech for the 2013 AEARU–LERU meeting with this line of thought. Yet I know that these ideas of supercontinent and neo-renaissance at the time of my delivering the speech in December 2013 were novel thoughts — certainly they were for me. This was the reason why I felt great trepidation in delivering it. Indeed, had I learned about just a few months before my speech, President Xi expounding on the Belt and Road Initiative, I would not have been as timid as I was. This is truly why today I am so enthusiastic about BRI because I believe it is one of the few human initiatives which could lead us out of our current dilemma!

I would like to make a slight detour here from the main subject matter, but I think it is an important one. As I mentioned, neo-Renaissance could be created by East–West cultural mind crisscrossing, admixing and colliding. There is one pre-condition which is critical: both sides must face each other with sufficient inherent self-confidence. To me, the words of Allison and Skinner are spoken not with self-confidence, but a lack of it.

Very recently, in the Conference on Dialogue of Asian Civilizations in Beijing, China, held on May 15, 2019, President Xi Jinping said with confidence in his keynote speech that[15]:

> China today is more than the country itself; it is very much a part of Asia and the world. In the time to come, China will open its arms wider to embrace the world and contribute the dynamic achievements of Chinese civilization to a better world in the future.

In 2009, right after the financial tsunami, I was invited to deliver a summary speech at a conference organized by the Asian Development Bank with the title "Industrial Reconstruction after the Financial Tsunami." I used the opportunity to stress the importance of Asians' inherent self-confidence.

> Throughout the 20th century, Asia has been psychologically "coupled" to the West, and understandably so. With superior economic and intellectual strengths, it is quite natural that Asia viewed the West as the 'standard of excellence.' However, after such a period as this with the West so palpably exposing its social & economic weaknesses, this may be the first time in the modern global economy that Asia can psychologically "DECOUPLE" from the West. This is not to suggest that Asia should decouple economically and intellectually from the West; rather, I am talking about a "psychological decoupling" to undo a sense of reliance on the West, without which it is unlikely that Asia will develop a deep sense of inherent self-confidence and without which the 21st century is surely not to be the Asian Century.

---

[15] Ministry of Foreign Affairs of the People's Republic of China. (May 16, 2019). *Full text of Xi's speech at opening of CDAC.* Retrieved from https://eng.yidaiyilu.gov.cn/qwyw/rdxw/90754.htm.

In the past several decades, especially in the post-2008 disaster era, the inherent confidence of Asians is on the rise. With that, and with the vigorous pursuit of the BRI, I am confident that the condition is now ripe for a BRI induced neo-renaissance to emerge to tackle the existential challenges facing humanity.

Chapter 4

Cultural Communication: An Ultimate Challenge of Chinese Culture

A fundamental point about BRI is "cultural communication (文化相通)." Indeed, only through cultural communication can one establish a communication paradigm, and only then can one realize BRI's development strategy, pushes forth BRI's constructions and creates projects in reality![1]

Charles Dickens' *A Tale of Two Cities* was undoubtedly one of my favorites, if not my favorite English novel. In reading the book, I was immediately captured by its beginning sentence:

It was the best of times, it was the worst of times, it was the age of wisdom, it was the age of foolishness ....

Clearly, as a great novelist with deep understanding of human behaviors, Dickens was able to capture not just the profound human sentiments of that era, but also palpably capture how Britain and

---

[1] The Insurance Institute of China. (November 9, 2016). "Yidai Yilu bairen luntan yanjiuyuan chengli ji xueshu yantaohui" zai jing zhaokai. Retrieved from http://www.sohu.com/a/118543983_492761.

France were fundamentally different in their respective cultures. For me, it is particularly interesting that while Britain and France were both countries who had and still are standing solidly on the Western civilization platform, culturally they were and still are vastly different.

Obviously, geopolitically, socially and culturally, the 21st century bears much resemblance to Dickens' 19th century in that "it was the best of times, it was the worst of times."

Regarding the "best of time," what Fareed Zakaria, the host of CNN's GPS program wrote in his recent article published in the *Washington Post* on January 31, 2019 is perhaps best reflecting this sentiment:

> On the simplest and most important measure, income, the story is actually one of astonishing progress. Since 1990, more than 1 billion people have moved out of extreme poverty. The share of the global population living in these dire conditions has gone from 36 percent to 10 percent, the lowest in recorded history. This is, as the World Bank president, Jim Yong Kim, notes, "one of the greatest achievements of our time." Inequality, from a global perspective, has declined dramatically.[2]

What Zakaria reported in his article is good news for the world, especially when some of the 800 million people lifted out of poverty were Chinese, according to the World Bank President Jim Yong Kim. For me, it is indeed a joy to see that in this respect, China can assume a lion's share of the credit.[3]

As regards to the "worst of time" part, what I have emphasized in the previous chapter on Supercontinent, humanity is now faced with existential challenges, such as the melting of the ice caps in the Arctic, which is a frightening manifestation of global warming (see

---

[2] Zakaria, F. (February 1, 2019). We have a bleak view of modern life. But the world is making real progress. *Washington Post*. Retrieved from https://www.washingtonpost.com/opinions/we-have-a-bleak-view-of-modern-life-but-the-world-is-making-real-progress/2019/01/31/6ee30432-25a8-11e9-ad53-824486280311_story.html.

[3] China lifting 800 million people out of poverty is historic: World Bank. (October 13, 2017). *Business Standard*. Retrieved from https://www.business-standard.com/article/international/china-lifting-800-million-people-out-of-poverty-is-historic-world-bank-117101300027_1.html.

diagram below). This enormous challenge is most transparent when the leader of the Western world, President Trump, wrote in his tweet on January 28, 2019 (where the word "Warming" was spelled erroneously) that:

> In the beautiful Midwest, windchill temperatures are reaching minus 60 degrees, the coldest ever recorded. In coming days, expected to get even colder. People can't last outside even for minutes. What the hell is going on with Global Waming? Please come back fast, we need you![4]

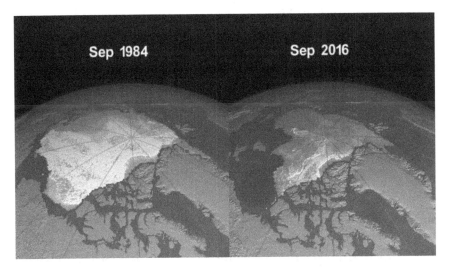

A composite image from NASA showing how the ice has receded in the Arctic from 1984 to 2016.

Source: Retrieved from https://fox2now.com/2018/02/26/nasa-releases-time-lapse-of-the-disappearing-arctic-polar-ice-cap/.

In his novel, Dickens discusses the profound difference between British and French cultures. The novel ended with a glorious line uttered by the main character Sydney Carton on his way to the guillotine: "It is a far, far better thing that I do, than I have ever done; it is a far, far better rest that I go to than I have ever known."

---

[4]The Daily Show's response to Trump's global warming tweet is. *Grist*. Retrieved from https://grist.org/article/the-daily-shows-response-to-trumps-global-warming-tweet-is-%F0%9F%91%8C/.

In the 21st century, the beginning phrase of the novel could very well be utilized to describe the Western and Eastern civilizations. I had mentioned in my last chapter the words of Kiron Skinner of the United States State Department, namely "China posed a particularly unique challenge as it represented the first time that we will have a great power competitor that is not Caucasian." These words manifest the conflict between the East (China) and West (United States) which, at the fundamental level, is a conflict between the two dominant civilizations!

So, one may ask at this point, why have the Eastern and Western civilizations which have existed for more than a millennium waited until now for the collision?

This tantalizing question deserves a closer examination. In my opinion, it is only happening because of the following reason. For the Western civilization, the Renaissance was the engine that propelled it to move upward and eventually reached its pinnacle after World War II, in which the United States became the undisputed leader.

There are a multitude of reasons why the United States became the leader. One of them was because before and during WWII, the unspeakable brutality of Adolf Hitler nearly drove the entire European intellectual elite, developed on the platform of the Renaissance, from science to technology to music to arts and whatever else, to the United States.

The book by Jean Medawar and David Pyke titled *Hitler's Gift: The True Story of Scientists Expelled by the Nazi Regime* gives an excellent account of this massive intellectual migration from Europe to North America, especially to the United States! There is no doubt that this lock, stock and barrel intellectual migration from one continent to another had never happened before in human history. There is also no doubt that the beneficiary of this migration catapulted the United States to the forefront in many dimensions of global leaderships and transformed the nation to become a global leader in the post-WWII era.

For the Eastern world, it is especially interesting that when the Western world began its rise in the 14th century, especially from the 18th to 20th centuries, it began to show serious decline. In China,

Book cover of *Hitler's Gift: The True Story of the Scientists Expelled by the Nazi Regime.*
Source: Retrieved from https://www.amazon.com/Hitlers-Gift-Scientists-Expelled-Regime/dp/1559705647.

which was the dominant nation in the Asia-Pacific region nearly throughout its entire history, a rapid decline was seen, especially in the 15th century when the Ming Dynasty shut its doors to the outside world. Later on, it declined precipitously from the 18th century onwards during the Qing Dynasty.

The reversal of East Asia's decline only began in the second half of the 20th century. Almost immediately after WWII, Japan with US assistance, began to reverse the trend. The "Four Tigers," namely Singapore, Hong Kong, Taiwan and South Korea, started their reversals toward the last third of the 20th century. For China, it happened only in the 21st century.

Japan and the Four Tigers began their rise before China by almost half a century and 30 years, respectively. Yet, even by combining them,

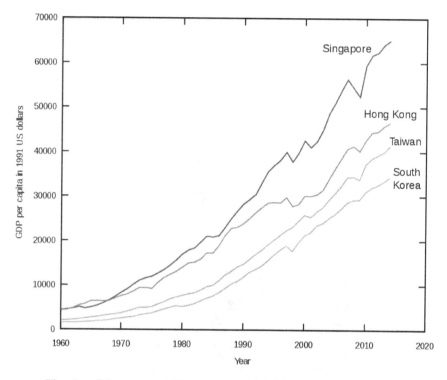

The rise of the so-called "Four Tigers of Asia" from the 1960s onward.

Source: Retrieved from https://en.wikipedia.org/wiki/Four_Asian_Tigers#/media/File:Four_Tigers_GDP_per_capita.svg.

they did not have sufficient strength, economies and otherwise to raise an alarm in the Western world that a "non-Caucasian civilization competitor" was in the making. In fact, it was not until China began to rise in the first decade of the 21st century and accelerated in the second that the alarm was raised.

Indeed, as I have mentioned earlier, the Chinese GDP, since 1997, had risen an astounding 12 times the year Hong Kong reversed its sovereignty back to China. Once China in the 21st century began to palpably rise in economic prowess, and especially in what Martin Jacques mentioned in a different form of modernity,[5] even if it were only perception-wise, and for sure perception is reality, it naturally became

---

[5]Jacques, M. Key Arguments & Synopsis. Retrieved from http://www.martinjacques.com/books/when-china-rules-the-world/synopsis/.

the leader. This is why today the two civilizations, represented by United States for the West and China for the East, respectively — with comments such as those uttered by Ms. Skinner mentioned in the chapter on Neo-Renaissance that *"the first time that we will have a great power competitor that is not Caucasian"* — vividly underscores the deep potency of the East–West collision!

The two speeches delivered by the leaders of the most powerful nations on earth today, President Donald Trump of the United States, representing Western civilization and President Xi Jinping of China, representing Eastern civilization are good representations of the abovementioned East–West enmity.

On January 27, 2017, at his inaugural speech delivered to the world, President Trump made the unabashed global declaration that[6]

> From this day forward, a new vision will govern our land. From this moment on, it's going to be America First.

In contrast, 10 days earlier on January 17, 2017, President Xi Jinping in his speech at Davos, Switzerland to the World Economic Forum said that[7]

> From the historical perspective, economic globalization resulted from growing social productivity, and is a natural outcome of scientific and technological progress, not something created by any individuals or any countries. Economic globalization has powered global growth and facilitated movement of goods and capital, advances in science, technology and civilization, and interactions among peoples.

The tone of the US President is explicitly aggressive, even with a touch of "in your face, the world," while the one from the Chinese President takes a softer tone to "treat the world with subtle strength and gentle care." It is remarkable that in the 21st century, Trump is "pulling

---

[6] Politico Staff. (January 20, 2017). Full text: 2017 Donald Trump inauguration speech transcript. *Politico.* https://www.politico.com/story/2017/01/full-text-donald-trump-inauguration-speech-transcript-233907.

[7] Jacques, M. Key Arguments & Synopsis. Retrieved from http://www.martinjacques.com/books/when-china-rules-the-world/synopsis/.

back" and signaled that United States, despite the fact that the country today is a multiracial nation, in his mind is the most powerful nation in the world representing Western civilization, will from now on be "inward-looking." On the contrary, the warm embracing tone of Xi is for people of all civilizations. It clearly outlined that people from all corners of the world need to understand and respect each other for the betterment of humanity. Comparing the two speeches, to say that they are "absolutely poles apart" may be an understatement!

From the last decade of the 20th century to the 21st century, the world has experienced a profound transformation, a transformation driven by the paradigm shift of technology, which was neither conceivable nor possible in the Renaissance era. Such a transformation is best and succinctly described by the book written by Thomas Friedman, with the title *The World is Flat*!

Book cover of *The World is Flat: A Brief History of the Twenty-First Century*.

Source: Retrieved from https://en.wikipedia.org/wiki/The_World_Is_Flat#/media/File:Worldisflat.gif

The central reason why Thomas Friedman concluded that the world became "flat" was through the amalgamation of the three technologically innovative "trinities," namely, superfast computers, superfast network (such as 5G of today) and the ability to intelligently archive massive amount of data, which in today's lingo would be "big data." Such a trinity gave rise to the rapidity of how a single human being can connect with many others, almost in real time and from any distance. Whimsically, this is as close to being "omnipresent" as a human can get.

It is especially interesting that when Friedman wrote the book in 2005, the world as we know it today in 2020, with Facebook, YouTube, WeChat, and what have you, had not even been invented yet. In the flat world of 2005 and the flatter world of 2020, there is no doubt that the interactions, even conflicts, between people, nations, cultures and ultimately civilizations can be carried out with unprecedented intensities and frequencies. Against this background, conflicts of civilizations can be ferocious, and may even be brutal! It is, therefore, absolutely critical that humanity should and must find a way to mitigate such a conflict, or face unimaginable existential consequences.

Hence, within the 21st century's best and worst of time landscape, BRI from China appeared on the horizon. On January 18, 2017, President Xi delivered a speech at the United Nations' Office in Geneva. The title of his talk was "Work Together to Build a Community of Shared Future for Mankind." For the present context, the relevant passage in his speech is as follows[8]:

> From the historical perspective, economic globalization resulted from growing social productivity, and is a natural outcome of scientific and technological progress, not something created by any individuals or any countries. Economic globalization has powered global growth and facilitated movement of goods and capital, advances in science, technology and civilization, and interactions among peoples.

Such a soft and far-reaching comment regarding the current situation by a Chinese President should alert the world. There is no doubt that on the one hand, since the Renaissance, China is for the

---

[8]Xi, J. P. Full Text of Xi Jinping keynote speech at the United Nations Office in Geneva. *China Global Television Network.* Retrieved from https://america.cgtn.com/2017/01/18/full-text-of-xi-jinping-keynote-speech-at-the-united-nations-office-in-geneva.

first time a modern and economically vibrant nation in its own right. In the past four decades, China with a population of 1.4 billion has emerged with dizzying speed, moving from its third-world status to second-world status of today. Indeed, China by all estimation is rapidly approaching the first-world status within the next one or two decades. Yet it is also a nation with significant depth since it has been bestowed continuously with five millennia of history.

By nature, China now is *de facto* one of the few, if not the only, massive nation that encompasses modernity with an ancient historical touch. With this as preamble, it is a sobering thought that in the 21st century, a Chinese leader could profess such a grand and unifying vision and can do so eloquently to encourage not just for China, but for all nations to increase "interactions among peoples." Furthermore, just as all important suggestions, President Xi also proposed a solution with accompanying resources to enhance such interactions. The solution is BRI which sits on the foundation of cultural communication!

In fact, the idea of "interactions among people" was already lurking around in BRI conversations in China ever since it was introduced in 2013. One of the clearest declarations of this concept which I was able to uncover was pronounced in a BRI forum in Beijing which was held on November 5, 2016. At that forum, the former deputy director of China Insurance Regulatory Commission (中国保监会) Mr. Zhou Yanli (周延礼) gave a keynote speech, in which he uttered a phrase which essentially captured the fundamental principle of "cultural communication (文化相通)." What he said was that standing on the BRI platform, how people from all corners of the globe could and should interact. Mr. Zhou said that[9]

> A fundamental point about BRI is "cultural communication (文化相通)." Indeed, only through cultural communication can one establish a communication paradigm, and only then

---

[9] The Insurance Institute of China. (November 9, 2016). "Yidai Yilu bairen luntan yanjiuyuan chengli ji xueshu yantaohui" zai jing zhaokai. Retrieved from http://www.sohu.com/a/118543983_492761.

Mr. Zhou Yan-Li.

Source: Retrieved from https://m.baidu.com/sf?pd=image_content&word=周延礼%20中国保监会照片&tn=nohead&atn=mediacy&fr=alawise&sa=vs_ala_img&imgpn=4&imgspn=0&localli mit=0&browseala=0&bdtype=0&limitcount=0&tt=1&di=51590&pi=0&cs=1755657183%2C912 102531&adpicid=&objurl=http%3A%2F%2Fi0.sinaimg.cn%2Fcj%2Fhy%2F20111103%2FU2 104P31T1D10748225F46DT20111103121203.jpg&imgos=2170376675%2C3420427020&imgi s=0%2C0&imgtype=0.

can one realize BRI's development strategy, push forth BRI's constructions and create projects in reality!

In those few but truly weighty words, Mr. Zhou Yan-Li succinctly pointed out that cultural communication must be and is the core issue. It is also the fundamental challenge of the BRI.

The Difference Between Ancient Silk Roads and Modern Silk Roads

By carefully reading President Xi Jinping's 2013 speeches in Kazakhstan and Indonesia, one can surmise that the theme of BRI is to revitalize the ancient silk roads, whether it be land-based or maritime-based. The ancient silk roads and the modern silk roads, which we now refer to as the BRI, are separated in time by several millennia. In those millennia, the world has gone through unimaginable sociological transformations, and scientific and technological innovations, such as the Renaissance, the scientific revolution of the 19th and 20th centuries, and the modern communication technology era in the 21st century. In nearly every conceivable dimension, such transformations and innovations could and did alter — completely — human's ways and means. In discussing the BRI, especially if one were to project its impact on humanity today, one simply cannot avoid comparing it with the meaning of the ancient silk roads: how are they fundamentally different?

In many of the speeches I delivered all over the world regarding BRI, I often asked the audience a whimsical question:

> What is the fundamental difference between ancient and modern silk roads?

The answers I received from the audience could usually be characterized as long discussions about how the BRI could have geopolitical and/or geoeconomic impacts while the ancient ones could not. While such answers do capture some of what I would consider as the essence of the difference, to me the most significant difference in the form of an "elevator comment" should simply be:

> In the ancient silk roads, there was NO Xi Jinping!

Although such a "humorous" answer could and often did induce a great deal of laughter from the audience, it nevertheless has a very serious implication. Indeed, even to the most casual observer, the starkest difference between BRI and ancient silk roads is that the latter arose entirely organically! In fact, when the ancient silk roads were in full swing, China, despite its convoluted history, was unquestionably the most modern and sophisticated nation in the world at that time. In ancient silk roads, which spanned over several millenia across many dynasties, such as Han (汉), Tang (唐) and Song (宋), China was culturally, economically and militarily all powerful. One could borrow the words of the US president Ronald Reagan by referring to China for most of that era as the "shining city on the hill"!

Indeed, with example after example, people across Asia and Europe would take the very long and arduous trips to the Far East, *à la* China, to seek and develop better opportunities. Yet curiously, in reverse, as far as I could surmise, due to lack of incentives, there were essentially no Chinese entrepreneurs who would venture out of the boundary of China in search of new opportunities. Individuals such as Zhang Qian (张骞) in the Han Dynasty were so rare that they could be singled out in history books.

It would appear that Chinese would much prefer to remain in their "comfort zone," which was, of course, China — the most economically advanced nation in the world at the time. As a result, the Chinese in ancient times would simply not have the necessary incentive to propel themselves to leave China. After all, if they had done so, they would need to learn about the history as well as the ways and means of people of other civilizations in order to prosper, if not to survive. They would truly then be out of their comfort zone, which they preferred not to be.

An Example That the Ancient Silk Roads Did Not Have "Two-way Traffic"!: Jews in China in the Song Dynasty

One of the most remarkable examples of the ancient silk roads' traffic asmmetry between East and West would be the presence of a less-known, but robust and flourishing Jewish community in China in ancient times. From as far back as the Han dynasty, Jews from the West, probably in what today would be places like Israel, Palestine, Syria, Iraq, Iran and so on, began making the arduous trip to China. Indeed, the First Chief Minister of Singapore between 1955 and 1956 (which was way before Singapore's independence) was an individual known as David Marshall, an Iraqi Jew.

The Jewish migration had reached its peak in the Song dynasty. Even currently, there are Jews living in Kaifeng. In fact, a faculty member from Tsinghua University communicated with me, informing me that he is a decedent. Of course, they are utterly assimilated by now. The Chinese Jews today would fit perfectly in the New York Jewish joke, which is "funny, they don't look Jewish"!

During the Han Dynasty, which was one of China's most robust and long-lasting dynasties, that lasted over four centuries (206 BC–220 AD), Jews in Western and Southern Asia somehow became aware of the economically robust China. Many made the remarkable and arduous trip via the silk roads to come to China, in search of opportunities. As friends, relatives and other compatriots learned about the "good news" for those who went and were successful doing businesses in China, many later were also attracted to travel the long hard silk roads to China as well. By the time the Sung dynasty (960 AD–1279 AD) rolled around a thousand years later, there were enough Jews in the capitol city Bianjing (汴京), now known as Kaifeng (开封). Kaifeng is now the provincial capital for the province of Henan (河南), which is some 670 kilometers directly south of Beijing. At that time, the Jewish community became very vibrant, living the ways and means of the Jewish culture, which included religious practice.

In 2007, my good friend Professor Aaron Ciechanover, Nobel Laureate in chemistry in 2004 and a professor at the Ruth and Bruce Rappaport Faculty of Medicine of the Technion, Israel Institute of Technology, and I, assisted by Professor Luo Qingming of Huazhong University of Science and Technology, visited Kaifeng. The details of our trip are described in Chapter 6.

Photo of a Jewish street sign in Kaifeng.

My friend Aaron Ciechanover and I had an unforgettable meal with a Jewish family in Kaifeng.

In my mind, the story of Kaifeng Jews raised two truly gripping issues.

The first is less relevant to the current discussion but is nevertheless of great human interest. As far as the historical accounts I could uncover, the ancient Jews who came to China assimilated rather amiably into the Chinese societies while still being able to maintain their traditions. In fact, despite the Chinese societies were very set in their ways and despite the fact that the Jewish community was rather large and palpably having very different ways and means from the Chinese, there was no record of the Chinese preventing the Jews, directly or indirectly, from practicing their lifestyle, which included their religious practices. Perhaps most notable was the fact that the Jews were even able to construct worship houses known as "synagogues." In fact, it was recorded that the first synagogue in Kaifeng was built in 1163.[10]

---

[10] Kaifeng Jews. (n.d.). In *Wikipedia*. Retrieved September 1, 2019, from https://en.wikipedia.org/wiki/Kaifeng_Jews.

This means that as far back as a millennium, when the Jews were facing anti-Semitic pushbacks nearly everywhere, and even today, such as the horrible event the world witnessed recently on October 18, 2018 in Pittsburgh, Pennsylvania, USA, where a white nationalist massacred eleven Jews in a synagogue (see photo below), the Chinese in the Song dynasty did not display any such hostility toward this group of "foreigners" who had lived and flourished among them.

Memorials to victims outside the Tree of Life Jewish synagogue in Pittsburgh in 2019.

Source: https://en.wikipedia.org/wiki/Pittsburgh_synagogue_shooting#/media/File:Tree_of_Life_Synagogue_Memorials_10-30-2018_01.jpg

For the present context, the second point is even more profound in that if the ancient silk roads were indeed a "two-way street," then logically one would expect that there should be as many Chinese at the Western end points of the silk roads as there were Westerners, such as the Jews in Kaifeng, in the Eastern end. After all, there is a well-known joke which says that "Chinese are

Jews of the East." This joke implies that the Chinese were (and still are) known to have great entrepreneurial skills. It is a fact that there was no known record that throughout the past several millennia, Chinese had seldom, if ever ventured out and/or searched for opportunities in the Western destination points of the silk roads. This surely implies that for millennia, the concept of "going out" was and still is not ingrained deep in the Chinese mindset.

Clearly, without a forceful incentive, the deeply ingrained inward mindset of the Chinese cannot and will not transform, or even alter to the slightest extent. This is another reason when I learned that China was initiating the BRI, it seems to me that this could just be such an incentive to modify, if not change, this millennium Chinese mindset.

The Fundamental Importance of "Cultural Communication": The BRI Challenge Posed by India

In the first and second "Belt and Road Forum for International Cooperation" held in Beijing in 2017 and 2019, respectively, a significant number of Asian leaders participated in the forums. Unlike the first forum where there were some prominent individuals from Asia absent, the second forum witnessed the presence of all 10 leaders of the nations from Southeast Asia. In particular, Singapore's Prime Minister Lee Hsien Loong and Malaysia's Prime Minister Mahathir Bin Mohamad, who both were absent in the first forum for different reasons, enthusiastically proclaimed respectively in the second forum that:[11]

> Singapore hoped to be able to play a constructive role in financial services, third-country investments and human resources development.

---

[11] Cheong, D. (April 23, 2019). Singapore can make 'modest contribution' to China's Belt and Road Initiative: PM Lee Hsien Loong. *The Straits Times*. Retrieved from https://www.straitstimes.com/asia/east-asia/singapore-can-make-modest-contribution-to-chinas-belt-and-road-initiative-pm-lee.

Singaporean Prime Minister Lee Hsien Loong addressed the high-level meeting of the Second Belt and Road Forum for International Cooperation held at Beijing, China, April 26, 2019.

Source: Retrieved from http://en.people.cn/n3/2019/0427/c90000-9573116-21.html.

and[12]

> I am fully in support of the Belt and Road Initiative. I am sure my country, Malaysia, will benefit from the project,

However, there is one important nation from Asia who was not only absent at both forums, but also openly declared that it was "boycotting" them. That country is India, an Asian neighbor of global importance, and is geographically directly south of China.

---

[12]Lo, K. (April 26, 2019). Malaysia's Mahathir backs China's belt and road but insists on open trade routes. *The Straits Times*. Retrieved from https://www.scmp.com/news/china/diplomacy/article/3007874/malaysias-mahathir-backs-chinas-belt-and-road-insists-open.

A media center's screen shows Malaysian Prime Minister Mahathir Mohamad delivering a speech at the opening ceremony for the second Belt and Road Forum, next to a replica of a Chinese high-speed train, in Beijing on Friday.

Source: Retrieved from https://www.scmp.com/news/china/diplomacy/article/3007874/malaysias-mahathir-backs-chinas-belt-and-road-insists-open.

It should be emphasized that while India as a nation was absent, as private citizens, there were quite a number of individuals of great influence from the country attending the second forum. They include:

(a) Bali Deepak, a renowned Professor of Chinese and China Studies at the Center of Chinese and Southeast Asian Studies from Jawaharlal Nehru University, Delhi, India. Besides contributing to many editorial publications in major India newspaper on the China–Indian issues, he also has to his credit a voluminous amount of scholastic work, including translating the profound "*The Four Books*, 四书" the collective name of "*The Analects* 《论语》," "*Mencius* 《孟子》," "*Great Learning* 《大学》" and "*The Doctrine of the Mean* 《中庸》." As is well known, the four books literally defined the core of Chinese philosophical doctrines for many millennia;

(b) Manish Chand, Founder and Editor-in-Chief of the renowned "Indian Writes,"[13] and

(c) Manoj Joshi, Distinguished Fellows of the Observed Research Foundation.[14]

Photo taken at the 2nd Belt and Road International Cooperation Forum in Beijing on April 24, 2019. Standing on my left and right are Professor Bali Deepak of JNU from India and Professor Edward Cunningham, Harvard University, respectively.

In a recent report from the *Diplomat,* one of the most influential Indian news media, it stated that[15]

---

[13] http://www.indianwrites.org

[14] http://www.orfonline.org

[15] India Signals to Boycott China's Belt and Road Forum for Second Time. (March 20, 2019). *The Economic Times.* Retrieved from https://economictimes.indiatimes.com/news/politics-and-nation/india-hints-wont-attend-aprils-belt-and-road-forum/articleshow/68494152.cms?from=mdr.

India, on Wednesday, signaled that it will boycott China's second Belt and Road Forum for a second time, saying no country can participate in an initiative that ignores its core concerns on sovereignty and territorial integrity. India boycotted the first Belt and Road Forum (BRF) in 2017 after protesting to Beijing over the controversial China–Pakistan Economic Corridor (CPEC) which is being laid through the Pakistan-occupied Kashmir (PoK) overriding New Delhi's sovereignty concerns.

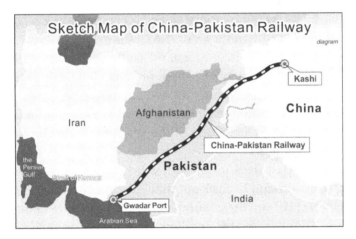

A depiction of CPEC. India is protesting that the Corridor goes through the yellow patch of this map, which is the India–Pakistan contested area known as Kashmir.

Source: Retrieved from https://www.chinausfocus.com/finance-economy/the-china-pakistan-economic-corridor-indias-dual-dilemma.

A Few Details About the "Non-Cultural Communication" Between India and China

Since they are two of the largest nations in terms of landmass and population, and are adjacent to each other geographically, one would have assumed that the cultural communication between India and China should have been a many-millennia interaction. In fact, nothing can be further from the truth. In this section, I will discuss this "non-cultural communication" between the two nations.

The maritime BRI project is the twin of a similar land-based project. To discuss maritime BRI, there is simply no way one can ignore or go around India. Yet, despite their geographical proximity, both countries — as I will demonstrate here — seem to not only have no understanding of one another, but also, considering the present situation, have no well established channel of cultural communication between them. Therefore, whether it be BRI or any other effort, the less-than-optimum condition which currently exists between India and China is not only diabolical for Asia, it is diabolical for the world.

Although I know of no official statistics taken, there is a common understanding that in India's vast 1.33 billion population, only at most a few thousands can understand Chinese. Within India, the Jawaharlal Nehru University's Chinese program led by Professor Bali Deepak, who has been carrying out a yeoman's work, ensures there is at least some minimum understanding of China in all aspects in India. As far as I know, he is one of the very few, if not the only one who has been doing so.

Also, in the past decade, there has been a very active program emerging from Taiwan. It turns out that Taiwan's National Tsing Hua University (NTHU) in the second decade of the 21st century has established a number of the so-called "Taiwan Educational Centers" in a few Indian higher education institutions, such as the Indian Institute of Technology Madras in Chennai, O. P. Jindal Global University and Amity University. The aim of these centers is not political, but is for introducing the rich Chinese culture to Indians.

I have visited India several times when I was a Senior Vice President of NTHU, and during these visits I was informed that with great foresight, an intention from the Indian government to plan — or at least a desire — to institute a national K-12 program to teach Chinese as the third language (the first two being English and one of the Indian languages) throughout India. Unfortunately, the effort never had a chance to take off because of the tiny number of people in India who understand Chinese. Also, ever since the 1962 border conflict between the two nations, relations were so strained that there is no appetite to import a vast number of Chinese language teachers. Indeed, for a nation with a population of 1.33 billion, using the phrase "a drop in the bucket" accurately sums up India's effort to understand China — is a truly dismal situation.

The situation in China is hardly any better. The lack of interest regarding anything Indian is clearly manifested in the 3000 or so Chinese tertiary institutions where there are at best a handful of institutions with "South Asia" programs and/or interests. For example, the Department of South Asian Studies of Peking University and the Institute of South Asian Studies of Sichuan University are a few such institutes with interest in South Asia.

Photo of Sichuan University's Institute of South Asian Studies.

Source: Retrieved from https://baike.baidu.com/item/%E5%9B%9B%E5%B7%9D%E5%A4 %A7%E5%AD%A6%E5%8D%97%E4%BA%9A%E7%A0%94%E7%A9%B6%E6%89%80/ 10923144?fr=aladdin.

Again, for a nation with a population of 1.4 billion, "lack of interest" in its close and massive neighbor may be too weak a phrase to describe the situation.

As I have mentioned earlier, India and China are massive Asian nations. In terms of population, according to 2016 data, the two nations have a people strength of 1.33 billion and 1.4 billion, respectively.[16] This means, together, these two nations are home to nearly 40% of the world's population. Their landmasses are 3.3 million and 9.6 million square kilometers, respectively. Geographically, India sits directly south of China and have 3300 kilometers of border. Separating the two nations is the world's tallest mountain range: the Himalayas.

China Is a "Homogeneous" Country and India Is an "Inhomogeneous" Country

Perhaps the most remarkable aspect about India and China is that these two countries, despite being neighbors *ad infinitum*, are vastly different.

As far as modern history is concerned, India is different from China in one very critical aspect: Politically and administratively, it was subjugated by over 400 years of British influence and rule. The British essentially controlled India between 1612 to 1858 through the East Indian Company. After 1858, Britain officially absorbed India, which then became a British colony till it gained independence nearly a hundred years later in 1947.

The "father of the nation" of India was the world-famous Mahatma Gandhi and the first Prime Minister was Jawaharlal Nehru. Despite both being passionate about "India's independence," both were profoundly influenced by the British culture owing to their education in the top institutions there: Nehru was a student at the famed Trinity College of Cambridge University, where epoch-changing individuals of historical importance, such as Newton and Maxwell, were students; Gandhi, on the other hand, was a law student at the prestigious University College of London. Many subsequent leaders of India, such as Indira Gandhi

---

[16]China Vs India by Population. (July 7, 2018). *Statistics Times.* Retrieved from http://statisticstimes.com/demographics/china-vs-india-population.php.

(Oxford University,) Rajiv Gandhi (Cambridge and Imperial College) and Manmohan Singh (Cambridge and Oxford) all received a through and through British education. Surely having vast and profound scholastic experiences as well as having United Kingdom's *crème de la crème* as fellow classmates would surely have made a deep impression on these Indians, and most of their countrymen would agree that they have been epoch-changing leaders of the nation.

A remarkable photo of Jawaharlal Nehru laughing with Mahatma Gandhi.
Source: Retrieved from https://en.wikipedia.org/wiki/India#/media/File:Nehru_gandhi.jpg.

I think there is no doubt that after nearly 450 years of British rule and colonization, Britain as a pivotal country following Western civilization, an indelible footprint in this regard was made on India's ways and means. Therefore, while India has had its own rich and robust history and culture, it is probably not difficult even for a casual ovbserver to detect the Western civilization lurking underneath the surface of Indian culture. This makes Indians easier to appreciate and understand, and even accept the Western ways and means than the Chinese.

India as a Case Study of Cultural Communication

Compared to India, China is its antithesis. In the past 450 years while India was under the rule of a Western power — the British Empire — and for the past 150 years, as a colony, China was never one.

Of course, one might argue that for the Yuan Dynasty (1271–1368 AD) and Qing Dynasty (1644–1912 AD), when the country was ruled by the Mongols and the Aisin Gioro clan (爱新觉罗族) of Manchuria, respectively, it was de facto a form of "colony." In China, it is not difficult to often find that there is a touch of Han chauvinism (汉族沙文主义) when one refers to those two dynasties as outside clans' domination (外族统治.) No doubt, the cultures of the Mongolians and Manchurians were and still are vastly different from the Han culture. Yet what is remarkable is that after nearly one hundred and three hundred years of ruling, respectively, for the people of China, the Mongolian and Manchurian cultures did not replace the Han culture. This is especially true for the Qing Dynasty where with more than 300 years of rule, the Manchurian cultures were essentially overwhelmed by the Han culture, and in its own diminutive way, the Han culture may even have flourished under the Manchurian rule.

For example, in modern-day China, there are still quite a significant proportion of Chinese, especially in the Northeast part of the country, who would identify themselves as Manchurians. A few years ago, I had the pleasure of visiting Harvard University's Fairbank Center of Chinese Studies. During my visit, I met Professor Mark C. Elliott, a Manchurian scholar whom I was informed could speak the Manchurian language with great fluency. I was quite surprised that he learned it not from a Chinese scholar but from a Russian scholar at the University of Washington in Seattle. This means that the number of people who could speak the Manchurian language is now reduced and confined to some distinguished scholars worldwide, such as Elliott.

I also learned from him that after the Chinese revolution of 1911, since the Chinese just totally demolished the Qing Dynasty controlled by Manchurians, the general interest within China in maintaining the Manchurian language, even from the perspective of an intellectual exercise, had sunk to an all-time low. I mentioned to

Professor Elliott that as someone who has a deep Chinese heritage, the fact that a significant part of the comprehensive Chinese culture is diminished is indeed a source of embarrassment for me.

During my past four decades of interaction with many friends in China, there is a small fraction of them who would claim to be of Manchurian decent. However, none can speak the language. I did mention to Professor Elliott that as someone with deep Chinese heritage, I am astonished that he had to learn one of the languages of China not from a Chinese, but from a Russian. He jokingly mentioned to me that another Harvard colleague, Professor Michael Szonyi, the director of the Fairbank Center for Chinese Studies was the one who had written the definitive book about Quemoy, with the title *Cold War Island*!

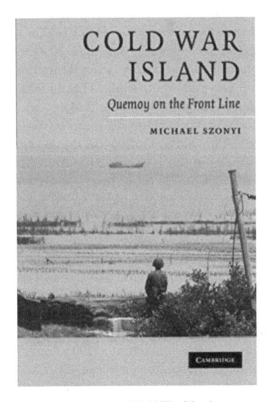

Book cover of *Cold War Island*.

Source: Retrieved from https://www.amazon.com/Cold-War-Island-Quemoy-Front/dp/0521726409.

I should emphasize that I am not here to argue the pros and cons of having outside clan domination. What I am arguing is that such dominations of the Mongolians and Manchurians are fundamentally different from the manner the British ruled India as a colonial power! Indeed, I think I am on fairly solid ground in saying that China was not a colony under such rules.

India has another characteristic that makes it profoundly different from China. It is known that 95% of Chinese belong to the Han clan (汉族). Within the Han clan, it is known that there are many dialects spoken from one end of China to another, and sometimes even from one end of a Province to another. For example, the dialect spoken in Shanghai, known as "Shanghainese," is completely different from the dialect spoken in Fujian Province, known as "Min-Nan 闽南话." Likewise, the dialect spoken in Hong Kong, Macau and most of the so-called Pearl River Delta region of Guangdong Province is Cantonese (广东话), which is very different from Shantou (汕头) and Chaozhou (潮州) even though both these cities are located within Guangdong Province. Having said that, it should be mentioned that although the spoken dialects can be completely different — so much so that one person who speaks one of the dialects cannot understand what another person is saying in another dialect — they can all use the written "Chinese" to communicate. In order words, nearly all Chinese from the Han clan, from one end of the country to another, can communicate in writing as long as they are not illiterate.

What this tells us is that except for the minorities, such as Zhuang clan 壮族 (17 million in population) and Uyghur clan 维吾尔族 (10 million,) the majority of the Chinese people have a mindset that is quite uniform. Not only can a person from Guangdong Province easily identify with someone from Shantou, he can also identify with someone from Wuhan (1000 kilometers away,) Lanzhou (2300 kilometers) or even Changchun (3100 kilometers.)

From the language perspective, it is also very interesting to compare China with India. In this respect, the two countries cannot be more different. China has language homogeneity to a significant extent while India does not. Indeed, not only is India a massive nation in population, it is also one that has a vast number of languages, not dialects. According to Wikipedia,[17] there are some

> 29 languages (that) have more than a million native speakers, 60 have more than 100,000 and 122 have more than 10,000 native speakers.

Most of these languages, such as Hindi, Bengali, Tamil and Punjabi, which must not be confused as dialects, even have their own alphabets. With different languages, it is natural that there will be different literatures and cultures. In some cases, even the religions are different. An Indian friend once jokingly told me that "Indians belong to one nation only when we are playing cricket with a foreign team!"

It is quite remarkable that India does not have a "national language' *per se*. There is a common perception that two of India's languages, Hindi and English, are known by most Indians. In reality, since only 57% and 11% of Indians, respectively, can understand these two languages, such a perception is at best erroneous.

The complexity of the Indian languages is a profound reflection of the internal social, political and cultural structures of India. In this respect, India is more similar to a collection of European nations than it resembles China as a single entity. For example, it is a nation where one area with over 91 million in population in the State of West Bengal (whose dominant language is Bengalis) and another area with nearly 71 million in the State of Tamil Nadu (whose dominant language is Tamil) have utterly different languages, cultures and even ways and means, and these differences could either be subtle or obvious. It is known that there is no European nation with a population of 100 million, and only one — Germany — has a population slightly larger than Tamil Nadu. Hence, for all practical purposes, if language is the identity of a nation, then the States of West Bengal and Tamil Nadu would more closely resemble independent countries than being states of India. Hindi, which supposedly is commonly understood in India, is only

---

[17]Languages of India. (n.d.). In *Wikipedia*. Retrieved September 1, 2019, from https://en.wikipedia.org/wiki/Languages_of_India.

understood by some 57% of the population. There are 43% of Indians who cannot understand this presumed common language.

The above discussion clearly delineates how India is fundamentally different from China. For an Indian growing up in India, he/she is cognizant that the language he/she speaks as mother tongue in all likelihood is not understood by a large percentage of his/her fellow compatriots. Therefore, appreciating and respecting the different languages and cultures of his/her fellow compatriots, even within India, is the norm and not the exception. Growing up in this environment and with the skill of appreciating compatriots who have totally different cultures renders Indians more ready and flexible in interactions with people who are different from them. It is this aspect that the Chinese mindset is profoundly different and, to a large extent, simpler than the Indian one!

Indians Lead the World in the Leaderships of Global Higher Education and Corporation

In recent years, there is a phenomenon that is only now beginning to receive some attention in China, and that is Indians have an indelible presence in the educational and corporate worlds. Before I explain this further, I would first like to set the stage with three Indians in the United States, who do not belong to either the two worlds I mentioned earlier, but whose deep presence in the American society is a palpable example of what cultural communications can bring.

First, every Sunday, in one of the world's most viewed global television station — Cable News Network, or CNN[18] — there is a program on geopolitics named Global Public Square (GPS), which the world watches. The host of GPS is a gentleman named Fareed Zakaria, who is a Konkani-Muslim Indian, Yale- and Harvard-educated, and is a very articulate individual. In all the programs,

---

[18]CNN. (n.d.). In *Wikipedia.* Retrieved September 1, 2019, from https://en.wikipedia.org/wiki/CNN.

Zakaria will first discuss in elegant English language what he considers is the week's most important issue and provide the audience with his analysis. Mr. Zakaria is also a self-described secular Muslim.[19] Having been an avid fan of GPS, I would be absorbed by the elegant content in my mind that his ethnicity and his slight Indian accent English were pushed to the background every time I watch the show.

Second, whenever CNN has a program which is either directly or indirectly related to health matters, the host would inevitably be an individual named Sanjay Gupta. At the moment with COVID-19, Sanjay Gupta appears at least four to five times a day! Mr. Gupta was born in Michigan and was educated at the University of Michigan Medical School. Before becoming a television personality, he was a practicing neurosurgeon. And more times than not, except for his name being clearly Indian, if one were to make him stand behind a veil, one would think that this was just another "standard" reporter.[20]

Third, in the past 12 years in the US CBS television network, there was a very popular comedy series known as The Big Bang Theory.[21] The series is based on a group of brilliant and goofy scientists and engineers from the California Institute of Technology. The show portrays their interactions with the society at large. There are six main actors and actresses. One of them has the show name Raj Koothrappali, and he is supposed to be an Indian astrophysicist. In real life, his name is Kunal Nayyar, and he is an Indian-born actor and comedian.

These three individuals outline for me the broad and deep relationship between the Indian community and the American society — a relationship which is clearly not shared by the Chinese community. One of the fundamental reasons why they have done so is via a conscious or subconscious cultural communication.

---

[19]Fareed Zakaria GPS. (n.d.). In *Wikipedia.* Retrieved September 1, 2019, from https://en.wikipedia.org/wiki/Fareed_Zakaria_GPS.
[20]Sanjay Gupta. (n.d.). In *Wikipedia.* Retrieved September 1, 2019, from https://en.wikipedia.org/wiki/Sanjay_Gupta.
[21]The Big Bang Theory. (n.d.). In *Wikipedia.* Retrieved September 1, 2019, from https://en.wikipedia.org/wiki/The_Big_Bang_Theory.

Of all the so-called minorities within the United States, I find it very difficult to accept the fact that it is simply an accident that CNN and CBS picked three Indians for very important roles in these globally visible programs. Of course, one should not and cannot take away the fact that all three individuals are truly talented in their respective professions. After all, not every Indian American, or American in general, can be as thought-provoking and as articulate as Fareed Zakaria. The same is true of Sanjay Gupta, whose presentations on health issues show he has deep understanding of healthcare issues facing the American society. Since Sanjay Gupta's screen presence normally does not last more than a few minutes, he has clearly mastered the skill to be surgically to the point and convey his thoughts with the least amount of words.

The same is true of Kunal Nayyar, who obviously is inherently a talented actor. Being an academic for a significant part of my career, I am especially intrigued by the selection of him beyond his acting talent. Although I do not have precise data, I know that the number of Chinese and Chinese Americans who are faculty and students at Caltech is as abundant as the number of Indians and Indian Americans there. For example, in 2018, out of 948 undergraduate students, 40% were Asians. If history is any guide, I am confident that of this 40%, a large fraction would be Chinese Americans and Indian Americans, and maybe a small number of Chinese and Indians from their respective countries. In fact, in the physics program which I know well, there are more Chinese American faculty members than Indian American faculty members.

So why is an Indian and not a Chinese chosen for the role in the Big Bang Theory. I do not believe that it came from "flipping a coin"! In my opinion, the deep-seated reason is because for this particular character, the scenario which he is embedded in is a "highly educated but mainly White" society. The interpersonal relationships between this character and rest of the cast must truly be accepted by the viewers, and must also deeply penetrate into the soul of a different civilization: the American society. In watching these three Indians week after week, year after year, I became convinced that not only how and what they say are exemplary in their own rights, but they have *de facto* entered into the "comfort zone" of the American society.

Besides the above three Indians, there is a large community of Indians whose impact in the U.S. society may be more profound than these three individuals. While their public presence may not be as media-visible as Zakaria, Gupta and Nayyar, they have quietly reached the pinnacle of their chosen careers, namely as leaders of higher education and the corporate world in the United States.

Take the example of higher education. Here, a significant number of Indian Americans have become leaders of some of the best institutions of higher learning. Nearly all began their tenure during the second decade of the 21st century. Some outstanding institutions that have or had Indians (probably most are Indian American US citizens) at the helm include the following:

1. University of Texas at Arlington (Vistasp Karbhari, whose tenure began in 2013).
2. Cooper Union in New York City (Jamshed Bharucha whose tenure was between 2011 and 2015. Since he completed his presidency at Cooper Union, he became the Vice Chancellor (the alternate name for the "president" in many Commonwealth universities) of SRM University in India.
3. Carnegie Mellon University (Subra Suresh, whose tenure was between 2013 and 2017. Since he completed his presidency at Carnegie Mellon University, he was recruited to be the president of Singapore's Nanyang Technological University, one of the fastest growing universities in Asia).
4. The University of California at San Diego (Pradeep Khosla, whose tenure began in 2012).
5. State University of New York at Buffalo (Satish K. Tripathi, whose tenure began in 2011).
6. University of Massachusetts at Amherst (Kumble R. Subbaswamy, whose tenure began in 2012).
7. Lawrence Technological University near Detroit (Virinder K. Moudgil, whose tenure began in 2012).

8. University of Houston (Renu Khator, whose tenure began in 2008).
9. Western Washington University (Sabah Randhawa, whose tenure began in 2016).

It also should be noted that there are now a significant number of Engineering and Business Schools in the United States that have Indian Americans at the helms. For example, the Dean of the most prestigious business school in the United States — Harvard Business School — is Nitin Nohria. Another example is Sunil Kumar, Dean of the Booth School of Business at the University of Chicago. Both Nohria and Kumar, like many of their compatriots, are graduates from the top Indian universities, Nohria from IIT Bombay and Kumar from the Indian Institute of Science in Bengaluru.

In my experience, I learned that many such individuals can and will be headhunters' targets for positions such as chancellors and presidents of universities. I, therefore, am confident that a number of such Indians will eventually go on to become university presidents in the United States.

I visited Chancellor Pradeep Khosla at his UCSD office in 2013.

Photo taken with President Karbhari when I visited the University of Texas at Arlington in 2016.

It is worth mentioning that before he became the president of Carnegie Mellon University, Subra Suresh was the Director of the National Science Foundation as well as Dean of Engineering at MIT. After he completed his term at CMU, he was hired by one of Asia's top universities, Nanyang Technological University of Singapore, as its president. It is worth mentioning that another outstanding Indian academician, Professor Sethuraman Panchanathan from Arizona State University was recently nominated to become the next director of the National Science Foundation.

By contrast, there are only two known Chinese Americans who are currently at the helm of universities. They are Henry Yang, Chancellor of the University of California Santa Barbara (UCSB), and Wallace Loh, President of the University of Maryland. It must be underscored that Chancellor Henry Yang has proven to be such a remarkable leader for one of the Chancellorships of the 10 campuses that form a

Subra Suresh.
Source: Retrieved from https://www.nsf.gov/news/mmg/mmg_disp.jsp?med_id=73767&from=.

part of the University of California System. In his 25 years at the helm, six faculty members became Nobel Laureates and he has lifted the university to great heights, thus enabling UCSB to emerge as one of the best in the world. And remarkably, he is still going strong!

A photo with President Henry Yang of UCSB when I was visiting him in 2017.

In an article on this phenomena, it was reported in *Inside Higher Ed,*[22] Ilene H. Nagel, who is the head of the education practice at

---

[22] Kiley, K. (March 21, 2013). Came for Grad Work, Rose to Top. *Inside Higher Ed.* Retrieved from https://www.insidehighered.com/news/2013/03/21/academics-born-india-see-growth-presidential-ranks.

Russell Reynolds Associates, a search firm that assisted for the SUNY-Buffalo and UT-Arlington searches, said that "*They often have an accomplished record of academic administration.*"

The term "accomplished record of academic administration" is worth expanding. If one were to walk into any random outstanding higher education institutions in the United States, one would easily notice there are as many Chinese Americans who are outstanding faculty as Indian Americans. Yet once you reach the administrative levels, be it department heads, deans and so on, you would find fewer Chinese Americans.

I can give a personal example of the rarity of Chinese Americans in the administrative positions in universities in the United States. When I first became the Vice President for Research for the University of Texas at Dallas in 2000, I wanted to locate other Chinese Americans who were in the same position in other universities. I had assumed that since there were an abundance of Chinese American faculty members in nearly every university and college in the country, quite a number of them would be in the same administrative position as I was. I was astounded that after an exhaustive search, I could find only one other person with the same administrative title. He was my friend and fellow physicist Professor Chuan-Sheng Liu of the University of Maryland. Not long after I discovered that he was my only counterpart, he left and assumed the position of the president of a university in Taiwan.

In my many decades of academic experiences, I discovered that most Chinese American colleagues, just like me when I was a cocoon professor, tend to prefer to remain in their professional "comfort zone" within their (narrow) professional lives and the people associated with their offices, that is other faculty members with similar intellectual interests, and of course, students and postdoctoral fellows.

I have often heard that many would claim that the lack of Chinese Americans moving up the academic administrative ladder is simply due to the racial glass-ceiling imposed on them by the American society. While there is certainly an element of truth in such a claim, I think that it should also be pointed out, and maybe as a more important element, that while the ceiling is there, often it is self-imposed. After all, to move up the administrative ladder, one needs to have a genuine interest and greater intellectual bandwidth to appreciate other people's issues. In a sense, that is also a form of cultural communication. The great discrepancy between Indian leaders and Chinese leaders in the education arena may simply be the fact that there is much room for improvement in the realm of cultural communication among the Chinese communities.

Dr Vincent Yip is a good friend of mine, who is a lecturer at Stanford University Continuing Studies, a fellow Singaporean, as well as a highly successful entrepreneur in the Silicon Valley. He told me that when he was teaching a management course at Stanford's business school, he would invariably find many students who were engineering and science graduate students. What surprised him was that among such students, there were always Indian and Chinese students in the mix. In discussing with the students, he soon found out that the Indian students generally felt that when the question arose as to whether they would continue an academic or corporate life, they would be interested to expand their intellectual bandwidth by moving up the management ladder and stepping out of their intellectual comfort zone. To prepare themselves for such eventualities, arming themselves with knowledge of management, which in a multi-racial society in the United States, must surely include understanding the ways and means of people of other cultures and civilizations. To the dismay of my friend who has a Chinese heritage, such visions and sentiments seemed to be missing among his Chinese students who tended to be far more inward looking than their Indian counterparts.

The dominant situation in the global corporate world for Indians is, unquestionably, even more spectacular. The tech website "Gatgets Now" published an article on January 26, 2018, with the title "Meet 9 Indian-origin CEOs "ruling" the technology industry."[23]

The 9 CEOs are the following:

1. Sundar Pichai, CEO of Google,
2. Satya Nadella, CEO of Microsoft,

---

[23] Gadgets Now Bureau. (January 26, 2017). Meet 9 Indian-origin CEOs 'ruling' the technology industry. *Gadgets Now.* Retrieved from https://www.gadgetsnow.com/slideshows/meet-9-indian-origin-ceos-ruling-the-technology-industry/sundar-pichai-ceo-google/photolist/53708166.cms.

3. Rajeev Suri, CEO of Nokia,
4. Shantanu Narayen, CEO of Adobe,
5. Sanjay Jha, CEO of Global Foundries,
6. George Kurian, CEO and President of NetApp,
7. Francisco Di'souza, CEO of Cognizant,
8. Dinesh Paliwal, CEO of Harman International,
9. Ashok Vemuri, CEO of Conduent Inc.

A photo of Sundar Pichai, CEO of Google. Like many outstanding Indians all over the world, Sundar, just like Subra Suresh, is a graduate of the Indian Institute of Technology.

Source: Retrieved from https://www.livemint.com/Industry/ck7SIuZBOnRRCcIYR5DfSJ/ Google-wants-to-train-other-companies-to-use-its-AI-tools.html.

I should add that while there is no data I could find, I do know that in the "non-tech world," the former CEO of Pepsi-Cola corporation, a company with an annual revenue of some $63 billion, was Indra Nooyi, who is an Indian lady. Ms. Nooyi made a famous quote which I thought could be the definition of "cultural communication," and that is

> I'm very honest — brutally honest. I always look at things from their point of view as well as mine.[24]

---

[24]Indra Nooyi. Brainy Quote. Retrieved from https://www.brainyquote.com/ quotes/indra_nooyi_416323.

Indra Nooyi.

Source: Retrieved from https://www.beveragedaily.com/Article/2018/10/03/Indra-Nooyi-Five-lessons-I-ve-learned-as-PepsiCo-CEO.

I am sure there are other examples of people in the global corporate world who are Indians but not on my radar screen. I am equally sure that if Chinese were to exist in such positions, they are few and far in between.

In the global tech world, as far as the Chinese community is concerned, it is stunning that there seems to be no counterpart holding positions equivalent to those held by the Indian community. At one point, Silicon Valley, because of the nature of the business, was given the name IC (or integrated circuit) world. Then by further examining the technical people there, IC whimisically stood for "Indians" and "Chinese." It is now obvious that in terms of corporate top leadership positions, the domination of Indians over Chinese is overwhelming.

To be a successful leader, either in the educational arena or in the corporate world, possessing a narrow area of knowledge superiority is necessary but hardly sufficient. Such an individual generally remains within his/her narrow comfort zone. Leadership requires someone who has developed a wide intellectual bandwidth, can respect other people's ways and means, and communicate with clarity and vision. Indeed, as the president of a university, whether it be in East or the West, having a wide range of knowledge as well as a broad human touch are the norm, not the exception. All of this would require the individual to have the propensity to develop "cultural communication" with other individuals, people of other disciplines, other institutions and maybe even other nations.

The fact that the Indians in the United States have so successfully climbed the administrative ladder, both in the educational and corporate arenas, surely implies that they inherently possess the necessary skillset to engage in "cultural communication" with the American society. As I have mentioned earlier, within India is a collection of many different cultures; thus, learning how to interact with a myriad of different cultures is the norm for an Indian and not the exception. Armed with this background, these individuals are able to fully appreciate, and in fact respect, the cultures and ways and means of other people and leverage — as my good friend David Naylor, former President of the University of Toronto would say — something almost identical to what Ms. Noori had uttered, namely,

understand other people's challenges with other people's cultures.

Indeed, to understand other people's culture would require stepping into other people's mindset. That again is the definition of cultural communication.

It is in this sense that the Chinese, who for millennia tended to be inward-looking, are not in competition with the Indians, and the outcome of the selection of high-level corporate and university leaders fully demonstrates this fact.

If China and India hold together, the future of Asia is assured. — *Jawaharlal Nehru, January 20, 1946.*

It is clear that the BRI pushes Chinese "to go out." It means that now, more than ever, China will have to deeply be involved in "cultural communication" with many countries. I will use this section to illustrate one example which I believe may be one of the

Photo taken with President Naylor when we both attended the centennial celebration of Hong Kong University.

most challenging examples. That country is India, which occupies a special place in my heart, being my birth country.

Going forward, China needs to culturally communicate with many countries and peoples. I hope that utilizing India as an example, one can realize the enormous challenges and excitement that the BRI can bring to China in particular, the world in general.

In October 2005, at the Annual Convention of the Indian Institute of Technology North Texas Alumni Association in Dallas, I was invited to deliver a keynote speech. After thinking long and hard about what I would say, I gave the speech with the title "India, US and China: Tripartite or Trinity in the 21st Century?" I discussed about how pivotal these three nations can and will be for the world in 21st century and how that will surely depend very much on the intertwined relations between them.

As I have mentioned earlier, at the beginning of this book, I was born in New Delhi, India. The whole family was there because my father (an NYU JD in 1937, who never practiced law but practiced

In 2003, I led a delegation from the University of Texas at Dallas to visit three top Indian universities: The Indian Institute of Technology at Bombay, Delhi and Roorkee. The photo was taken at one of the New Seven Wonders of the World, the Taj Mahal in India. In the middle is the late Professor Alan MacDiarmid, Nobel Laureate in chemistry 2000.

journalism) was the chief English editor of the Kuomintang's Central News Agency. A few weeks after my speech in Dallas, my son Ian was also admitted to NYU's law school. During his admission interview where he visited the university, he somehow was able to dig up some information about my father, such as the names of the JD graduating class in 1937. Since my father passed away in 1950 in a tragic air-crash, it pained my mother so deeply that she seldom mentioned him. Thus, my father in all those years was seldom in my cognizance. In fact, in looking back, until the moment that my curiosity about my father got the best of me, the fact that I was born in India, which nearly everyone I knew would find it curious, did not seem to have any relevance or any impact on any decision I needed to make in my life. Clearly, my son's action at NYU propelled a surge in my interest in my father — the desire to know more about him was a turning point for me.

Soon after my son's actions at NYU, on a subsequent Saturday morning, while I was surfing the Internet, I suddenly could not resist the inner urge to know more about my father. Unfortunately, by then, my mother had passed away and I had no direct or indirect way to learn more about him. In the end, as curiosity killed the cat, I did what a youngster would do: I "Googled" my father! Although I know his Chinese name, I was not sure how they were translated in English. Finally, in desperation, I simply typed in "Paul Feng" and "India" in Google and allowed it to search for me!

Photo of my family taken in Nanjing sometime before 1949. The man in the picture was my father Paul Feng. The baby was me.

I was convinced that such a search would be fruitless.

As usual, I started to search, and Google almost instantly gave me a whole bunch of websites. Most seemed to have nothing to do with what I was interested in or looking for.

Except one!

And that one absolutely astounded me!

This website[25] contains a spellbinding and beautifully written article by Mr. Manoj Das with the title "Forging an Asian identity." I later discovered that Manoj Das is a well-known Indian literary figure. The elegance of his writing certainly fits his reputation. According to Wikipedia,

Manoj Das (born 1934) is an award-winning Indian author who writes in Odia and English. In 2000, Manoj Das was awarded with Saraswati Samman. He was awarded Padma Shri in 2001, — the fourth highest Civilian Award in India for his contribution in the field of Literature & Education. Kendra Sahitya Akademi has bestowed its highest award (also India's highest literary award) i.e. Sahitya Akademi Award Fellowship.[26]

Photo of Manoj Das.

Source: Retrieved from https://upclosed.com/people/manoj-das/.

The article by Manoj Das was published on January 7, 2001, in one of India's most influential newspapers, *The Hindu*. It was written with such linguistic grace, flare and perfection that not only I was mesmerized by its every word, but I now feel compelled to encourage everyone with the slightest interest about the relationship between India and China to read it in its entirety.

---

[25]Forging an Asian identity. (January 7, 2001). Burma Library. Retrieved from https://www.burmalibrary.org/reg.burma/archives/200101/msg00016.html.
[26]Manoj Das. (n.d.). In *Wikipedia*. Retrieved September 1, 2019, from https://en.wikipedia.org/wiki/Manoj_Das.

In the article, there was a passage, given in the following, which utterly startled me:[27]

...We in India have debated as much as other Asian countries have, about issues like the desirability of Western influence on our culture, its inevitability or otherwise, and the relation between tradition and modernity. Like the May Fourth Movement in China which championed western values and ideals in the 1920s, we too had voices against our traditions and they were given a reasonable hearing. An exchange in experiences of this kind would no doubt be highly educative.

For quite some time, Indian literature for the common Englishman meant what Rudyard Kipling and the like wrote. For long, India's window as well as that of the West on Chinese life has been Pearl S. Buck's Good Earth. But when I read Lu Hsun, a number of his short stories and The True Story of Ah Q, I realised that despite the realism in the works of Pearl Buck and other gifted writers, Lu Hsun's work had an authenticity that could be expected only of a native of China. I do not propose to display my meagre knowledge of Chinese literature here, but what I propose is a strong and well-planned academy of Asian literatures to take care of the great need to know one another.

Photo of Pearl S. Buck.

Source: Retrieved from https://missionsbox.org/news/pearl-s-buck-insight-missions-chinese/.

---

[27]Forging an Asian identity. (January 7, 2001). Burma Library. Retrieved from https://www.burmalibrary.org/reg.burma/archives/200101/msg00016.html.

Photo of Lu Xun.

Source: Retrieved from https://supchina.com/2018/04/25/mingbai-lu-xun-father-of-chinese-literature-doctor-of-souls/.

And who could take any effective step in that direction? For me, the answer came in the form of the first Prime Minister of India, Jawaharlal Nehru. Speaking to Mr. Paul Feng of the Central News Agency, he said on January 20, 1946,

"If China and India hold together, the future of Asia is assured."

This holding together need not be confined to diplomacy; it can, by all means, be a psychological force that can work wonders in the realms of creativity...

To say that seeing the phrase (in italics here) caused me to immediately fall off my chair at that moment was an understatement.

The 12 words uttered by Nehru flabbergasted me not because Nehru, with his enormous reputation as a great statesman, said it. It is also not because the statement is truly visionary, which it clearly is. To be honest, I have known for quite some time that Nehru had made such a comment. But I have never until then had any deep personal feeling towards it, other than the fact that it was a forward-looking comment.

What caused me "to fall off my chair" is because Nehru, the world-renowned Indian statesman said those 12 words *to my father.*

At the moment when I read those 12 words, I experienced an instant adrenaline rush. Suddenly, those 12 simple yet powerful words were no longer just a profound voice at a distance, but deeply personal. From that moment on, I palpably felt that India and I are spiritually connected. To me, "holding" India and China together is now in my DNA.

I am also touched by what Manoj Das wrote, which was that "*Lu Xun's work had an authenticity that could be expected only of a native of China.*" These words, especially the word "authenticity," have succinctly captured the basic notion that for a native of India to truly understand China, he/she needs to seek the authenticity which could come about only if he/she could truly understand the underlying Chinese culture. The plea made by Manoj Das, which presumably was to both Indians and Chinese, was that there should be a "*strong and well-planned academy of Asian literatures to take care of the great need to know one another*" that "is loud and clear for both countries to seriously and comprehensively engage in "cultural communication" in the most profound manner.

It is equally true that for a Chinese to understand India, he/she also needs to seek authentic knowledge about the Indian culture and ways and means. This also could come about only if he/she could understand the underlying Indian culture! I am overwhelmed by someone in India who could utter words like "*to take care of the great need to know one another.*" And this happened even long before President Xi initiated the BRI, and "*to take care of the great need to know one another*" is precisely what "cultural communication" meant!

In going over and over those 12 words uttered by Nehru in my mind, I was also riveted by the word "hold." What and how to hold? In 1946, when Nehru uttered the phrase, although India was essentially untouched directly by the brutal WWII, it had just emerged from several hundred years of British colonial rule, and the country was undergoing an independence struggle, coupled with a lengthy and painful separation, which eventually rendered the countries we know now as India, West Pakistan and East Pakistan. China on the other hand had just painfully endured eight inhumane and nightmarish years of the "war of resistance" with the Japanese's brutal-beyond-belief militaristic regime. In all likelihood, "holding together" for India and China would not and could not have been the highest priority for leaders of both countries at that moment.

On October 1, 1949, the Chinese Communist Party led by Mao Zedong proclaimed on Tiananmen (the Gate of Heavenly Peace) the establishment of a "new" China — the "People's Republic of China or PRC." Between October 1, 1949 and December 31, 1949, many countries rushed to recognize the new Chinese government and established diplomatic relations with it. Not surprisingly, however, besides the Soviet Union, all were either the Soviet bloc nations or North Korea and Mongolia. In fact, the first country outside of the Soviet bloc or Soviet-influenced country to recognize the PRC was India, and this happened on January 1, 1950. It is notable that this was 6 days before Great Britain recognized the PRC (although the request was refused by the Chinese government). Being the first of the non-communist countries to recognize PRC, it appeared that Nehru's dream of "holding China and India together" saw a sliver of hope.

Yet that was not to be. Twelve years later, in 1962, the first and thus far only significant military conflict occurred between China and India. The conflict lasted only one month, from October 20, 1962 to November 20, 1962. It should be noted that the number of casualties in some of the major international conflicts in the 20th century, such as WWI and WWII, were in the many millions. In fact, even the 21st century Iraq war had close to half a million casualties. Adding the casualties on both sides together, the Sino-India 1962 conflict had far less than 10,000 casualties. Yet what is truly unfortunate is that while this conflict may have had a relatively small number of casualties, it became the main and long-lasting cause to inflict a deepscar on the mindset of both countries. It sent the relationship of the two nations into a deep freeze, diplomatic and otherwise, for the next 50 years.

In those 50 years, whatever little interest Indians had about China and Chinese ways and means were squashed almost to oblivion. The same was true for China. Although there were some minute signs of the thawing of the relations at the beginning of the 21st century, what happened at the First and Second Belt and Road International Cooperation Forum in Beijing — where India formally "boycotted" the meeting — was telling the world that "holding together" India and China, as Nehru so eloquently said in 1946, still has a long way to go.

Yet, it is undeniable that currently India and China have emerged as two of the most powerful nations not just in Asia, but the world at large. How they could interact with one another, how they could mutually work together to help themselves and the world to overcome challenges, especially when they are geographically so close, will have profound and long-term consequences for Asia and the world. To this end, for the sanity and future of Asia, if not the world, it is only a logical assumption that Nehru's 1946 dream of "hold" they must, and "hold" they shall.

Furthermore, both countries have long and rich histories, and both, for millennia, have not engaged in any form of blood feud. In fact, it was the historically famous monk Xuan-Zhuang (玄奘) who during the Tang Dynasty (A.D. 618 – A.D. 907) made the arduous trip to India to bring back many of the original Buddhist writings and translated them into Chinese. Such writings in the Chinese language allowed Buddhism to flourish in China, and eventually in other parts of Asia Pacific, such as Korea, Vietnam and Japan.

Route taken by Xuan-Zhuang.

Source: Retrieved from https://baike.baidu.com/item/%E7%8E%84%E5%A5%98/296302?fromtitle=%E5%94%90%E7%8E%84%E5%A5%98&fro mid=196059.

A depiction of Xuan-Zhuang.

Source: Retrieved from https://www.agefotostock.com/age/en/Stock-Images/Royalty-Free/ WR1916709 which includes the following depiction: "This very old Chinese illustration shows the Chinese Buddhist pilgrim Xuan-Zhuang (also spelled Hsuan-tsang and Xuan Zang) on his return home from India, where he searched for sacred books of Buddhism and studied with Buddhist monks, in A.D. 645, during the Tang dynasty. In a typical representation, it shows Huan Tsang carrying on his back many Buddhist texts, an oil lamp hanging from the backpack bundle, and straw sandals on his feet."

It is undeniable that much of the current animosity between the two nations is the consequences of contemporary and regional politics and/or geopolitics. It is geopolitics because there are palpable footprints of other global powers lurking in the midst. An excellent example of what will happen when India and China are left alone to solve a problem is given in the following. Take the tense military situation staring down at each other for more than 2 months in 2017 at the India–China border area known as Doklam (a region bordered by China, India and Bhutan.) Without outside interference, both sides were able to resolve the confrontations with cool heads.

Map of the region of Doklam.

Source: Retrieved from https://www.quora.com/What-is-the-Doklam-conflict-When-did-it-start.

Fundamentally, it appears that both sides came to the realization that (a) there is nothing to be gained by letting the confrontation drag on, which may indeed by accident lead to flaring up of accidents; (b) the example of the 1962 conflict reminded both countries, especially China, that even by "winning" a no-matter-how-minute blood-spilled conflict, could be too costly in the long run; (c) despite all their differences and animosities, India and China have been friendly to one another for millennia.[28]

I have often wondered out loud what would happen if indeed as Nehru said that "China and India can hold together." Would it mean that there will be one million Chinese — only 1 in 1400 Chinese, and one million Indians — 1 in 1200 Indians, while maintaining their

---

[28] 2017 China–India border standoff. (n.d.). In *Wikipedia*. Retrieved September 1, 2019, from https://en.wikipedia.org/wiki/2017_China%E2%80%93India_border_standoff.

respective national identities and dignities, who can truly understand each other's histories, cultures, political structures, even cuisines, and ways and means? Indeed, would it mean that both countries would have a significant number of universities who would engage in serious and large-scale research on each other's long and deep histories, cultures and ways and means? If that is what "hold together" means, then one could expect that for the first time in human history, two massive and profound nations can create an unprecedented cohesive force not just for mutual benefit, but for the benefit of the entire Asia. In fact, by their sheer magnitudes and global outreaches, they can together propel humanity to a new level of enlightenment.

Facing the current relationship between India and China, with all its convoluted geopolitical and geoeconomics entanglements, it seems that in order for them to "hold together," as Nehru would say, it would require a powerful incentive that is far beyond what normal geopolitics and geoeconomics can provide.

I began thinking about what could be the "hold" agent ever since I realized in 2004 the 12 immortal words of Nehru, which was long before President Xi initiated the Belt and Road Initiative. My firm belief all along was that if India and China could indeed hold together to be the driving force for the good of humanity, the world could literally undergo an unprecedented tranquil facelift.

With the BRI being launched in 2013 with the mantra "interactions among people," and when I knew about it in 2016, I inherently felt that this was exactly what I had been waiting for, namely holding India and China together was given a chance to succeed. After all, to render the BRI successful, to engage in "cultural communication" with the outside world for China, in which there is no possibility of excluding India. In fact, I have said to myself, and have included it in my many speeches worldwide, that:

Would it not be a great irony of history, that after more than 70 years since Nehru uttered those 12 visionary words, it would take the profound vision of President Xi Jinping, who initiated the BRI to become the holding agent for India and China?

India Is the "Moon of China in the 21st Century" and China Is the "Moon of India in the 21st Century"

Clearly, the best destiny for Asia, and maybe the world as well, is for India and China, the two massive nations sitting geographically next to each other, to "hold," as Nehru had expounded on in 1946. Looking at the geopolitical and regional politics landscapes, one may not reach an optimistic view about such an outcome. However, being an eternal optimist, I remember the phrase in the famous poem by the Sung dynasty poet Luyou (陆游), which is "山重水复疑无路，柳暗花明又一村," which essentially means in the modern terms that "there is light at the end of a long dark tunnel"!

My optimism is derived from remembering a speech delivered by President John F. Kennedy.

President John F. Kennedy of the United States of America.

Source: Retrieved from https://www.immigrationdirect.com/blog/2013/11/in-remembrance-of-john-f-kennedy/.

On September 12, 1962, a year before he was assassinated, President John F. Kennedy declared to a stunned audience of 40,000 in the football stadium of Rice University (in Houston, Texas) that[29]

We set sail on this new sea because there is new knowledge to be gained, and new rights to be won, and they must be won and used

---

[29] We choose to go to the Moon. In *Wikipedia*. Retrieved September 1, 2019, from https://en.wikipedia.org/wiki/We_choose_to_go_to_the_Moon.

for the progress of all people. For space science, like nuclear science and all technology, has no conscience of its own. Whether it will become a force for good or ill depends on man, and only if the United States occupies a position of pre-eminence can we help decide whether this new ocean will be a sea of peace or a new terrifying theater of war. I do not say that we should or will go unprotected against the hostile misuse of space any more than we go unprotected against the hostile use of land or sea, but I do say that space can be explored and mastered without feeding the fires of war, without repeating the mistakes that man has made in extending his writ around this globe of ours.

There is no strife, no prejudice, no national conflict in outer space as yet. Its hazards are hostile to us all. Its conquest deserves the best of all mankind, and its opportunity for peaceful cooperation may never come again. But why, some say, the Moon? Why choose this as our goal? And they may well ask, why climb the highest mountain? Why, 35 years ago, fly the Atlantic? Why does Rice play Texas (I should add that was and still is because Texas football is orders of magnitude stronger than Rice University)?

We choose to go to the Moon! We choose to go to the Moon... We choose to go to the Moon in this decade and do the other things, not because they are easy, but because they are hard; because that goal will serve to organize and measure the best of our energies and skills, because that challenge is one that we are willing to accept, one we are unwilling to postpone, and one we intend to win, and the others, too.

Reading this eloquent and emotional passage in Kennedy's speech perked up my optimism considerably. From it, I learned that when a great nation, which China and the United States both are, intends to pursue an immense effort, usually it is not because it is easy, but because it is hard. For the United States then in the 20th century, when the nation was neither economically nor technologically ready for such a great venture as ensuring humankind going to the moon, President Kennedy stood on his presidential bully-pulpit to pronounce to the world that by doing so, it would open up an entirely new vista, never before attempted. By saying so with such conviction and passion and following it up with the prestige of his office, he as President of the United States (even though a year later he was assassinated) was able to garner tremendous all-round national energy, from sectors as diverse as science, technology and public policies and support, not to mention garnering the pride, to pursue such a lofty goal.

And on July 20, 1969, less than a decade later, two astronauts, Neil Armstrong and Buzz Aldrin, landed on the moon.

Buzz Aldrin stands beside the US flag at Tranquility Base on the moon.

Source: Retrieved from https://www.noted.co.nz/currently/history/myths-legends-of-moon-landing-first-man/.

There is an obvious lesson one can learn from Kennedy's 1962 "moon landing" declaration, which is the United States intended to go to the moon, and within a designated timeframe. The needed vision and courage, especially political courage, of President Kennedy were simply monumental. It appears that if the effort was worth pursuing with all the energy and might a country can muster, especially from a nation as powerful as the United States, elucidating the intention with utter clarity from its leader, I am convinced that the effort has already achieved half the success.

I do not have the slightest doubt that for China and India to "hold," the degree of difficulties facing both countries to achieve it will surely be as challenging, if not more so, than the United States' intention to send humans to the moon. But just as Kennedy was convinced that going to the moon was so very important not just to the United States but to the world that it was worth overcoming any challenges, and to boldly declare that his country will send humans to the moon within a decade, President Xi Jinping — in a similar vein — representing China in 2013 declared in Kazakhstan and Indonesia that China will "go out" via the BRI for the betterment of not just China but the world. To render BRI a complete success, to ensure that China and India "can hold together" is one of the many challenges the initiative must overcome, if not in the short run, then surely in the long run.

In many of the speeches I delivered around the world regarding BRI, I made the whimsical but heartfelt statement that

for China in the 21st century, its moon is *India.*

Likewise,

for India in the 21st century, its moon is China!

A Summary of Cultural Communications

The BRI is such a profoundly important initiative for China. Once again, I cannot emphasize enough that it is entirely a Chinese initiative, unlike the ancient silk roads which were organically formed. Therefore, it should and must have placed on China as a country, and the Chinese as a people, an unprecedented and unimaginable demand to alter the millennium mindset of "not going out," and comprehensively and proactively "thinking and acting in an outward manner"!

Furthermore, the fact that China today is a nation that has many dimensions of significant importance, which has taken actions as profound as this is, would have global impacts. Such a mindset transformation could very well be another turning point for human history. Hopefully, such a turning point is for the better. Finally, for the Chinese to "think and act in an outward manner," this upstream of upstream challenge is precisely what I have emphasized from the beginning of this chapter, which is what Mr. Zhou Yanli mentioned in 2016, namely before anything else, there must be "cultural communication"!

Propelled by the BRI, China will look to and interact with the outside world in a multidimensional manner. By that I mean before any interactions with foreign countries can take place, be it economical, technological, regional, political, geopolitical and cultural, China must be fully ready to *a priori* appreciate, understand and respect the cultures which embody the "entire being" of foreign countries and civilizations. In reverse, China also needs to welcome and assist the outside world to understand China far deeper and far more comprehensively than those countries had ever before!

On April 27, 2019, President Xi Jinping in the inaugural speech of the Second Forum of the Belt and Road International Collaboration reemphasized the critical importance of cultural communication. He said that[30]

> We need to build bridges for exchanges and mutual learning among different cultures, deepen cooperation in education, science, culture, sports, tourism, health and archaeology, strengthen exchanges between parliaments, political parties and non-governmental organizations and exchanges between women, young people and people with disabilities in order to facilitate multifaceted people-to-people exchanges. To this end, we will, in the coming five years, invite 10,000 representatives of political parties, think tanks and non-governmental organizations from Belt and Road participating countries to visit China. We will encourage and

---

[30]Ministry of Foreign Affairs of the People's Republic of China. Working Together to Deliver a Brighter Future For Belt and Road Cooperation (April 26, 2019). Retrieved from https://www.fmprc.gov.cn/mfa_eng/zxxx_662805/t1658424.shtml.

support extensive cooperation on livelihood projects among social organizations of participating countries, conduct a number of environmental protection and anti-corruption training courses and deepen human resources development cooperation in various areas. We will continue to run the Chinese government scholarship Silk Road Program, host the International Youth Forum on Creativity and Heritage along the Silk Roads and the "Chinese Bridge" summer camps. We will also put in place new mechanisms such as the Belt and Road Studies Network and the Belt and Road News Alliance to draw inspiration and pool our strength for greater synergy.

One sees that in every word in this quote, President Xi was emphasizing the fundamental importance of cultural communication for the BRI to move forward.

With many millennia of wisdom embedded in the Chinese civilization, understanding the outside world was a part of it. In the 5th century AD, the military strategist Sun Tzu (孙子) wrote a treatise known as the "Art of War" (孙子兵法) in which he stated succinctly that "know thyself and thy competitors, hundred encounters hundred triumphs" (知己知彼, 百战不殆).

Book cover of *Sun Tzu's The Art of War.*

Source: Retrieved from https://titusng.com/2013/03/03/sun-tzus-five-characteristics-of-leaders/.

Although the intended readers of the monumental treaties by Sun Tzu were, as the title of his book would suggest, for military strategists, the implications of this statement indeed are so general that it is also appropriate for all forms of human interactions, and certainly it is for the BRI.

In the BRI, "*to know others*" must not and should not be a luxury. It must be an absolute necessity. Also, neither should it be interpreted as an intention for China to expand its influence beyond its border. Rather, it should be understood as China's genuine intention to assume the responsibility as one of the most successful nations on earth to achieve with other nations multiple wins or at least a dual win through "cultural communication." In this way, China can assist all nations, and with it itself, to enable betterment of humanity.

For example, some of the BRI activities would be Chinese companies investing in foreign countries or developing economic corridors. At the core, such activities are all intense interactions between human beings, and for such interactions to be successful and sustainable, they must be based on a firm foundation of "cultural communication."

The Chinese name for China is "Zhong Guo (中国)," where "zhong" means "center."

Zhong.

Source: Photo retrieved from https://www.pinterest.com/pin/558446422522622197/.

As was mentioned, for millennia, the Chinese mindset had a profoundly inward-looking view of themselves and their nation. Such a mindset prevented the nation from truly reaching the comfort zone of other civilizations.

The magnificent Chinese Pavilion at the 2010 World Trades Fair in Shanghai was mentioned by Wikipedia as "The 63-metre high pavilion, … is dubbed 'The Oriental Crown' because of its resemblance to an ancient Chinese crown."[31]

Chinese Pavilion at the 2010 World Trades Fair in Shanghai.
Source: Retrieved from https://en.wikipedia.org/wiki/China_pavilion_at_Expo_2010.

To me, another way to view this pavilion is that it seems to spell out to the world that "the world comes to China" and not "China embraces the world." This underscores the millennium Chinese-rooted mindset.

The BRI, unlike the ancient silk roads, is an entirely Chinese creation. Therefore, its ultimate success must be hinged on a deep-seated mindset transformation of China as a nation of immense

---

[31] China pavilion at Expo 2010. In *Wikipedia*. Retrieved September 1, 2019, from https://en.wikipedia.org/wiki/China_pavilion_at_Expo_2010.

dimensions, with a modern and robust economy and possessing a rich and ancient civilization. Therefore, one must not underestimate the level of global difficulties which the BRI will encounter. To institute global "cultural communication" is on the one hand enormously difficult and on the other an absolute necessity.

In this regard, education, especially higher education, should and must play a yeomen's role. The 3500 tertiary institutions in China today, and hopefully all the universities in the Supercontinent, should and must shoulder this responsibility, to educate an entirely new generation of intellects worldwide to carry out this arduous task which has a lofty goal in rendering the world to face the existential challenges and make it a better place for humanity.

The BRI will change the global rules of the game, and one of the critical new rules is "cultural communication." As one of the most robust nations in the world today, the BRI introduced by China will give unprecedented implication to the meaning of the term "a powerful nation." It is perhaps because the Chinese have learned from their own history, in which they were once the most powerful nation in the world, and from the more recent history, where the Western world defined power as military and economic might and dominance, that in the 21st century, gentleness, modesty and integrity should be its definition. Indeed, I dare say that with the success of the BRI, this will be the first time in human history that a nation is leveraging noble demeanors to be the definition of "power."

To personally visit foreign lands and study in depth the people there is the only way to carry out cultural communication. In the next three chapters, I will give three case studies of the importance of cultural communication. In Chapter 5, I will discuss how my good friend Lee Hong-Fah formed a motorcade and bravely drove from Singapore to London. The trip was *de facto* a modern-day Zhang Qian exploration. In Chapter 6, I will discuss in detail my visits to Kaifeng, Henan Province, to understand in-depth the situation of the Jews there in the Sung Dynasty. The chapter also explains how the Jews and Chinese interacted so palpably during that period in history. In Chapter 7, I will point out what my understanding of

Canada is as a nation, and ways for China to culturally communicate with it. Finally, I will present a visit report of mine regarding Malaysia, as this was my attempt to understand one of the pivotal Southeast Asian nations.

Ultimately, with cultural communications, this is why the success of the BRI should not and cannot merely be the success of China, it must be the success of humanity!

Chapter 5

Case Study 1 of "Cultural Communication": A Conversation With Lee Hong-Fah (李洪发), the Modern-Day Zhang Qian (张骞)

I found it remarkable that even for the Western part of Malaysia, from Penang to the State of Johor (a State of Malaysia which is just north of Singapore) which is a mere 800 kilometers, the cuisines, cultures and not to mention politics, could differ noticeably. What was particularly interesting for me was to observe the gradual transition, which was only possible by land travel.

As I have mentioned in the Preface of this book, during my research about the meaning of BRI, I was deeply impressed by Zhang Qian (张骞). In the Han Dynasty of China (202 BC–9 AD and 25 AD–220 AD), one of the Emperors, Han Wu-Di (汉武帝, 156 BC–87 BC) dispatched a military general Zhang Qian to carry out various expeditions to the so-called "Western region," which is Central Asia of today. According to records, Zhang Qian went as far west as the Caspian Sea, which is bounded in today's geopolitics by Kazakhstan, Russia, Azerbaijan, Iran and Turkmenistan. The careful and accurate reports made by Zhang Qian, using the present-day vernacular, rendered him one of the first, if not the first, Chinese who was able to understand and appreciate people with profoundly different cultures, histories and lifestyles, i.e. cultural communication.

According to Baidu, Zhang Qian was gloriously honored as being "第一个睁开眼睛看世界的中国人," or "the first Chinese to observe the world with open eyes"! In this context, I am truly honored to know one of the few men whom I would refer to as the Zhang Qian of the 21st century. He is a Malaysian Chinese named Lee Hong-Fah (李洪发). What Lee Hong-Fah had accomplished could indeed be a case study of "cultural communication."

A Bit of Background on Lee Hong-Fah

During my three and a half years as Senior Executive Vice President of Cheng Kung University (成功大学) in Tainan, Taiwan, I became aware that this university, during the second half of the 20th century, recruited a significant number of outstanding students of Chinese heritage from Malaysia. With that as preamble, I had the great pleasure of meeting one such alumnus — Lee Hong-Fah. In the following, I shall give the reasons why I made the previous claim about him.

In the post-WWII era, Malaysian secondary school students with Chinese heritage could either enter the "English-stream" schools where English was the language of instruction or the "Chinese-stream" schools where the language of instruction was primarily Chinese. For a variety of reasons, the opportunities for post-secondary education for the latter group were exceedingly limited. Except for those whose families were well-to-do and therefore could afford to go abroad, such as United Kingdom, Australia and, to a lesser extent, Canada, Taiwan became a target attraction for this cohort with a high-quality higher education system.

During the 1960s through the 1980s, the number of students from Malaysia who studied in Cheng Kung University was in the many thousands. Also, except for a relatively small percentage who made the decision to stay in Taiwan after they completed their education, most returned to Malaysia.

Lee Hong-Fah and I took this picture in Port Klang, Malaysia, with his cross-country van in the background.

In Taiwan, these Malaysian students mostly pursued disciplines of science, engineering or business. At that time, the Malaysian government did not recognize Taiwan's academic degrees, and thus such a large number of technologically highly educated returnees were all blocked from entering the government-related or -sponsored opportunities. Hence, they were forced to enter various forms of private businesses. Armed with excellent education and diligence, it was not surprising that many eventually became financially highly successful. With wealth, some were able to play a significant role, political and otherwise, in Malaysia.

One could easily imagine that had the Taiwanese educational opportunities not been available, the future of this cohort of Malaysian Chinese would in all likelihood be dismal. Therefore, deep in their hearts, they appreciated the life-changing Taiwan educational opportunities. So, it was not surprising that thousands of alumni from Cheng Kung University formed a very powerful and active Malaysian alumni association whose missions were, and still are, to promote goodwill among themselves and, more importantly, to uphold the wellness of their *alma mater.*

Almost as soon as I took up my position as Senior Executive Vice President at Cheng Kung University in 2007, I came into contact with the leadership of Malaysia's Cheng Kung University Alumni Association. At that time, one of the leaders was Lee Hong-Fah. Partly because of my position in Cheng Kung University and partly because I grew up in Singapore, forming kinship with him was quite natural. In time, we became close friends.

Like many of his compatriots, Lee Hong-Fah came from a poor family. He completed his secondary education with good grades in 1968. As he told me, *"I wanted to study mechanical engineering, and back then, Cheng Kung University was already very interested in Malaysian Chinese students, and therefore was most interested in recruiting me."* Thus, he was admitted to Cheng Kung University. There were then only a few universities in Taiwan, and fewer still offering mechanical engineering as a discipline, and one of the best, if not the best, was Cheng Kung University.

During my time at Cheng Kung University, I had the good fortune of meeting with the former Dean of Engineering and a retired Professor of Mechanical Engineering, Professor Lee Ke-Rang (李克让). In my extensive interactions with Professor Lee, who is an expert in rheology, i.e. the study of non-Newtonian flow materials, I learned about how meticulous and demanding a teacher he was. I could surmise that students like Lee Hong-Fah, who always mentioned Professor Lee with such reverence, must have had a first-class undergraduate engineering education, probably comparable to anywhere in the world at that time. Thus, this education became the solid underpinning which Lee Hong-Fah stood on to build his career later in Malaysia.

Standing next to me are Mrs. And Mr. Lee Ke-Rang.

After Lee Hong-Fah completed his undergraduate studies in 1973, he stayed briefly in Taiwan to work for one year to gain additional practical experience, before returning to Malaysia. Leveraging his solid theoretical and practical mechanical engineering knowledge, he first worked for a German company in Malaysia whose business was to manufacture sophisticated electric cranes. He did so well in that job that the company made the decision to send him to Germany for an intense three-month training. By 1983, he was ready and able to begin his own entrepreneurial and successful career of building a company to design, market, fabricate, install and service electric cranes. In the subsequent 25 years, which was also the period when Malaysia saw enormous growth, his company became one of the most important ones in this field in Malaysia. Then in 2007, the year before I met him, he sold his company and entered the next and maybe more exciting phase of his life: exploring Asia and Europe.

By the time Lee Hong-Fah and I met, while he was still only in his mid-50s, he had already retired and sold his company. The retirement gave him more free time and significant means which he never had before. He then began to devote time to develop and promote the activities of Cheng Kung University's Alumni Association as well as began seeking other activities that could fulfill his intellectually active mind.

As our friendship blossomed, whenever the opportunities arose, Lee Hong-Fah and I would engage in serious discussions about a multitude of issues surrounding the development and evolution of Asia Pacific. I found the discussions with him always exciting and enriching due to his wide range of experience and knowledge. Mind you, our discussions were never your usual chit-chats. They were generally serious and in-depth, and he was always highly analytical in his geopolitical analysis, which an excellent engineer should be able to do.

Lee Hong-Fah's Entourage Undertook Land Travel to China Ten Times

Lee Hong-Fah, during my phone conversation with him to write this chapter, said that in 2007, he had felt for several decades, mentally, intellectually and physically constrained, because of the enormous demand on his time for his business. Indeed, one of his passions in life was to travel. He noticed that Malaysia is "land-linked" to China, a country of his ancestry, and not surprisingly he had an irrepressible urge to "travel by land" to China. For obvious reasons, such a concept was not only unusual, it was thought to be impossible. Therefore, as soon as he was unconstrained from his responsibilities because of his retirement from the business, he began planning such a trip to travel by land to China.

In 2008, Lee Hong-Fah finally acted on this deep desire and organized the first motorcade entourage of 30 individuals with a similar inclination. Together, they bought 10 high-performance cross-country vans and made the trip from Singapore to China and back. In the subsequent several years, this entourage made a total of 10 such trips. Undoubtedly, with such trips under their belts, he and his team gained an enormous amount of experience, technically, culturally and politically, through making such arduous trips to faraway lands. Although 2008 was merely twelve years ago, for

China's transportation system, it was an era that was significantly different from today. By 2008, China already had a sophisticated national superhighway system and today, it has supplemented it with a high-speed rail system.

A typical birds-eye-view of China's modern superhighway system.

Source: Retrieved from https://medium.com/shanghaiist/china-starts-work-on-worlds-first-super-highway-that-can-charge-electric-cars-as-they-drive-9f29b1459977.

Without knowing it, what Lee Hong-Fah *de facto* did was to carry out in-depth, what my two good friends Michael Szonyi, Director of Harvard University's Fairbank Center and Haiming Liang, Chair of China Silk iValley Research Center, would refer to as "field research." What Lee Hong-Fah learned from observing, discussing with people of all nations and cultures, staying in living quarters which no tourists are willing or able to stay in, and last but not least, appreciating the local cuisines, was an in-depth learning of the ways and means that few people in the world would encounter or had encountered.

In 2008, social media was in its infancy. Therefore, neither Lee Hong-Fah nor I were familiar enough to use this platform for communications. Thus, except for a word or two I heard from him about the ten trips whenever we met either in Tainan or Kuala

Lumpur, without anything tangible, those words did not register significantly on my radar screen.

Quite recently, in order to write this chapter, I engaged in several long telephone conversations with him about those ten trips. I began by asking him what motivated him to make such a trip.

> "By nature, I just love to travel," he said. "Even before the ten driving trips to China, whenever opportunities arose, I preferred to drive back and forth to many cities in Malaysia. By doing so, I found that I could inevitably gain a deeper understanding of the geography, the people, the culture and even the food for a country as small as Malaysia. I found it remarkable that even for the Western part of Malaysia, from Penang to the State of Johor (a State of Malaysia which is just north of Singapore) which is a mere 800 kilometers, the cuisines, cultures and not to mention politics, could differ noticeably. What was particularly interesting for me was to observe the gradual or sudden transition, which was only possible by land travel."

Regarding his ten trips to China, he said that:

> Yunnan province was always our entry point into China. From there, we would go westward to Tibet, Qinghai, and Xinjiang. These are landmass-wise, enormous provinces, with 1.22, 0.72 and 1.66 million square kilometers, respectively. They are also highly underpopulated whereby one could travel a very long way and see nature in its virgin form. Yet mind you, by 2008, China's nationwide superhighways were already fairly extensive and mature. Because the land was so desolate, our knee-jerk expectation of the road conditions would be from modest to poor. But to our surprise, we found most of the roads to be quite adequately maintained. As a civil engineer, I know well that construction is "easy," but "maintenance" is hard. From what we saw regarding the road conditions, we concluded that once China had the means to do so, significantly upgrading the country's transportation infrastructure was way up in its priority. Clearly, this tells us that there are people in engineering management that understood this fundamental principle well!

After Xinjiang, the entourage went eastward, through Gansu, Ningxia, Shanxi, Hebei, and ended up in Beijing.

As I probed deeper about the entourage's experiences, he told me something that startled me. Lee Hong-Fah said,

> Back then, we realized that whenever we needed mechanical work because our cross-country vans took a beating in China, we had never failed to find local technicians who could fix them with sufficient knowledge. We noticed that China was, and I am sure still is, dotted with technical institutes, whose primary purpose was to educate a vast number of capable technicians. These technicians were literally dotting the entire landscape of China. We are sure that as China was constructing significant number of superhighways, the top planners realized that it was imperative to maintain a large cadre of capable auto-mechanics nationally to ensure seamless logistics was a reality. I am quite certain this was one of the reasons why the country's supply chain did not break down, even in the most remote regions.

During many of their pit stops, they met and chatted with Chinese long-haul truck drivers. Lee Hong-Fah said that:

> In 2008, this was especially true in the remote provinces, where we found that people were quite reticent to converse with us. Such behavior was probably because there were very few foreigners in those remote areas of China, especially driving on highways. Yet, from our few interactions, I could already tell that they seem to know quite a bit about the world outside of China. For example, I was, in fact, surprised to learn how much they seemed to know about Malaysia. In reverse, I am quite sure that a Malaysian long-haul truck driver would know nothing about the interior of China!

Lee Hong-Fah also discussed with me briefly some of the ways and means of Thailand — the country through which the entourage had to travel to and from China. What was most interesting to him was that when they first made the trip, compared to the Chinese, the Thais demonstrably had a more refined demeanor, according to him. As time went on, however, he noticed that the Thais became increasingly "ruder" while the Chinese seemed to move in the opposite direction. Lee Hong-Fah conjectured that for

Thais, this could be a direct consequence of the gradual upheaval resulting from the political and social disorder, leaving them increasingly frustrated and dissatisfied with the condition of their nation. On the other hand, in the past two decades, while China still faces enormous challenges, the social disorder and the level of dissatisfaction has appeared to be dampened somewhat. He made the comment that:

> Had I not made ten trips to Southeast Asia and China over a couple of years, I am sure I could not possibly had observed this phenomenon!

Finally, due to the fact that Tibet shares borders with India and other nations like Nepal, it was not uncommon for the entourage to go through numerous military checkpoints. It was interesting that as soon as any military personnel at the checkpoints noticed their Malaysian car license plates, they would immediately switch languages and speak with them in good to excellent English. Furthermore, they were always polite and professional. Lee Hong-Fah said that:

> I think China understands how sensitive the border areas are, and therefore the very large number Chinese military personnel sent to guard these exceedingly long borders had good English language ability and were highly trained in social manners!

This comment reminded me of the time when Hsinchu's Tsing Hua University was establishing the Taiwan Education Centers, and we were contacted by the Indian military personnel. They expressed great interest in having the Centers teach Chinese to the Indian military. The reason for this was because at the border, all the information gathered from China would be in Chinese and no one could understand it. On the other hand, from what Lee Hong-Fah told us, since most of the Indian information is in English, it is no wonder the military sent to the border has a good command of the English language!

The route taken by Lee Hong-Fah's entourage, from Singapore to London!

Lee Hong-Fah's Entourage Undertook Land Travel to China, Central Asia and Europe in 2015

Sometime in 2015, from our Facebook communications, I noticed that Lee Hong-Fah appeared to be organizing another major trip. Just as with his previous ten China trips, this time it also involved about ten enormous heavy-duty cross-country vans and some 30 like-minded individuals. As they started to make the trip, I could literally follow them as time went on while they were driving through Malaysia, Thailand, Laos and then entered China. Unlike his former trips to China that I could only hear about when we met in person, this time I could observe it in real time!

I noticed that in the vast western part of China, they drove through Yunnan, Tibet, Qinghai and Xinjiang.

These are photos given to me by Lee Hong-Fah. They were taken at the Himalayan ridge.

He also posted on his Facebook page, some truly spectacular and breathtaking photos of the people, the scenery, the culture and, most remarkably, even their moments of struggles, mechanical and otherwise. He also mentioned that unlike the 10 trips in 2008, this time they found that nearly all the roads were paved and that there were numerous hotels along the way in these enormous Western Chinese provinces. Of course, most importantly, the quality of the toilet facilities had also improved noticeably! In general, the facilities available for tourists were more abundant and in better condition this time around. Perhaps what is most noticeable is the old saying "cleanliness is next to godliness!"

Unlike the previous 10 trips to China in 2008, this time the entourage did not terminate their trip in China. In fact, at the Xinjiang border with Kyrgyzstan, they made their grand entrée into Central Asia. They travelled through two former Soviet, now independent, countries — Kyrgyzstan and Kazakhstan — that have landmasses of 200 thousand square kilometers and 2.7 million square kilometers, respectively. As a point of reference, this means that these two countries are one-third or 2.6 times the largest Province of China, Xinjiang. The distance from one end of Kyrgyzstan's border with China to the other end of Kazakhstan's border with Russia would be close to 1600 kilometers. Yet from the pictures posted on Facebook, the endless multi-lane highways, as Lee Hong-Fah told me later on, "were mostly constructed and maintained by China." From the enclosed photos, these highways, which reminded me of the highways of Texas, though they may look desolate are nevertheless well maintained.

A well maintained four-lane highway near the Xingjiang–Kyrgyzstan border.

With regard to Kazakhstan, Lee Hong-Fah told me an experience they had in Almaty, the largest city in the country. For one

Border between Kyrgyzstan and Kazakhstan.

reason or another, when they arrived at the city, they could not find lodging for the entourage. In the end, the only place they could find to rest their tired bodies was in the dormitories of a local university. According to Lee,

> We were glad not because we found a place to rest, but because we were able to meet and interact palpably with many students of the university. To our surprise, we discovered many of them came from every corner of the world, from Africa, Europe and South America. They were all very enthusiastic about the education they had received there. This gave us the first indication that these central Asian countries were not as remote and desolate as one would think!

According to Lee Hong-Fah, his entourage could feel the presence of China in these two Central Asian nations. In fact, according to him, China had played, and probably is still playing, a major if not critical role in these countries' economic transformations. They were accomplished either with Chinese assistance or directly with Chinese laborers. Lee Hong-Fah told me that since the entire entourage could speak Mandarin, the locals who understood Chinese in both Central Asian countries would sometimes assume that they were also Chinese from China. He said with a whimsical smile:

> After all, they could not tell that our Mandarin has a heavy Malaysian accent!

Lee Hong-Fah emphasized that the locals were very friendly and helpful towards them and that they would inevitably utter the word "*Chinese*," following up with a thumbs-up gesture. There were other instances where the locals realized that Lee Hong-Fah and his entourage came from Malaysia. Apparently, they knew enough about Malaysia being a "Muslim country," and therefore automatically assumed that the people in the entourage were also Muslims. Such a mistake seems to have a positive effect of breaking down any initial interaction barriers.

It is worth mentioning here that one could feel the Russian ambiance in these two Central Asian nations. Most people whom Lee Hong Fah and his entourage encountered could speak fluent Russian. This is of course not surprising since these two central Asian countries were once part of Soviet Union, whose culture and political systems for many decades had made deep inroads.

After Kazakhstan, the entourage entered Russia, where they had to travel approximately another 1600 kilometers before entering Finland. While in Russia, they made an extended stopover in two of Russia's major metropolitan cities, Moscow and St Petersburg. According to Lee Hong-Fah:

> We noticed that the Russian highways, unlike those in Kyrgyzstan and Kazakhstan, are noticeably poorer in quality. In fact, at times, they were simply dirt roads!

The border checkpoint to enter Russia, unlike all previous borders, was exceptionally tight. A two-hour immigration procedure was quite common. "*Talking to some of the truck drivers at the border,*" Lee Hong-Fah said, "*they told me that some time it was so laborious that it would take half or a full day of wait for them!*" Also, the level of corruption was noticeable. In fact, according to Lee Hong-Fah, it was customary for anyone crossing such checkpoints to hire a Russian travel agent before entering, as the agent's primary role would be to "facilitate" the crossing of the border into Russia.

In Russia, what was most noticeable was the level of scientific knowledge among the locals. According to Lee Hong-Fah,

> Russians seem to be a very scientific population. Regarding our discussions with many people, on any topic, generally they could back up with scientific and logical reasons. In many ways, they were very German-like, very logical minded indeed! I think this must be a reflection of the overall educational quality of the country.

This comment is completely in agreement with my several trips to Russia in the first decade of the 21st century. In Appendix B, I discussed a visit wherein I leveraged my interaction with the top theoretical physicist in Moscow, Vitaly Ginzburg, and had broad discussions with him on the scientific ambiance in Russia.

As soon as they entered Scandinavia, the entourage immediately noticed a different level of affluence. No matter how remote the destination in Scandinavia, one could notice that the roads were well maintained. Travel infrastructures such as high-quality hotels were ubiquitous. Of course, for the entire Scandinavia, everything was extremely expensive!

The entourage touched all four countries: Finland, Norway, Sweden and Denmark. In Finland, they drove close to a thousand kilometers all the way north to the Arctic Circle, where Finland borders Norway. There they entered Norway and drove southward for another 1000 kilometers before reaching Sweden. They drove through Sweden until they reached the magnificent Oresund Bridge which links Sweden with Denmark.

It is worth noting that when I was spending a year as a visiting professor at the Niels Bohr Institute in Copenhagen in the late 1970s, this Bridge did not exist. This was one of the reasons why I did not had the opportunity to visit Sweden, despite its proximity. Having such a bridge now, it is clear that in the past several decades, Scandinavia has made significant improvement in its transportation infrastructure. This reminded me what the longest bridge China had built, to link up Hong Kong, Zhuhai and Macau, had done to the region, economically and culturally.

Photo of the HK–Zhuhai–Macau Bridge.

Source: Retrieved from https://www.discoverhongkong.com/au/see-do/culture-heritage/modern-architecture/hong-kong-zhuhai-macao-bridge.jsp.

From Denmark, the entourage drove to Germany, then Holland, and finally went on a boat to England. From England, they shipped their automobiles back to Malaysia and flew home.

Unlike Central Asia and most of Russia, which most people from Asia and North America are unfamiliar with, Scandinavia and northern Europe are well known to all. Indeed, companies such as Nokia from Finland and Ericsson from Sweden, to name a few, are known in every corner of the world. I am particularly familiar with these two companies because when I first settled in Dallas, Texas, in the year 2000, the North American headquarters of these two companies were there.

Something quite interesting about Scandinavia according to Lee Hong-Fah:

Three things that truly astounded me about Scandinavians. (1) They are truly socialistic states; (2) They are absolutely law abiding and (3) There are no religious fanaticism!

I could personally identify with these three observations. Regarding the first, I noticed that when I was in Denmark in the late 1970s, nearly every public function, such as local transportation, health facilities, operas and other music concerts, were either free or very nearly free. It was there that I was able to attend many concerts and ballets for free. As regards his second observation, I personally noticed how the Danes paid exquisite attention to the red no-crossing sign. Late one evening, I was at a crossroad. Next to me was an old lady. It was the middle of the winter and there were absolutely no automobiles in sight. I was extremely surprised that she still waited for the light to turn green before crossing the street. For someone who has spent many years in New York City, the urge to "jaywalk" was quite difficult to resist! Regarding the third observation, I heard from a good friend in Italy, who was brought up as a Roman Catholic, that he would only go to church three times in his life. The first was for his baptism, the second was when he got married, and the third would be his funeral! Living in many areas of the United States, I have noticed the rise of religious fervor, if not fanaticism. Unfortunately, according to the news, even peaceful Scandinavia is nowadays affected by "popularism," and religion fanaticism is now on the rise!

The entire trip, from Singapore to England and back to Malaysia took approximately two months!

Summary

In the past 10 years, I have learned one common and irreplaceable aspect regarding the fundamental of social science research from three individuals. The first is Professor Michael Szonyi (宋怡明), who is now Director of Harvard's Fairbank Center for Chinese Studies. The second is Professor Chen Yi Yuan (陈益源), the former Head of the Chinese Department of Taiwan's Cheng Kung University. The third is Dr. Liang Haiming (梁海明), Director of China's Silk Road iValley Research Institute. Although these three individuals have different intellectual interests, they stood on one common platform, which was that the outcome of their research did not merely arise from dissecting and digesting information contained in articles of other intellects, but in the distillation of information from in-depth and long-term "field research!"

Although Zhang Qian, as far back as the Han Dynasty, was "the first Chinese to observe the world with open eyes," it means that it wasn't the *modus operandi* before him or any other Chinese, for that matter. Unfortunately, neither was it the *modus operandi* of Chinese in the subsequent millennia. Thus, the profound observations made by Lee Hong-Fah during his 10 overland trips to China, which in reality turned out to be dry runs to gain experience so that he could successfully make the truly arduous Asia–Europe land trip later on, contained invaluable and rich information for China to render the BRI "to go out" (走出去) mission to be ultimately successful. The information contained in this chapter, which is collected using their observations and interactions with a large number of people from various points on their trip, is unquestionably still the tip of the iceberg of what they had observed through their "field research."

When Lee Hong-Fah made this trip, BRI was still at its initial phase. So, in his mind, BRI had nothing to do with his trip. For him, it was merely a personal desire to explore a world he knew little or nothing about. Ironically, what he and his entourage have accomplished, in my mind, had everything to do with BRI. After all, in order to pursue BRI in Asia, Europe, Africa and beyond in the coming several decades, China would need to have not just one entourage like Lee Hong-Fah's but hundreds, even thousands and maybe millions, so that the information absorbed, understood and collected could be analytically, systematically and structurally analyzed, intelligently archived, and nationally and internationally distributed, thus serving as treasures for humanity.

Every new civilization, language and legal system encountered, and every new cuisine tried and enjoyed — such "big data" (using today's popular vernacular) — could provide guidance and understanding for the urgently needed cultural communication. In this way, if China could nurture many millions of modern-day Zhang Qians to observe the world with open eyes, the BRI will surely be one of the most, if not the most, thrilling human initiatives that could bestow benefits not only to China but to humanity in general.

I would like to add here that Lee Hong-Fah made another road trip recently. This time from Malaysia, to Thailand, Myanmar, India and China. I hope, in a future book, I can write a chapter about this trip.

Chapter 6

Case Study 2 of "Cultural Communication": Search of Jewish Heritage in China

According to Xu, there are now 11 Judaic Research Centers scattered in Chinese universities. When I learned about this, I was a little dismayed that if there were 11 centers of this nature, why is it that in the Chinese academic world, the level of intellectual interest for its significant neighbors in India and the 10 Southeast Asia nations nations is not the same as that of the Jewish culture?

Cultural communication is a complex and multidimensional form of human interaction. The more one understands the history and ways and means of another culture and civilization, the better can human interactions take place. This was why from the start of BRI, it places cultural communication on such a high pedestal!

In this chapter, I will present a discussion of how, almost by accident, I discovered that during the Song Dynasty nearly a thousand years ago, in a city in China known as Kaifeng, there was a vivacious Jewish community. In the previous chapter, I mentioned briefly how this community that comes with all the "bells and whistles" of Jewish livelihood, was one of the evidences that the land-based ancient silk road was a "one-way street" — it was primarily going from outside to inside China. This experience, in hindsight, allowed me to further appreciate the invulnerable Jewish culture.

From the cultural communication viewpoint, this experience went deeper than I had expected. It is an excellent example which shows that to have a true cultural communications, one needs to develop understanding of all facets of a culture and civilization. Indeed, the more you learn, the more you need to learn. It is like an onion: With each layer, it will bring you closer to tears!

Nowadays, thinking back about my multiple cultural heritages, I would have to admit that first and foremost, as I have emphasized in the preface of this book, my heritage is Chinese. Secondly, I cannot deflect from the fact that United States is a country I am eternally grateful to because it is where I have stayed the longest and built my family and career. As such, even by osmosis, I have inherited a great deal of the American culture in my DNA. Finally, as I would tell everyone, I have also inherited a great deal of Jewish culture, albeit superficially. This came about because in my over three–decade career as an active physicist, many of my teachers, a large percentage of my collaborators, colleagues, postdocs and students were Jewish. My doctoral thesis advisor, Benjamin Bayman of the University of Minnesota and the Department Chair, the late Morton Hamermesh, are both world-renowned theoretical physicists and Jewish. My fellow Ph.D. classmate who was 3 years my senior — Professor Stuart Pittel — is also Jewish. Two of my three office mates in graduate school are Canadian Jews. In many of our long night discussions in the office, I learned the difference between Jewish and Chinese families. My *de facto* mentor in nuclear physics throughout my research career, through which I learned a great deal of technical calculational tools, came from reading the book with the title *The Shell Model*, authored by two great Israeli physicists, Amos de Shalit and Igal Talmi of the Weizmann Institute of Science in Rehovot, Israel. Talmi eventually became a lifelong friend.

From the perspective of cultural communication, my multiple interactions with the Jewish world, scientific and otherwise, could be regarded as a case study! This chapter is one of the many stories that vividly describes my personal "cultural communication" with the Jewish world, from the past to the present. I hope the readers could take away from my experience and grow their own cultural communication with other civilizations.

This is the distinguished Israeli physicist and a household name in nuclear physics, Professor Igal Talmi. This photo was taken at the Weizmann Institute at Rehovot, Israel, where Igal works, even at the advanced age of 94! Professor Talmi had a deep scientific impact on me.

As I mentioned in Chapter 4, where I touched upon the issue that a millennium ago, there was a significant Jewish community flourishing in China. This group of "outsiders" first started to arrive in China sometime during the Han dynasty via the Silk Roads from faraway lands, which today are known as the Middle East, or more precisely, Israel, Palestine, Syria, Iraq, Iran and so on.

For me, this story of the Jews appearing in China began nearly 20 years ago, when my dear friend, the late Professor Joseph Birman of the City University of New York, who was Jewish and a prominent theoretical physicist (who unfortunately passed away in 2016), once mentioned to me in passing that "there is a Jewish legacy" in a city called Kaifeng (开封) in Henan Province (河南).

Professor Joseph Birman (1927–2016).

Source: Retrieved from https://www.ccny.cuny.edu/news/PROFESSOR-BIRMAN-TO-RECEIVE-SAKHAROV-PRIZE-FOR-HUMAN-RIGHTS.

Map of Henan Province.

Source: Retrieved from https://www.chinahighlights.com/henan/map.htm.

From the Chinese history that I learned in schools in Singapore, I knew that during the Song dynasty, Kaifeng, the capital then, was known as Bianjing (汴京). At its prime, Kaifeng[1] was a vibrant city, full of commercial and intellectual activities.

---

[1]Kaifeng. (n.d.). In *Wikipedia*. Retrieved September 1, 2019, from https://en.wikipedia.org/wiki/Kaifeng.

A renowned Song Dynasty painter Zhang Ze-Duan (张择端) created a well-known painting known as "Along the River During the Qingming Festival (清明上河图)." This painting depicted in a very animated and detailed manner how the population in Bianjing during the Song dynasty celebrated this deeply meaningful ancestral tomb sweeping festival — a festival that is still being celebrated in all corners of greater China today, namely, the Mainland, Taiwan, Hong Kong and Macau. In fact, in recent years, using advanced digital techniques, the painting has been turned into an animated video!

Painting of "Along the river during the Qingming Festival."
Source: Retrieved from http://art.ifeng.com/2017/0811/3368562.shtml.

Having such a grand and profound artistic and intellectual landscape for Bianjing, to have an active Jewish community that is historically known to be culturally robust existing in the midst of this lively Chinese city a millennium ago could surely be an excellent example of the profound meaning of cultural communication.

Until Professor Birman came along, as far as I could remember, the history I had learned never mentioned that Kaifeng, or Bianjing, had such an important historical legacy. It was for this reason when Professor Birman first mentioned to me regarding this history, I thought that he, who was known to have a jovial nature, was simply kidding. I did ask him how he became aware of this history? To that he could only give me a less than convincing answer. He did say, however, that he learned about it during his many trips to Israel. During a visit, a historian from the Hebrew University of Jerusalem mentioned this fact to him in an offhand manner. Unfortunately, he said that he did not have time to discuss this fact in more detail with that historian.

I knew Professor Birman since the mid-1980s. He was Jewish and a scientist with an intense interest in Chinese culture and history. He was also an absolutely gender-neutral person who told me often that his wife's accomplishments were far greater than his. He said that this was not because he was modest! Professor Birman said that he admires Chairman Mao's quotation that "women hold up half the sky." Of course, the fact that his wife Joan Birman, who is also Jewish, is a world-renowned mathematician in low-dimensional topology made his claim credible!

In particular, he was always telling me that there were many aspects in which Jews and Chinese were alike. His favorite joke was that "if you take the 'o' out of Cohen, a common Jewish family name, it will become Chen, a common Chinese family name!" It was, therefore, not surprising that he wanted me to discover more about the Kaifeng Jews in my future trips to China.

That, of course, prompted me to first Google this issue. I am not sure why Professor Birman did not do that himself. Perhaps he belonged to an older generation that was "technologically challenged!" Upon searching, I was directed to the following website,[2] which, to my surprise, confirmed what Professor Birman had learned from his historian friend in Israel was indeed true. Unfortunately, for many years after Professor Birman mentioning the issue to me about Kaifeng, since I had no connection to Kaifeng or to Henan Province, academic or otherwise, there was no opportunity for me to visit the city.

The opportunity finally came when the following two serendipitous occurrences happened all at once.

First, in 2006, I was invited by the director of the Britton Chance Center for Biomedical Photonics of Huazhong University of Science and Technology at Wuhan, Professor Luo Qingming (骆清铭), to be the Vice Chairman of the Scientific Advisory Board of the Center.

---

[2]Kaifeng Jews. (n.d.). In *Wikipedia*. Retrieved September 1, 2019, from https://en.wikipedia.org/wiki/Kaifeng_Jews.

Wuhan (武汉) is the provincial capital of Hubei (湖北), a province which is directly south of Henan Province, and is 600 kilometers south of Kaifeng. In 2007, we decided to hold the Board's inaugural meeting on April 12 and 13 in Wuhan. The geographical proximity of Kaifeng and Wuhan spurred my interest to try and see whether I could visit the city.

Second, what really tipped me over to visit Kaifeng was that one of the Board members was Professor Aaron Ciechanover, who was not only the 2004 Nobel Laureate in chemistry, but was also a professor of the medical school of the Technion, Israel Institute of Technology. This means he is Jewish. Aaron is a man who profoundly cherishes his Jewish heritage and history. Apparently, he, like me, had heard about the Kaifeng legacy. Such a legacy was simply too alluring for him not to explore it further. When he was trying to set up his trip to Wuhan, he informed me and Professor Qingming Luo that despite his unbelievably stressful schedule, he absolutely wanted to spend a few days in Kaifeng before or after our meeting in Wuhan, in order to explore this remarkable Jewish legacy.

Qingming, who is almost a "magician" when it comes to organizational ability, was able to assist us in connecting with the leadership of Henan University in Zhengzhou (郑州), the provincial capital of the Province of Henan. Zhengzhou is only about 80 kilometers west of Kaifeng. Thus, our visit to Kaifeng was officially hosted by Henan University, one of the best comprehensive universities with 40,000 students in Henan Province. Of course, having Aaron be a Nobel Laureate did not hurt either. Qingming even asked two of his most able assistants, Hua Shi and Dawson Han, to accompany us to Kaifeng. In fact, Dawson went to Kaifeng two days earlier to ensure the logistics was all sorted out. I can say now that it was indeed perfect.

I would be remiss if I did not give credit to another important individual. That person is Professor Xu Xin (徐新), a well-known and extraordinarily rare Judaic scholar from Nanjing University (南京大学).

Since March 2004, when I was bestowed the honor of becoming an Honorary Trustee of Nanjing University, I often would receive information from that university. Roughly 3 months before the Wuhan board meeting, when I realized that we were about to go to Kaifeng, I noticed an announcement that one of Nanjing University's faculty

Photo of the Advisory Board of the Britton Chance Center for Biomedical Photonics of Huazhong University of Science and Technology on the occasion when Professor Aaron Ciechanover received his honorary doctorate degree.

members had received an honorary doctorate from Bar-Ilan University in Israel. After a bit of searching, I found out that the individual was Xu Xin (徐新), a distinguished professor and director of the Institute of Judaic Studies of Nanjing University. Over the past 18 years, Xu has unquestionably become a top authority of Judaic studies in China. His extensive visits to United States have allowed him to build up warm friendships with truly prominent Jewish leaders in the United States, such as Diana and Guilford Glazers of Los Angeles. Obviously, Xu Xin's effort of bringing the Jewish culture into China impressed the US Jewish community. In fact, the Glazers bestowed an endowment to set up the Institute in Nanjing University in their names.

Needless to say, I was flabbergasted when I learned that Professor Xu is a Jewish scholar. It was clear that he became interested in the cultures of the Jews not because it would bring him wealth and fame. In fact, at his time, it would have been just the opposite. He did so because, as he told me later on, he felt that while the worldwide Jewish community which has only around 15 million people[3] may be tiny, its global impact could be significant. I have to say that Xu Xin is an excellent example of how China today with the BRI effort could engage in cultural communication.

Professor Xu Xin with Guilford and Diana Glazers.
Source: Retrieved from http://www.chinadaily.com.cn/cndy/2008-11/04/content_7170318.htm.

Through his intellectual effort, Xu Xin had already produced quite a number of scholars. One of his postdoctoral fellows in this "unusual" area of research is Professor Zhang Qianhong (张倩红), who became Dean of the College of History and Culture of Henan University in Kaifeng. Professor Zhang herself is already a distinguished researcher in Jewish culture in China.

According to Xu, there are now 11 Judaic Research Centers scattered across Chinese universities. When I learned about this, I was a little dismayed that if there were 11 centers of this nature, why is it that in the Chinese academic world, the level of intellectual interest for its significant neighbors in India and the 10 Southeast Asia nations is not the same as that of the Jewish culture?

---

[3]Jewish population by country. (n.d.). In *Wikipedia*. Retrieved September 1, 2019, from https://en.wikipedia.org/wiki/Jewish_population_by_country.

Photo with Professor Zhang Qianhong (张倩红) and Aaron Ciechanover at the Jewish Studies Center of Henan University.

On April 14, Aaron Ciechanover, Hua Shi and I arrived in Kaifeng after a 7-hour drive from Wuhan. To my surprise, the trip was quite pleasant, driving along the well-maintained and, more importantly, well-manicured superhighway. Upon arrival, we were met by Professor Xu Xin who took time out from a conference he was attending in Beijing and came specifically to meet Aaron and myself.

Thus, the stage was set for the visit.

Kaifeng Jewish Legacy

It can be said with absolute certainty from looking at historical relics that the Jews undertook arduous travel along the silk route all the way from the Middle East to China even as early as the Han dynasty. By the 10th century, they had settled in Kaifeng. If one were to look into the history of that era, one would learn that it was a time where robust commercial activities existed and advanced forms of technology were developed. In fact, it was during this era that gun power was invented. I also learned that this was when paper money was used for the first time in human history. Presumably because of the great commercial activities occurring in China at that time, and the Jews by nature being truly outstanding entrepreneurs, they naturally found Kaifeng to their liking, and thus stayed there.

According to Xu, at its peak, there were more than 5000 Jews living in Kaifeng. There were synagogues and a flourishing Jewish tradition and active cultural life in this city. What is most interesting is that despite the fact that they had very different ways and means from the local Chinese, there was no hint — not even the slightest — according to Professor Xu, that among the Chinese there was any display of anti-Semitic feelings toward their Jewish neighbors in Kaifeng. Indeed, the Chinese appeared to have totally accepted the Jews, their ways of life, their culture and even their religion. Thus, for 700 years, until the Qing dynasty completely shut the door of China to the outside world, Jews from the Middle East continued to come to China, especially to Kaifeng.

Unfortunately, since the close-door policy was instituted, the number of Jews arriving in China began to dwindle. Coupled with the fact that great turmoil occurred in China in the 19th and 20th centuries, the Jewish community virtually disappeared from Kaifeng. Indeed, if one were to nonchalantly visit Kaifeng today, without the expert guidance of Professors Xu of Nanjing University and Zhang of Henan University, there would be no obvious trace of that particular aspect that one could detect in Kaifeng. That there was once a flourishing Jewish cultural life, community and heritage has been deeply buried.

In fact, by now, there is at best only very slim evidence that Jews were ever in Kaifeng at one time. Aaron and I saw a little bit of that when on the evening we arrived in Kaifeng, we were invited to dinner by a Zhao family (whom Dawson was quite familiar with) who was one of the 10 or so families with a direct Jewish lineage. This family lives a Spartan lifestyle, and it is obvious that they are not well to do. Yet, Aaron and I, especially Aaron, were so overwhelmed by their hospitality. The family prepared a 10-course dinner for us once they found out that Aaron came from the Holy Land. Most of the dishes

I could recognize as "Chinese," but one was akin to the famous Jewish "matzo bread" that I could easily find in the United States.

Interestingly, it was not until we were ready to depart from the Zhao's that they discovered that Aaron was a famous scientist, a Nobel Laureate no less! This was quite a contrast to how any Chinese university would treat Aaron. His Nobel Prize–winning status usually precedes his arrival! Apparently, for the Zhao family, Aaron being a Jew was far more important than the fact that Aaron was a Nobel Laureate. Aaron, who was quite accustomed to the overwhelming treatment he usually received in China, was extremely pleased by this fact!

It is worth underscoring that this Jewish family has the family name Zhao (赵). This was because the Song Dynasty was ruled by the Zhao family — the first emperor of the Song Dynasty was Zhao Kuang Yin (赵匡胤). Xu Xin informed us that Jews were allowed to assume seven Chinese family names and one of them was Zhao!

Although the Zhao family who were so gracious to host us with great warmth do celebrate Jewish holidays, such as the Passover, we

Portrait of Emperor Zhao Kuang Yin.

Source: Retrieved from https://baike.baidu.com/item/%E8%B5%B5%E5%8C%A1%E8%83%A4/61716?fr=aladdin.

suspect that they were taught such traditions by Jewish visitors from the West only in recent years. Still, one cannot help but be impressed by the fact that they have kept their Jewish cultural heritage almost intact, and their desire to identify themselves as "Jewish" is indeed palpable!

Henan University

Since Aaron is a Nobel Laureate in chemistry, our host — Henan University — naturally did not allow the opportunity to slip by without a fanfare for such a celebrity. With rapidity and extreme efficiency, the university organized a public lecture to be given by Aaron. Even though our visit fell on a Sunday, the lecture was attended by well over 500 enthusiastic students and faculty members. Aaron was treated like a rock star!

Still, the highlight to Henan University was our visit to the Jewish Research Center of Professor Zhang Qianhong. Both Aaron and I

The auditorium of Henan University. It sits in the middle of this beautiful campus.

Source: Retrieved from https://en.wikipedia.org/wiki/Henan_University.

were impressed by the fact that there were 11 graduate students pursuing their master's degree here. As in most Chinese universities, these students tended to be on the shy side. When Aaron and I were taken to the library of the Center (which has only several thousand books about Judaism), this group of students, who were very interested in meeting Aaron, were quietly standing in the hallway hoping for a glimpse of this great scientist. Once I noticed them, I immediately invited them into the room to meet with Aaron.

Although Aaron had won the Nobel Prize, this did not diminish his deep interest in being a teacher. He immediately took the opportunity to interact with the students and asked each what they were working on. One student, for example, was working on the topic "displaced Jews after the holocaust"! However, all of them expressed their dismay because of the enormous difficulty in locating and having sufficient access to the requisite literature to carry out their research. One of the students told us, with a sparkle in her eyes, that she had won a scholarship to go to "the Hebrew University" for 8 months in the fall that year! She said to Aaron and I that "*when I am in the Hebrew University, I intend to bury myself in the library so that I can absorb as much information regarding my research as possible!*"

To say that the meeting with Aaron "made their day, or year" would be a massive understatement! I am quite sure this meeting with Aaron will forever be etched in their memories.

I took the opportunity to tell this group of students that without knowing it, they could be an extremely important group of intellectuals in China in the 21st century. This is because China and United States will be two of the most important nations in this century. The influence of the Jewish community in the United States, be it intellectually, economically or politically, is profound. Therefore, understanding the Jewish heritage could be exceedingly important for China in order to appreciate the mood of the United States, directly or indirectly. Since this group of students, for whatever reason or reasons, had chosen to study in an area where few were, and still are, doing so in China, their appreciation and understanding of the Jewish heritage could and would have a profound impact on the relationship between China and the United States.

Obviously, when I mentioned the above points to the students in 2010, I had no inkling that towards the end of the second decade of the 21st century, with the US and China being in a state of increased animosity, these comments would become even more meaningful and relevant. I could see this group of bright-eyed and bushy-tailed students all lit up from the inside after my comment. This was, in all likelihood, a view from the window into their future that they had probably never heard of.

In many ways, this trip to Kaifeng is *de facto* "field research" on an ancient interaction between the Chinese and the Jews, an interaction which seems to map out how these two ancient cultures were able to culturally communicate with one another and create a significant amount of mutual and positive energy between them. One of the most important takeaways of this exercise is in developing cultural communication is that one should never assume that history does not play a role. It does, and palpably so.

Once again, cultural communication comes in the most unexpected manner. I was deeply impressed by Aaron's interest in the Kaifeng Jews. Obviously, when comparing the Kaifeng Jews to the Jews of modern times, the ancient ones only have a very minor role to play in today's global Jewish platform, if any. For example, as close to the Jewish heritage as Joseph Birman was, he had not learned about such compatriots until much later in his professional life. Yet remarkably, what happened to the ancient Jews' existence in China provided a valuable lesson to Aaron about how modern Jews could exist in China. No wonder that Aaron, after visiting Kaifeng, exclaimed that it was "unbelievable and unforgettable!"

Besides holding his position at the Technion, little did Aaron know then that 14 years later, he would be holding the position of Vice Chancellor of a Chinese university known as Technion-Guangdong Institute of Technology in Shantou in Guangdong Province. I am sure that making "contact" with the ancient Jews in China had given him a deeper appreciation and a far better way to culturally communicate with the Chinese as to how best to perform in his current role as a modern-day Jew in China. If that is not cultural communication, then I don't know what is!

Chapter 7

Case Study 3 of "Cultural Communication": "Small Nations" Like Canada Need to Understand *Realpolitik,* Especially Now!

Preamble

Understanding Canada, for United States and China, is difficult. Being so close to the United States, both mindset-wise and geographically, and home to such a small population, it is difficult for both China and the US to perceive Canada as a stand-alone nation. Of course, perception *is* reality!

Until fairly recently, there has been essentially no news of any substance, or anything at all, regarding the interaction between China and Canada. Indeed, ever since the BRI was proposed in 2013, there has never been any discussion within Canada showing the slightest interest in participating. The fact that the United States had a lukewarm response in the beginning, and now is downright against it, probably has something to do with the Canadian attitude towards the BRI. Within China, Canada is also not high on anyone's priority list, not economically, not scientifically, not in terms of education, not anything. So, what is the point of having a chapter on Canada?

However, it needs to be underscored that China and Canada had a long and meaningful relationship, which, unfortunately, is now all but forgotten by both the Chinese and Canadian leadership as well as the general public. For example, the former Prime Minister Pierre Trudeau (1919–2000), a worldly leader, was a friend of Chairman Mao. Indeed, as soon as the "reform and opening up" era was unveiled in China, there was establishment of diplomatic relations with China, even before the United States! As my friend Ruth Hayhoe of the University of Toronto told me:[1]

> The United States Agency for International development (USAID) could NOT offer any formal development aid to a Communist country, so no significant aid was offered. But Canada signed a development agreement with the Chinese government, to substantially support the rebuilding of the universities across key areas — first management, then many others — health, environment, engineering etc. At the same time, the World Bank offered $1.3 billion in largely interest free loans to rebuild infrastructure.

Canada is a nation with an enormous landmass that sits just north of the United States. Yet, Canada only has a population of 38 million, ranking number 38 among all nations of the world. On the other hand, spanning 10 million square kilometers in terms of landmass (Russia spans 17, China 9.6, the United States 9.8 and Australia 7.7), Canada is the second biggest nation in terms of landmass. Geographically, it sits directly north of the United States, the undisputed most powerful nation in the world, and shares a 9000-kilometer border. Furthermore, after the European Union and China, Canada is the 3rd largest trading partner of the United States.

With this geographical proximity and owing to its financial importance, one would have assumed that living in the United States, one could, on a daily basis, be fed with, if not pounded by a massive amount of news as to what is happening in Canada. Nothing can be further from the truth.

---

[1] Private communication. See also https://www.oise.utoronto.ca/cidec/UserFiles/File/Research/CIDEC_Projects/Conference2014/Yongming_ZHOU_presentation.pdf and https://www.oise.utoronto.ca/cidec/UserFiles/File/Research/CIDEC_Projects/Conference2014/Dilantha_Fernando_presentation.pdf

Until I came to Asia in 2007, for the previous 43 years, I was essentially living and building my career in the United States. Before 2006, my cognizant of Canada were confined to except at one point I had a fairly intensive scientific collaboration with some of the physicists at McMaster University, an outstanding Canadian University not far from Toronto, and also undertook some short touristic visits (not to mention eating the absolutely delicious Chinese food in northern Toronto and Richmond, Vancouver) such as to the famous Niagara Falls on both sides of the US and Canada borders, and that the French spoken by the French Canadians was considered as "bad French" by the Parisians, I knew very little about Canada, its people, its politics and its geopolitical postures. Living in the US, unless one makes a concerted effort to learn about Canada, there was essentially no information about this important neighbor either on a daily basis in the news, or on any basis.

On December 1, 2018, the situation saw a sharp change. This came about because of the news that was splashed across the globe that a Chinese, the Chief Financial Officer of technological giant — Huawei — Ms. Meng Wanzhou (孟晚舟) was apprehended in Vancouver airport by the Canadian government, on the request by the US Government. Almost overnight, one could feel the collateral impact of what was a rather tranquil, steady and low-key relationship between Canada and China took a hard nosedive. Until that day, there was no known dispute or animosity between the two countries. On the media in the US and China, and presumably all across Canada, all of a sudden, the amount of information about Canada and its relationship with China in political and economic arenas came into sharp focus.

Although the situation of Ms. Meng of Huawei is, of course, unique for China and Canada, Canada's challenging and long-term relationship with China and the United States is not. A good Canadian friend who has considerable influence in Canada and who knew that I grew up in Singapore startled me by telling me that:

Although Canada is a massive country land wise, maybe because its existence from the start was under the umbrella of its enormous "big brother" in the south, therefore in its mindset, it may not even have the same level of self-confidence and sophistication as your hometown Singapore.

Hearing such words, I inherently felt it rang true because Singapore, just as Canada, is now existing in a precarious situation where in the 21st century, having China its largest trading partner and the United States having the most powerful military presence in the region, it too had to find an optimum geopolitical pathway in dealing with the United States and China.

Facing this reality, the Prime Minister of Singapore Lee Hsien-Loong (李显龙) made the following eloquent comments in his keynote speech, delivered at Asia's most important geopolitical forum, the 2019 Shangri-La Dialogue on May 31, 2019, as to how a "small" nation like Singapore needs to navigate an optimum path when it is confronted with such a complex challenge. Indeed, just as his father, the late Lee Kuan-Yew who needed political wisdom of his era, Lee Hsien-Loong seemed to have found a totally different wisdom — the fundamental understanding of and navigation in *"Realpolitik"* in the 21st century.

Prime Minister Lee stressed that as a small nation, even for Singapore which is recognized as progressive and forward-looking,

Prime Minister Lee Hsien Loong of Singapore.

Source: Retrieved from https://www.straitstimes.com/singapore/spore-must-help-all-to-get-good-start-pm.

if it had to deal bilaterally with a large power such as China or United States, it will probably end up at the short end of the stick.

With that in mind, Prime Minister Lee made the following sensible suggestion:[2]

> Being small, we are naturally disadvantaged in bilateral negotiations. We need to reform and strengthen multilateral institutions, not cripple or block them. More fundamentally, confining ourselves to a bilateral approach means forgoing win-win opportunities which come from countries working together with more partners. We need to build a broader regional and international architecture of cooperation. When groups of countries deepen their economic cooperation, they will enhance not just their shared prosperity but also their collective security. With more stake in one another's success, they will have greater incentive to uphold a conducive and peaceful international order. This will benefit many countries big and small.

Facing the current United States political reality, one cannot but be pessimistic that these words of wisdom and the suggestion from the leader of a "small" country would be heard, let alone acted on. On the other hand, with China's deep and proactive interest in vigorously promoting the BRI, with "going out" and creating "common future for humanity" as its missions, it is likely and more probable that China can, and hopefully will, pay attention to such a suggestion in its interactions with small countries like Singapore and, by extension, Canada.

In fact, as one of the two most economically powerful nations in the world, with Eastern civilization as its foundation, it is reasonable, even expected, that China could take the high road of exhibiting a magnanimous nature in its interactions with small countries. After all, the comments made by Prime Minister Lee of Singapore suggesting that powerful nations should and must develop sustainable cultural communication with all nations seem to resonate with what President Xi summarized in his keynote speech at the second Belt

---

[2]In full: PM Lee Hsien Loong's speech at the 2019 Shangri-La Dialogue (May 31, 2019), CNA. Retrieved from https://www.channelnewsasia.com/news/singapore/lee-hsien-loong-speech-2019-shangri-la-dialogue-11585954.

and Road International Cooperation Forum held in Beijing on April 24, 2019, in which he said:[3]

> The Belt and Road Initiative is rooted in the ancient Silk Road. It focuses on the Asian, European and African continents, but is also open to all other countries. All countries, from either Asia, Europe, Africa or the Americas, can be international cooperation partners of the Belt and Road Initiative. The pursuit of this initiative is based on extensive consultation and its benefits will be shared by us all.

Obviously, what President Xi said here should be a high priority for China in BRI projects in the coming years. The lesson one learns from Singapore can be applied to Canada and all other small nations in the world as well. To do so, China must understand the fundamental necessity to culturally communicate with all countries, especially the "small" ones.

I have lived in the United States for a long time. As someone who has deep interest about the world I live in, I have always had a special interest to have in-depth cultural communications with the two neighbors of the United States — Canada and Mexico. When I became the Vice President of Research at the University of Texas at Dallas (UTD) in 2000, because of geographical proximity (Texas has over 1200 kilometers of border it shares with Mexico), the opportunity to learn about our southern neighbor, Mexico, opened up for me.

During my tenure at UTD, I made frequent visits to cities like Mexico City, Guanajuato (the home town of the former President of Mexico Vicente Fox) and Monterrey in order for UTD to further develop close ties with counterpart institutions. Such visits also gave me a deeper understanding of Mexico, albeit still superficial. In fact, from my multiple visits, I developed a very close relationship with the then director of Centro de Investigación en Matemáticas (CIMAT), Professor José Carlos Gómez Larrañaga, and the Vice President for Research of the Instituto Tecnológico y de Estudios Superiores de

---

[3]Xi, J. P. Full text of President Xi's speech at opening of Belt and Road forum. *Xinhuanet.* Retrieved from http://www.xinhuanet.com/english/2017-05/14/c_136282982.htm.

Monterrey (Tech Momterrey), Professor Francisco Cantu. CIMAT is one of the most prominent mathematics institutes in Latin America, and Tech Monterrey is the top private university in Mexico.

In fact, in 2004 when I led the Vice Presidents of Research from Texas, Oklahoma, Louisiana and Mexico as part of a delegation on a visit to China, because I was so impressed by his global inclination to higher education and his transparent open-mindedness, I specifically invited Dr. Cantu to be a member of the delegation. I am pleased to learn that quite recently, Tech Monterrey has formed an "innovation alliance" with the city of Hangzhou (杭州). This is a truly exciting development because Hangzhou, which is where China's e-commerce giant Alibaba is located, is the next tech-hub of China in the 21st century, after Shenzhen. Such a Mexico–China technological collaboration will surely bring about a win–win situation for both nations. My many-year interactions with Mexico have

The 2004 Delegation of Vice Presidents from Texas, Oklahoma, Louisiana and Mexico meeting with counterparts of various universities at Peking University. The second person on the right front row is Dr. Cantu.

made me a firm believer of the so-called aspect of "field research" to enable true understanding of a nation or a region.

With regard to Canada, unfortunately, for a long time I did not had the opportunity to carry out an in-depth exploration about this northern neighbor of the United States. Even though there are significant physical similarities between the two nations, there is virtually no information about Canada transmitted to the United States via the news media on a daily basis.

As I have mentioned earlier, Canada is a vast nation. Besides its more well-known major metropolitan cities such as Greater Toronto in the Province of Ontario, Montreal in the Province of Quebec and Vancouver in the Province of British Columbia, there is enormous amount of landmass in between. For example, between Montreal and Vancouver, there are six Provinces, and a distance of 4600 kilometers separates them. To learn about Canada, one probably needs to learn not just about the famous cities. This is akin to learning nothing about China beyond Beijing, Shanghai and Guangzhou!

With that in mind, the opportunity to study this further came to me when during December 1–5, 2006, I was fortunate to have an excellent opportunity to better understand the "middle of Canada" when the then president of the University of Calgary, Dr. Harvey Weingarten, invited me in my capacity as the Vice President of Research of the University of Texas at Dallas, to visit his university. The mission of my visit was to seek opportunities for our two universities to collaborate. Thinking back, getting to know Dr. Weingarten *de facto* opened the Canadian *Pandora Box* for me!

Dr. Weingarten's university is located in the city of Calgary in the Province of Alberta. Alberta is one of the Provinces in the middle of Canada. In distance, it is 1000 kilometers east of Vancouver and 3300 kilometers and 3500 kilometers west of Toronto and Montreal, respectively. In the past decade, because of the discovery of its enormous so-called "oil sands reserve," which is estimated at 1.7–2.5 trillion barrels,[4] it has become a wealthy and fast growing Province.

---

[4] Oil Sands. *Fuel research and development for the 21st century.* Retrieved from https://www.ems.psu.edu/~pisupati/ACSOutreach/Oil_Sands.html.

Over the weekend that I was there, I took the opportunity to also play the role of a tourist and visited the truly breathtaking and magnificent Banff National Park and Lake Louise. The Banff National Park is a part of the massive mountain range in the Western part of North America, starting from the Canadian side in the Province of British Columbia, running through Alberta in Canada and the states of of Idaho, Montana, Wyoming, Utah and Colorado in the United States and ending at New Mexico. In Alberta and Colorado, the scenery is simply majestic! The crown jewel of the majestic views would be Lake Louise in Alberta.

Panoramic view of Lake Louis in the Banf National Park.

Source: Retrieved from https://www.tripadvisor.com/Hotel_Review-g154912-d186815-Reviews-Fairmont_Chateau_Lake_Louise-Lake_Louise_Banff_National_Park_Alberta.html.

During that visit to Calgary, I was able to develop a close personal relationship with Dr. Weingarten. Dr. Weingarten was a well-known Yale-trained psychologist and a former Provost of McMaster University. After Dr. Weingarten completed his tenure at the University of Calgary in 2010, he assumed the position of Chief Executive Officer of the Higher Education Quality Council of Ontario (HEQCO), an educational think-tank for the Province of Ontario. There he entered the world of geopolitics and higher education policymaking, and developed a broader appreciation and understanding of how and why higher education is so critical and fundamental in today's 21st-century world. In particular, he maintained his strong interest in promoting the interactions between Canada and Asia.

Over the past decade, we have remained in close contact, and often engage in lengthy discussions on matters of higher education and geopolitics of Asia and North America. We even wrote an editorial together with the title "Why Canadian universities should collaborate with Asia."[5]

A photo I took with Dr. Harvey Weingarten.

Dr. Weingarten is a gracious, utterly altruistic and confident individual. During the past decade, he was gracious enough to introduce

[5]Weingarten, H. and Feng, D. H. (October 24, 2012). Why Canadian universities should collaborate with Asia. *In My Opinion*. Retrieved from https://www.universityaffairs.ca/opinion/in-my-opinion/why-canadian-universities-should-collaborate-with-asia/.

to me two important and highly influential Canadians — the Governor General of Canada, David Johnston, and the former President of the University of Toronto, Dr. David Naylor. I always say that once you get to know truly outstanding individuals, your life will be deflected. I can safely say that these two individuals did precisely that.

Governor General of Canada, His Excellency David Johnston

The position of the Governor General of Canada is Canada's counterpart to the Monarch of England — namely Queen Elizabeth II. Therefore, technically, just like the Queen, the individual holding this position is *de facto* Canada's head-of-state. A few weeks before October 13, 2013, on China's CCTV, I saw President Xi Jinping officially

Dr. David Johnston, Governor General of Canada was accompanied by President Xi Jinping during his State visit to China.

Source: Retrieved from https://www.cbc.ca/news/politics/gov-gen-david-johnston-trots-the-globe-to-boost-canadian-trade-1.2500876.

receiving the "head-of-state" of Canada, and at that point in time I had no idea who the distinguished, white-haired gentleman was.

Little did I know that a few weeks later, when I was speaking at a HEQCO conference organized by Dr. Weingarten in Toronto, the keynote speaker was none other than the Governor General of Canada, His excellency David Johnston himself.

Since I was one of the few invited speakers of the Conference, that morning I was given the great honor of having breakfast with Mr. Johnston. In fact, I was even fortunate to be seated next to him. I must say that I was quite reticent to receive such an honor, not knowing what I possibly could say to a national head-of-state, whom I believe must be an outstanding politician.

Well, nothing can be further from the truth. As soon as we sat down, Mr. Johnston turned to me and said:

> My assistant told me that you are the Senior Vice President of National Tsing Hua University in Taiwan. I was for many years the President of McGill University and the University of Waterloo. So, I can tell you that deep down in my heart, we are both university professors!

That broke the ice! I never would have dreamt that the leader of a nation was a university president, and a professor no less! Mr. Johnston and I found a common platform — both being university professors — to interact. I also discovered that he was a Harvard- and Cambridge-trained lawyer. In the subsequent 15 minutes, Mr. Johnston and I were able to engage in a substantive conversation regarding higher education, especially how Canadian and Asian universities could work together. He said something that seemed to be particularly poignant in this day and age:

> I was deeply impressed by China during my recent visit. There is so much China and Canada can work on together. Of course, Canada is not a powerhouse like the United States, but in many specific areas, especially in higher education, it has some internationally well-known and substantive institutions. What Canada needs to do is to learn how to let the world know about us!

In our discussion, I found Mr. Johnston, being the leader of a nation notwithstanding, to be a truly amiable, humble and engaging individual with a wide intellectual bandwidth. In my interactions with a large number of Canadian academics, I found that Mr. Johnston's demeanor was more the norm than the exception. With his knowledge of the world, people like him — and there are many such individuals — could be important bridges for China and Canada to build a sustainable relationship.

A meeting we had with the Director General of Canada Dr. David Johnston. standing next to me is Dr. Harvey Weingarten, and standing next to him is Dr. Johnston.

Dr. David Naylor, Former President of the University of Toronto

During one of my visits to Canada, Dr. Weingarten introduced to me to the then President of the University of Toronto, Dr. David Naylor. The way we were introduced is worth repeating, because it shows how truly Canada believes in informality.

One evening, when Dr. Weingarten and I were talking in his office, dinner time was fast approaching. He suddenly made the suggestion, *"let's see whether David Naylor is available to join us!"* When Dr. Weingarten saw my bewildered facial expression, he shrugged his shoulders and said:

> Oh, he is the president of the University of Toronto, the best university in Canada, even better than the University of Calgary! He is very knowledgeable and I am sure you will greatly enjoy meeting him!

With that comment, he made a phone call to Dr. Naylor, and we proceeded to a neighborhood pizza joint.

Dr. Naylor came about 20 minutes later than the agreed time. The moment he arrived, he apologized profusely and said he had to *"walk the dog"* and just could not be on time. Before becoming the president of the University of Toronto, Dr. Naylor was the former Dean of Canada's top-notch medical school. Besides receiving

The Naylor building on campus at the University of Toronto.

Source: Retrieved from https://www.acotoronto.ca/show_building.php?BuildingID=10520.

whatever honor Canada could bestow on an individual, Dr. Naylor is also a world-renowned clinical epidemiologist. Just as Dr. Weingarten, Dr. Naylor is a man of great humor and global sophistication. He is so famous in the University of Toronto in particular, and Canada in general, that there is a building on campus named after him!

Since that day he was late because he had to walk the dog, we became very good friends.

In fact, we were such good friends that he was gracious enough to write a foreword for my book *Edu-Renaissance: Notes from a Globe Trotting Higher Educator*. The paragraph he wrote in that forward poignantly manifested his deep concern for the world that he foresaw was coming[6]:

> It is trite to observe that the late 20th and early 21st centuries have been a period of accelerating 'globalization'. I use that term neutrally, to signify simply the movement, variously physical or virtual, of goods, services, ideas, and people across national borders. But sadly, at a point in human history when international ties and cross-cultural understanding should be deeper and stronger than ever, we have also witnessed the emergence of counter-forces in the form of renewed tribalism, fundamentalism, and sectarian violence.

These words, although written in 2016, well before the tribalism of President Trump, are warnings even in 2020! Clearly, only a truly globally minded university president with deep concern for humanity could utter such words of profound wisdom.

On the day that Dr. Naylor stepped down from his presidency, he invited me to be there to witness the transition. At that event, I met nearly all the presidents of Canada's universities. I deliberately went around and struck up conversations with many of them. What I discovered was that a number of them originated from foreign countries. For example, I met and discussed quite a lot of topics with Dr. Indira Samarasekera, the then President of the University of Alberta, who came from Sri Lanka and Dr. Amit Chakma, the President of the University of Western Ontario, who came from Bangladesh.

---

[6]Naylor, C. D. (2016). Foreword I. In Feng, D. H. *Edu-renaissance: Notes from a Globetrotting Higher Educator*. Singapore: World Scientific, xii.

Dr. Naylor led a large entourage to visit the National Tsing Hua University in Hsinchu, Taiwan in 2014.

A "class" picture of all the senior administrators (presidents and vice presidents) representing the entire corp of Canadian universities on the day when David Naylor stepped down as president of the University of Toronto.

After we met at the pizza joint, Dr. Naylor invited me to visit Canada again one year later, to deliver a speech entitled "Globalization or Internationalization: Challenges for Asia Pacific Universities in the 21st Century" in the Munk School of Global Affairs of his university. The lecture was chaired by the Dean of the Munk School, Dr. Janice Stein, a well-known media personality in Canada who appears frequently on Canadian television stations to discuss geopolitics issues.

A picture I took with the Director of the Munk School of Global Affairs, Dr. Janice Stein. Dr. Stein is a well-known public figure in Canada.

To be perfectly honest, as a theoretical physicist, the Munk School was *terra incognita* for me. Hence, I accepted the invitation with some trepidation. Although I was familiar with Toronto as a city, I had never visited the University of Toronto before, and definitely, never given a talk in the Munk School, or any such institution of that nature, for that matter.

So to prepare for the talk, I looked into what relevance did Toronto or UT had, *vis-à-vis*, with the Asia Pacific. To my utter astonishment, I found out that the city had over 800,000 Asians at that point in time.

With this information, I started to ask myself the following question:

What makes a city "Asian"? Does it have to reside in Asia?

If a city existing in another continent has exceeded some threshold number that could render its mindset "Asian," would that not be an "Asian city"? For example, with 800,000 Asians, has Toronto reached the threshold of the mindset of being not just a great North American city, which it obviously is, but also a great "Asian city"? And if one pushes this topic further, could the University of Toronto be viewed not only as a great North American university, which it obviously is, but also an "Asian university." Such a mindset, if properly cultivated, could play a significant role in the cultural communication between China and Canada.

Chinese food in Toronto is simply out of this world. To me, food of a nation is one of the most important and fundamental manifestations of its culture. I remember on one afternoon of my visit to the city, as I was near the University of Toronto, I was quite

An absolutely delicious bowl of beef noodles I had in Toronto.

hungry. I then spotted a random Chinese restaurant. So, I went in for the purpose to just satiate my hunger, not expecting the most exquisite Chinese food. What I had, to my absolute pleasure and astonishment, was one of the best beef noodles comparable to any dish of beef noodles I had in Taiwan, Macau or Hong Kong.

Thinking back, such "trivial" yet important information may be what China needs to bear in mind while dealing with Canada.

Alberta

It is customary for me that whenever I visit a place for the first time, my *modus operandi* is to learn as much as I can about the place and compare the collected data with something or someplace that I am familiar with. I found that in this way I can inevitably gain a deeper layer of understanding about the place I am about to visit, even before visiting it. In this case, I did my homework about Alberta and compared it with the State of Texas where I was residing.

Some Comparisons Between Alberta and Texas

First, I know I have stated this several times already, and that is Canada is simply huge! For someone who had lived in Texas, it may

Maps of Alberta and Texas.

Source: Retrieved from https://greenwichmeantime.com/time-zone/north-america/canada/alberta/map/ and https://www.nationsonline.org/oneworld/map/USA/texas_map.htm, respectively.

sound strange! In Texas, people would go on boasting about how big their State is by mentioning that from one end of Texas (say Dallas) to the other end (say El Paso), the distance is half that to San Diego, California! Indeed, in terms of landmass, I cannot help but be startled to discover that the Province of Alberta is nearly as big as the State of Texas. In fact, most Canadian Provinces, such as Ontario, British Columbia, Alberta, Manitoba and Saskatchewan, are enormous, and some are even bigger than Texas.

I am sure I am not overstating that most, if not all, Americans (unless you are from the State of Alaska) regard Texas as simply big! Of course, Texas is indeed a state covering an enormous area of land. After all, it has an area of 690,000 square kilometers. On the other hand, the two Westernmost provinces of Canada, Alberta and British Columbia, have a landmass of 642,000 and 945,000 square kilometers, respectively. These data were eye-opening for me!

Second, putting human beings in this picture provides another interesting comparison. Canada is of course "population challenged"! This is not necessarily a bad thing. I am sure there are leaders in China who would prefer China to be slightly population challenged (but not age challenged)! Canada has only 32 million people, which is 10% the US population (300 million). Taking Alberta and Texas into consideration, both have nearly the same landmasses, but their respective populations are 4 million and 23 million. This means that Alberta has approximately 16 persons per square mile while Texas has 85 persons per square mile.

However, these two numbers are somewhat misleading because it does not take into account the distribution of the respective population densities. For example, most Albertans live in the southern part of the Province, and hence the population density for that region would be significantly higher than the Provincial average. A similar situation exists in Texas where the triangular region defined by Dallas–Forth Worth–San Antonio–Houston is home to some 70% of the 23 million people. I have a feeling that there can be a great deal of synergy between the Texas triangle and the Edmonton–Calgary corridor.

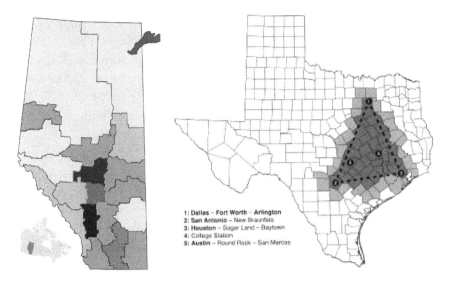

The Edmonton–Calgary corridor of Alberta and the Dallas–Houston–San Antonio triangle of Texas.

Source: Retrieved from https://en.wikipedia.org/wiki/Calgary%E2%80%93Edmonton_Corridor and https://en.wikipedia.org/wiki/Texas_Triangle.

Third, what is really interesting for me, coming from the higher education perspective, is that Alberta's two large and internationally well-known flagship universities, University of Alberta and University of Calgary are situated in its two large cities, Edmonton and Calgary, respectively. For Texas, its two large flagship universities, University of Texas at Austin and Texas A and M University, are not in the two most populated metropolitan areas, Houston and Dallas-Fort Worth. Of course, in Houston and Dallas, there are two good universities, University of Houston and the University of Texas at Dallas, respectively. But quality wise, it is well recognized that there is still significant room for improvement before these two universities can catch up with their counterparts in Austin and College Station. In fact, this is especially true for Dallas-Fort Worth, as it is the only "technological-intensive" region in the United States without an absolute first-class university.

While each scenario has advantages and disadvantages, I suspect that the advantages of Alberta (where the best universities in the province are right in Edmonton and Calgary, thus driving them economically and intellectually) far outweigh the disadvantages. For example, for the two of Provinces' best universities in its largest cities, their talent pools certainly are considered a definite plus. Imagine if the Silicon Valley in the greater San Francisco region was not home to Stanford University and the University of California Berkeley, it would then be questionable if this area could still lead the world in its supreme high-technology development and entrepreneurial activities.

Fourth, both Alberta and Texas are "energy" State or Province, respectively. It is well known that Alberta's oil reserves, known as "oil sands," is enormous. However, extraction of this natural resource was for a long time not commensurate with the low cost of fossil fuel extraction from the grounds of Saudi Arabia and Texas. Today, it is different. This, I am sure, is one of the reasons why Alberta is experiencing an "economic boom," as we would say! In fact, the moment you step into Calgary, you see people hustling and bustling, and you can almost feel the excitement of the town.

Calgary and Dallas-Fort Worth

The conventional wisdom about Calgary is that it is a "cow town" (some of that perception comes from its once-a-year world-renowned celebration of the "Calgary stampede.")

Photo of Calgary Stampede. It is interesting if in the above picture, the Canadian flags are replaced by the flags of United States, this could very well be a scenery in Texas.

Source: Retrieved from https://www.renfrewchrysler.com/blog/when-calgary-stampede-rodeo-calgary-ab/

The population of Greater Dallas-Fort Worth, known collectively as Metroplex, according to the census of 2019 is 6.8 million, and growing fast. Calgary is home to around 1.4 million, and also growing very fast. Just as the Metroplex which essentially sits on one enormous prairie, Calgary is also on a prairie, and therefore there is no natural inhibitor to restrict its growth. In fact, we saw earlier that there was rapid development of the Northern part of the city, which is very similar to the growth of Frisco, McKinney, the northern suburbs of the Metroplex. I am quite sure that if it is physically possible to shrink the Metroplex down in landmass and in population to the Calgary dimensions, you will end up with it becoming a Calgary, but with warmer weather in the winter in particular, and all year round in general!

The downtown area of Calgary bears great resemblance to downtown Dallas, with its usual skyscrapers protruding from the prairie. However, if you go on top of the TV tower of Calgary, you can see a "wall" on the western horizon — the magnificent Canadian Rockies, which is only about a 90-minute drive from downtown. Unfortunately,

A TV tower in Calgary and the Reunion Tower of Dallas, respectively.

Source: Retrieved from https://www.tripadvisor.com.my/LocationPhotoDirectLink-g154913-d155544-i110771991-Calgary_Tower-Calgary_Alberta.html and https://en.wikipedia.org/wiki/Reunion_Tower, respectively.

one will not see any big mountains standing on the TV tower of Dallas! I would be remiss if I did not state that during our visit, we actually did visit the Rockies. To say that the scenery there was spectacular is an understatement!

Although I did not have time to experience the cultural life of Calgary — unless one considers my going to the Calgary Flames hockey game and watching in awe 18,000 screaming Canadians a cultural experience — I was told that just like Dallas, it has the full array of orchestras, art museums, operas, rock concerts and so on. I believe for any region with aspirations of higher and better growth, a robust cultural landscape is a fundamental necessity.

Of course, no matter how busy we were, eating is an activity that is still and always needed. So, as usual, we did sample food at some of the Chinese restaurants in town. I would say that they are certainly as good those in Dallas, but definitely not even close to the supreme quality of Chinese food we encountered at Vancouver and Toronto! However, since it is recognized that the Chinese food in Vancouver and Toronto are almost as good as that available in Hong Kong, this was hardly a fair comparison!

Finally, I must say that I have never stayed in a hotel that was more comfortable and cozier than the one we stayed in Calgary. The hotel, called Kensington Riverside Inn, sits just north of Bow River, and therefore in the evening, the entire skyline of Calgary lit up like a gigantic Christmas tree in front of us. Indeed, it was a breathtaking view! I almost forgot to mention that each hotel room comes with a fireplace. With temperatures in Calgary routinely dipping well below zero Fahrenheit (−18°C) during the nights we were in town, I suspect it must have been one of the protective mechanisms the hotel provided for the clients if and when there would be a power shutdown!

A taste of Canadian higher education: The University of Calgary

As I have mentioned, my host was the University of Calgary, or UofC as is known. For any city or region, the reason for it to have a great university goes far beyond it simply being an educational institution for the youth. It began as a branch campus of the University of Alberta in 1908, but gained "autonomy" in 1966. Today, the university has 32,000 students and nearly 2000 faculty members. Even more important, it is intellectually standing shoulder-to-shoulder with some of the best Canadian universities, such as McMaster University, McGill University and University of Alberta. According to a particular global university ranking organization, the University of Calgary is ranked as 7th in Canada, with McMaster, McGill and Alberta being ranked 6th, 2nd and 4th, respectively. Also, there is a well-known number which is, in an aspiring region the number of universities should be around one for every 2 million people. This was true in Singapore, which has 2 universities for its population of 5 million. Having a population of 4 million, Alberta having two outstanding universities is right in the ballpark.

The rise of the University of Calgary reminded me of the kind of meteoric rise universities such as University of California at San Diego (UCSD) and Carnegie Mellon University (CMU) have had. Both achieved international reputation in roughly the same time span. It is worth noting that unlike UCSD and CMU, which now have global perception and reputation as bio-U and computer-U, respectively, (even though they both have other equally outstanding strengths), I am not sure I detected one area where UofC commands public perception (this is not to say that in reality it does not have one. Unfortunately, as one of my political friends from Washington would say, "perception is reality"!).

There is another area where UofC is improving rapidly, and that is the intellectual quality of its students, especially its undergraduates. According to its website, UofC's undergradutes' quality has improved markedly (using numbers that is equivalent to US's SAT score) in the past several years. Since I did not see that the amount of scholarships given out to students increased significantly in the same period (I call that "buying students"), it means that better qualified students were attracted to UofC almost entirely because of its increasing reputation. I have said this often: There is no such thing as a great university where the (undergraduate) students are not of the highest quality. This data tells me that UofC is rapidly attaining this fundamental characteristic of a great university.

Although in building a great university, having a strong financial underpinning is not everything, it is nevertheless true that "*vision without funding is hallucination.*" In this respect, there is one metric of measurement which can serve this purpose, and that is the amount and rate of increase of research contracts and grants coming into the university annually. Here, UofC is certainly making outstanding progress. According to its website, in 2000, the total research dollar in income for the university was around CAD$100 million, and in 2017, it shot up to around CAD$380 million. Indeed, a nearly 400% increase in 17 years is breathtaking for any university. One of the reasons for this "funding explosion" surely is due to the fact that in the past 20 years, UofC had made a concerted effort to recruit the best of the best from around the world to be its faculty members.

Of course, as in most universities, while it is not chump change, CAD$380 million is still somewhat on the low side for a university as comprehensive and large as UofC, especially since it has a medical school. Certainly, one sees that most of the top universities (I am using US universities as a guideline here since I am not familiar with other Canadian universities) with an in-house medical school would have significantly higher funding than USD$300 million, because the medical school alone will generally amass around a couple of hundred million dollars of research funding. For example, in some US universities, medical schools would bring in that much funding just from National Institutes of Health alone! On the other hand, since UofC research dollars is on such a fast-growing trajectory, I have confidence that soon, say within another decade, it will be on par with the world's best.

There is no doubt in my mind that having a powerful university can accelerate the growth of a city, especially one as exciting and robust as Calgary.

President Harvey Weingarten

I was most fortunate that I had two long but interesting conversations with the President, Dr. Harvey Weingarten, about this rapidly growing university. His office was an off-the-corner small room in the administration building. It was hardly palatial! His attire, while appropriate, was not immaculate! His hairdo reminded me of the style worn by the great movie director Peter Jackson. In fact, President Weingarten told me that the local newspaper once put his picture side by side with Jackson's to show their similarity. He also said, with a little sadness on his face, that "Peter is richer!", which I concurred with "probably just a bit!" These interactions and his body language gave me the warm impression that while he is serious intellectually, he does not take himself very seriously.

Before visiting the university, I read most of the public speeches Dr. Weingarten had delivered in the last couple of years. This is because I am a believer that a great university must have as its president one who can deliver elegant speeches about not just the importance of education but also what education can do to enhance the betterment of humanity. As a public university, the president must explain to the public why public money should support it.

In this regard, I was certainly not disappointed by what I was able to read from his speeches. In fact, one of them outlines what UofC has achieved thus far, where it is today, and where he would like to see it in the years to come. I was especially impressed with the statement where he outlines succinctly his realistic evaluation of UofC's position in the Canadian higher education landscape and his lament of "not good enough" attitude:

> I have no doubt that, given the trajectory we are on, we will have more than caught up to the likes of University of Toronto or University of British Columbia over our next 40 years. But if this is all we do it will not be satisfying. To be true to our namesake city, UofC is obliged to strive to be a leader in higher education. Leadership at a university means thinking about how the world should be, what our students need, and what we must do to serve

our students and public better. More of the same, even if we are doing the same better, is not good enough.

To me, such a vision, especially "what our students need, and what we must do to serve our students and public better," should not be confined to UofC only, but to all aspiring universities in the 21st century. Indeed, these are golden words that one seldom hears in higher education today.

I also took the opportunity to discuss with President Weingarten another sentence in his speech which I thought was especially poignant:

> .... Finally, but not least, a university enmeshed with its community has a significant physical presence in the heart of the community. So, as we announced at the Chamber in February 2004, we intend to build a downtown Urban Campus ...

In fact, the idea of having a downtown urban campus, even though the university is only a mere 10-minute drive from it, is quite significant. I can easily imagine that some may say that this could be viewed as an extravagant exercise. To me it is not. Just as Dallas, the economic and technological power of Calgary, which is growing daily because of Alberta's economy, is situated in the downtown region. In fact, President Weingarten said something so visionary that there are literally hundreds, if not thousands, of people holding doctorates in downtown Calgary and that it would indeed be a major resource right at the doorstep of UofC, which it can ill-afford to neglect. Reflecting on this fact, it is indeed true that while the downtown area of Dallas is where the economic, artistic and cultural pulse of the region is, it lacks the presence of a great intellectual center like a university which can galvanize and render the city truly vibrant.

In this regard, I am reminded of one of the top universities in Tokyo city which I had the privilege of visiting often many decades ago — the University of Tokyo. Once I got to know the university, it gave me the impression that it is omnipresent at all points of this metropolitan city. The heart of the university sits in its downtown campus in Hongo, while there are two campuses in the suburbs, one in the western end Komaba and one in the northeastern end Kashiwa. Each campus has a unique and non-overlapping characteristic, and each can draw together and add value to the University of Tokyo with the rich and robust resources of Tokyo.

Therefore, does it not make sense that having a downtown Urban Campus will be an intimate platform for UofC to interact with the folks there on a daily basis? In fact, it can, and for sure will, facilitate seamless "town and gown" interactions! As the only research university in a city of about a million, it is also the only game in town, and therefore President Weingarten had a gut feeling that the university has the added responsibility to be an integrated part of the city. To this end, the word "enmeshing" is particularly noteworthy.

To me, it is impressive that President Weingarten understood this at the gut level and seemed to articulate it as clearly as he can, in words and actions to the downtown crowd.

Running a university requires enormous financial resources. To this end, a great university president must be a great fundraiser as well. Fundraising must be carried out with sincerity and with charm. I was happy to learn that the week before meeting with me, President Weingarten was in Hong Kong, meeting with UofC's large alumni. I also learned from the website that one of Hong Kong's major philanthropists, Henry Fok (霍英東), made a significant contribution to UofC. What Henry Fok wanted to do was to assist the University of Calgary to attain the next level of globalization. From my discussion with Dr. Weingarten, I instinctively could tell that the fingerprints of President Weingarten were all over this effort.

This discussion with President Weingarten conjured up a phrase I heard from the president of another university nearly 12,000 miles away, which happens to be my hometown called Singapore. In a recent speech, the President of the National University of Singapore Dr. Shih Choon Fong said that "…. *A Good University Teaches, A Great University Transforms* …" This feeling was palpable in my discussion with Weingarten.

A picture I took with President Shih Choon Fong (on the left) and President Su Guaning. They were former presidents of National University of Singapore and Nanyang Technology University, respectively.

Institute for Sustainable Energy, Environment and Economy

I was also given the opportunity to meet with the director, Dr. Robert Mansell, of the Institute for Sustainable Energy, Environment and Economy (ISEEE). To ensure that this important institute, which is not only a horizontal silos integration effort within the university, but also one which will "enmesh" with the economic and intellectual effort of the Province, President Weingarten agreed to dip his hands into the project by being the titular lead.

According to the "propaganda" of the Institute,

> ... ISEEE builds on considerable strengths in research and academic programs in energy and the environment at the University of Calgary. ISEEE was established in 2003 to provide leadership

and coordination for developing and implementing energy- and environment-related initiatives at the University....

In discussing with Dr. Robert Mansell, who is an economist by training, it was not difficult to detect the uniqueness of the Institute. Unlike most research institutes within a university, which either deal with hardcore technologies or hardcore policy issues, this one brings together both as a tandem.

Again, I had a particular interest in visiting this institute. Just weeks before, I had the great experience of meeting with the leaders of two massive projects in China, the Shanghai high-speed maglev system and the Yangtze River Water Resource Commission. I was also a co-organizer for a workshop hosted by the Alan G. MacDiarmid Center for Renewable Energy of China's Three Gorges University. All are highly technologically challenging projects.

My only experience ever on the Shanghai Maglev system in 2006.

A visit I made to the Yangtze river water resource commission in Wuhan in 2006.

Picture taken in 2006 inside the hydraulic hall of China's Three Gorges hydraulic power plant.

However, I was amazed that all three groups I mentioned here in China, while being technologically intensive still face the primary difficulties of establishing "sustainable" and "meaningful" policies and devising the appropriate legal administrative architecture to enforce them. It is clear that all technologically innovative projects must be accompanied by sensible, comprehensible and enforceable policies. Therefore, the fact was that here was an institute which places high priority on policy studies in areas which are so very technologically demanding, and this is indeed more refreshing. Recently, I was disappointed to learn that because of internal bickering, ISEEE was shut down. Nevertheless, it seems to me that the idea of having such an institute pursuing policies for large-scale technological projects, be it inside a university or outside, is worth pursuing.

Schulich Engineering School

I had a wonderful meeting with the Dean of Engineering, Dr. Elizabeth Cannon. Dr. Cannon became the President of the University of Toronto when Dr. Weingarten stepped down in 2010.

I found that the school was in an upbeat mood because a well-known Canadian philanthropist named Mr. Schulich recently gave it a healthy dosage of funding, hence the name of the School. The funds provided by Mr. Schulich will significantly strengthen the teaching capabilities as well as adding sufficient funds to recruit top-notch individuals to fill the endowed chairs in various disciplines.

It is very interesting to me that while the School has the full array of departments, namely electrical and computing, mechanical and manufacturing, civil, and chemical and petroleum, there is also one very unusual department: geomatics engineering!

According to its website,

Geomatics Engineering is a modern discipline, which integrates acquisition, modelling, analysis, and management of spatially referenced data, i.e. data identified according to their locations. Based on the scientific framework of geodesy, it uses terrestrial, marine, airborne, and satellite-based sensors to acquire spatial and other data. It includes the process of transforming spatially referenced data from different sources into common information systems with well-defined accuracy characteristics.

I was especially intrigued by the "mission" of this department because just a few weeks before my visit, as was mentioned, I visited the China's Yangtze River Water Resource Commission, an organization whose mission is to manage this massive river as a "system" rather than merely a "river." To this end, the equipment and R&D facilities I saw throughout the mission, and the language of the technical staff were multidisciplinary, from GIS, to GPS, to massive data acquisition, to data mining, to remote sensing, and so on and so forth. All of this would fit the mission of geomatics engineering of UofC to the glove.

I detected a bit of understandable disappointment when a couple of years ago UofC was not selected as the site for Canada's national nanotechnology research center. The University of Alberta, which was up the street, was selected. For a country like Canada, it makes sense not to establish more than one nanotechnology center. When resources are limited, it is definitely more efficient and profitable to concentrate the effort in one place rather than diffusing it. It is not the most efficient thing to practice what I sometimes refer to as the ill-conceived $1/N$ model, when N is large. This may also imply that not being selected, the pursuit of this very hot topic of R&D in a big way in UofC needs to be put on the backburner, at least for the time being. Of course, these are my words, not Dr. Cannon's. Also, having a large national research center in this area in the same province could have some impact in this area of research in UofC.

Medical School

The Medical School of UofC is a massive branch of the institution. I had a most enjoyable meeting with its Associate Dean, Dr. Richard Hawkes, a jovial fellow with an excellent sense of British humor! Our discussions ranged from medical education, to medical ethics, to public health. We also talked about medical research and the fundamental importance of collaborations with other branches of the university. If memory serves me correctly, Dr. Hawkes was most enthusiastic about finding ways to work even more closely with the scientists and engineers of UofC. We both agreed wholeheartedly that the progress of modern medical research would be very difficult without the massive influence of basic science and engineering. He told me about a recent NIH panel he had participated in, wherein this point was emphasized by all panel members multiple times.

The Medical School, which has over 250 faculty members, half of them of a clinical nature, is sitting slightly outside of the main campus in a massive set of buildings — almost a separate campus. Both the University Hospital and the Medical School are in the same complex. There are also several new buildings, and one of them is a major, new but not quite complete research facility. When I was taken around the building, I saw the most modern "bells and whistles" one can find in such a facility.

Richard and I also discussed about the fundamental importance of medical imaging, and by extension biomedical photonics. According to Richard, this is a very strong area of focus in UofC. Of course, as a physicist, I told him that I am proud that this technology was known in the beginning as "nuclear magnetic resonance" until the word "nuclear" became politically incorrect. That is why today it is known as "magnetic resonance imaging."

I took the opportunity to "drop the name" of my good friend the late Britton Chance, who was without a doubt one of the greatest scientists of the 21st century, who pioneered the truly exciting field of biomedical photonics. I was of course not surprised that Richard was well aware of the profound contributions of Britton. Subsequent email exchanges with Richard had resulted in him agreeing to attend the workshop in spring 2007 held at the Brittan Chance Center for Biomedical Photonics at Huazhong University of Science and Technology in Wuhan, China.

In visiting this Medical School, I was reminded once again by the joke that when the seven presidents of the Ivy League universities sit down for a meeting, only one will have a smile on his/her face. That individual is the President of Princeton and the reason for that is because Princeton is the only university among the seven that *does not* have a medical school. This joke outlines the intrinsic difficulty of meshing a medical school, which usually has also one or a few hospitals associated with it, with the normal operation of a comprehensive university. Looking at the massive structure here, I think I can reconfirm the reason for the smile on the face of President of Princeton University!

I told Dr. Weingarten that I was most impressed by what the city of Shanghai did recently in changing the city's lack of science and technology perception. Riding on the vision of a good friend of mine, Yang Fujia (former President of Fudan University now Chancellor of UK's University of Nottingham), the city began successfully pushing the idea of constructing a state-of-the-art synchrotron radiation facility in Shanghai, which will make the city one of *the* centers for material research in the 21st century. This project, now completed, will make a real difference to a city that is home to as many as 20 million people.

So, I made the suggestion that while Calgary is now riding high economically, it may be time for it to consider, with UofC's leadership, building a significant and large project for the region, to transform its image from "cow-town" to "vibrant tech-town"!

Ariel view of Shanghai synchrotron radiation facility.
Source: Retrieved from https://epics-controls.org/projects/ssrf/.

Some Final Thoughts

Canada, unlike the United States, is a dual-language country, English and French are the languages spoken. It is absolutely a common misconception in Asia that due to its physical similarities with the United States that subconsciously, Canada is somehow an appendix or at least closely linked to its vast neighbor. It is not. Having said that, because of Canada's geographical proximity to the United States and because it has only one-tenth of the population of the US, it is natural that it will sometimes be overshadowed in more ways than one by its powerful neighbor.

As I have indicated, at one point in the late 1970s and early 1980s, I was collaborating intensely with the physicists at McMaster University. This university is in a city called Hamilton, which is very close to the Niagara Falls. During that period, I have noticed that McMaster University's physics department, just like many US universities, have a significant number of foreign faculty members. In fact, in the theoretical physics group, there were Indian, Chinese, British and French faculty members. I suspect that other parts and departments of McMaster would have the same characteristics. This was quite unlike the physics departments I was familiar with in European countries such as Germany, Britain and France where one would generally be hard-pressed to find a significant percentage of faculty members who are not natives. In this sense, Canada is a warm and welcoming country. It would indeed be very sad, in perception or in reality, if this were to change.

As I have mentioned in this chapter, from the many Canadians I have interacted with, especially those that I mentioned in this chapter, I have found them to generally be extremely friendly with the outside world. Unlike the United States, where there is noticeable religious fanaticism, Canada is not characterized by this phenomenon. In general, while the United States is turning inwards, I do not sense that Canada is doing the same. I hope this is not a trend that will be seen in the future.

Canada's geopolitical perspective is, or should be, closer to that of Singapore than the other G7 nations it belongs to. Although in terms of landmass it is considerably larger than France, Germany, Italy, Japan and the United Kingdom, in terms of global influence it is not. In many ways, just as Singapore is forever in search of a dynamic geopolitical pathway to deal with or handle the ever and fast changing US–China relationship, Canada needs to do the same. In this regard, it seems to me that Canada is "less fortunate" in that the United States is literally at its doorstep and has established historically, under strong persuasion from the United States, far tighter binational agreements, while Singapore has not and made sure it does not have. It is in this sense that Singapore can be less overpowered.

China should not and must not assume that the way it "culturally communicates" with the United States can simply do the same with Canada. This would be an utterly false assumption. Since Canada, though "small," is still a vital nation, I think it is important that China should "culturally communicate" with Canada in its own right and to truly appreciate the subtle differences between Canada and the United States. Of course, Canada should be brave enough to let the United States understand that it takes its sovereignty seriously. I hope that what I have discussed in this chapter, which obviously is only scratching the surface, would be an incentive for China to develop a deeper understanding of this nation.

Before ending, I would be remiss if I did not mention about Dr. Michael Stevenson, former President and Vice Chancellor of Simon Fraser University in Victoria, which is in the Province of British Columbia. Dr. Stevenson is an outstanding scholar who grew up in South Africa.

In 2009, President Michael Lai, my boss at National Cheng Kung University in Taiwan requested that I form a "Blue Ribbon Panel" to explore the possibility of the universities becoming autonomous from the Ministry of Education. In carrying out this task, I accidentally came upon a brilliant article with the title "University Governance and Autonomy: Problems in Managing Access, Quality and Accountability." I thought that the article was simply brilliant after I read it. I then remember saying to myself, I must invite the author to be a member of the "Blue Ribbon Panel."

I found out that the author was Dr. Michael Stevenson. We became friends.

A picture with some of the Blue Ribbon Panel members taken in my office at the National Cheng Kung University. Standing in the middle is Dr. Michael Stevenson.

There was a passage in his article which I thought would be relevant to understanding higher education, and in particular how people need to understand one another in general:[7]

> Before I bring my remarks to a conclusion, I want to make a general observation about the way universities are commonly perceived in my country (namely Canada) and possibly your own. They are often treated on the basis of a mix of ignorance and prejudice, as

---

[7]Stevenson. M. (April 26, 2004). University Governance and Autonomy: Problems in Managing Access, Quality and Accountability. *Autonomy of Public Universities Forum.* Retrieved from http://research.ncku.edu.tw/re/commentary/e/20090327/2.html.

hide-bound by tradition, given far too much autonomy with public funds, wasteful, and as I said earlier, filled with featherbedding "dead wood." This is not the reality in fact. The reason why universities have been the most durable institutions in history, practically speaking from the thirteenth century on, is that their unique combination of autonomy and decentralization creates exactly the modern type of institution which is able to innovate, which is able to manage change, in a far more effective way than either government bureaucracy or corporate hierarchy. In fact, corporate hierarchies are moving to flatter and more decentralized models of organization which mimic the university rather than vice versa.

This comment underlines the flavor of Canadian higher education! Finally, I am confident that the current animosity between Canada and China is a geopolitical dissension. As in all geopolitical dissensions, unless it is of a religious nature, which can last a millennium, if not longer, it is not long-lasting. I am also confident, that the warm friendship between Canada and China will resume after the dissension is over, which I am confident will happen sooner or later. Quite recently, I was dismayed to listen to a group of distinguished political analysts in Canada that their tone towards China was no different from the Neocons in the United States. At this point in time, Canadians need to take seriously the words of Prime Minister of Singapore Lee Hsien Loong regarding "realpolitiks." Indeed, my earnest hope is that the people of both countries should and hopefully can take a long-term view, learn much about each other, and rekindle the warm friendship which the first Prime Minister Pierre Trudeau created with China for mutual benefits. This chapter was written with that goal in mind.

To end a chapter dedicated to the discussion about Canada and China, and not to discuss the profound contribution of the Dr. Norman Bethune, a Canadian physician to China would be incomplete at best.

I first visited China in the spring of 1981. One of the universities I visited then was Jilin University (JLU), one of the important universities which I had established strong collaborative relations ever since the end of the "Cultural Revolution." JLU is located in the provincial capital city of Changchun. While there, the president of JLU, the late Tang Ao-Qing, graciously met with me. I remember distinctly that he said "besides Jilin University, I want you to visit a medical school in our city, which unfortunately is not affiliated to our university. I want you to visit this school, not because it is the best in China, but that it was created for the Chinese people to remember a great Canadian who dedicated his life to hold the peoples of China and Canada together."

Norman Bethune.

Source: https://en.wikipedia.org/wiki/Norman_Bethune#/media/File:Norman_Bethune_ graduation_1922.jpg

The university which was located not far from the downtown campus of JLU then, was known as Norman Bethune Medical University (白求恩医科大学).

According to Wikipedia, Norman Bethune[8]

"was a (University of Toronto trained) Canadian physician and medical innovator. Bethune came to international prominence first for his service as a frontline surgeon supporting the Republican

---

[8]Norman Bethune. (n.d.). In *Wikipedia*. Retrieved September 1, 2019, from https://en.wikipedia.org/wiki/Norman_Bethune.

faction during the Spanish Civil War. But it was his service with the Communist Eight Route Army during the Second Sino-Japanese War that would earn him enduring acclaim. Dr. Bethune effectively brought modern medicine to rural China and often treated sick villagers as much as wounded soldiers. His selfless commitment made a profound impression on the Chinese people, especially CPC's leader, Mao Zedong. Mao wrote a eulogy to him, which was memorized by generations of Chinese people. Bethune is credited for saving millions of Chinese soldiers and civilians during the Second- Sino Japanese War, and is known worldwide as one of the most influential doctors of all time."

With this, I think that at this critical moment between Canada and China, both Chinese and Canadians could do well to remember what this great Canadian had done for the friendship of these two great countries!

Chapter 8

Case Study 4 of "Cultural Communication": "Constructing" a True Supercontinent

I was born in India, but grew up in Southeast Asia. For that reason, Malaysia has always occupied a special place in my heart. That is one of the selfish reasons why I am writing this chapter.

When I was growing up in Singapore, the concept of "Sing-Ma 新－马" i.e. Singapore and Malaya in one breath, was always mentioned. In fact, my wife — who grew up in Hong Kong — while we were dating, referred to me as "a Sing-Ma kid" (新马仔) to her friends. In 1964, on August 21, when I left Singapore for the United States, I was a Malaysian citizen, holding its passport. In recent years, while living in Asia, I noticed Malaysia was receiving more and more attention from the Asian news media. As far as the BRI is concerned, Malaysia was also one of the critical nations constantly being mentioned in recent years. The necessity of China and Malaysia was engaging in cultural communication appears to be more imperative today than ever.

On May 9, 2018, a Malaysian national election was held that shocked Asia. By this time, Malaysia was already a Southeast Asian nation of fundamental geopolitical importance. For any outsider, this election and the results were truly convoluted and had all the signs of being an intriguing human drama.

After all, when was the last election anywhere on earth wherein a former Prime Minister, who led a new coalition of mostly new political parties could defeat the government which was also run by a coalition of many political parties? Furthermore, the defeated coalition had been in power since Malaysia became independent 61 years ago on August 1, 1957. What is stunning is that the new Prime Minister Tun Mahathir was actually a leader of that party and a former Prime Minister some two decades ago! To top all these intriguing aspects, Tun Mahathir now carries two "old" insignias: "old" as in former and "old" as in 95 years old!

Tun Mahathir led a new coalition known as Pakatan Harapan (PH or Alliance of Hope), which consisted of four political parties, Democratic Action Party, People's Justice Party, National Trust Party and Malaysia United Indigenous Party, to defeat the current government, which was also a coalition known as Barisan Nasional, or BN. The leader of BN was Najib Razak, the son of the former Prime Minister Tun Razak and who resigned after the defeat. As a coalition, BN consisted of three parties, the United Malays National Organization (UMNO), Malaysian Chinese Association (MCA) and Malaysian Indian Congress (MIC). From 1981 to 2003, when Mahathir was the Prime Minister of Malaysia, he was the leader of BN!

In the subsequent 12 months after PH won the election, Malaysia and China went through a series of uncomfortable geopolitical ups and downs. These came about because during Razak's era, his government worked with China's BRI and signed several important infrastructure deals. One of them was the East Coast Rail Link (ECRL), a 688-kilometer high-speed rail project linking Kota Bahru at the northeast end of Malaysia's peninsula with the port city Klang that lies about 34 kilometers south-west of the capital Kuala Lumpur. After PH took over the government, the ECRL became a rather hot potato, partially because of the price tag, and especially when the Western media made it to be an archetypical example of BRI's "debt traps." Regarding this issue, I had published two articles with my colleague Dr. Liang Haiming.[1] In April 2018, dusk seemed to have

---

[1]Feng, D. H. & Liang, H. M. (November 21, 2018). Is BRI road to a 'debt trap'? The numbers say no. *Global Times*. Retrieved from http://www.globaltimes.cn/content/1128434.shtml & (November 6, 2018). & Opinion: Is Malaysia involved in 'Debt Diplomacy' with China?. CGTN. Retrieved from https://news.cgtn.com/ news/3d3d514e78497a4d30457a6333566d54/index.html.

settled, and Malaysia and China finally agreed to continue the project. Understandably, there is no more mentioning of the Western media the conflict between Malaysia and China since then.

As far as ECRL and BRL are concerned, I recall a rather sobering and lengthy conversation I had with a longtime friend who is also one of Malaysia's most influential academic leaders. This was during the time Razak was still in power. His conclusion was that there was great necessity for China and Malaysia to understand each other comprehensively — namely they must culturally communicate with each other far better than they had been doing at that time.

My friend agreed that for Malaysia to become an important nation in the 21st century, constructing and/or upgrading its infrastructure was a must. It was also clear that without a real change in Malaysia's financial *modus operandi*, it simply did not have the means, financially or otherwise, to carry out these much-needed efforts. Having said that, he complained bitterly that although it was clear that China did treat the Malaysian BRL projects as reasonable international commercial transitions, as China should, the ECRL unfortunately was primarily a result of the corrupt practice of the Razak government. He told me that he had warned the representatives from China that Razak's corruption would bring about the downfall of his government. Unfortunately, he told me with sadness, that his warning fell on deaf ears.

Furthermore, he also mentioned that in dealing with Malaysia, China could use more help, or education, in understanding Malaysia's grass-root sentiments. It appears that the ECRL was mostly handled from the Chinese side, including the supply of materials and manpower. From China's viewpoint, this was understandable because for China to be successful in such endeavors, speed was crucial. To this end, from the Chinese perspective, it was certainly more desirable to bring in well-trained and well-seasoned Chinese workers for the project. After all, spending time and effort to train local workers for the project was time consuming and expensive. Thus, local Malaysians received little or no benefits. According to my friend, from the Malaysian perspective, this is, of course, a short-sighted view, because in the end, Malaysia will have an infrastructure that will render the country economically much stronger than it would have been otherwise. But one needs to appreciate that for the locals who were more likely to take on the view of "what's in it for me now," it was not easy to have such a vision. The lack of locals participating in the BRI effort could and did create widespread ill will.

In recent discussions I had with Lee Hong-Fah, whom I mentioned extensively in Chapter 5, he told me that in the past year and a half since the election, China had set up many training centers to get local workers up to speed with the project. Furthermore, projects are now outsourced to local industries. In Lee's words, there is significantly a far more mature attitude in the way China is now handling the ECRL project.

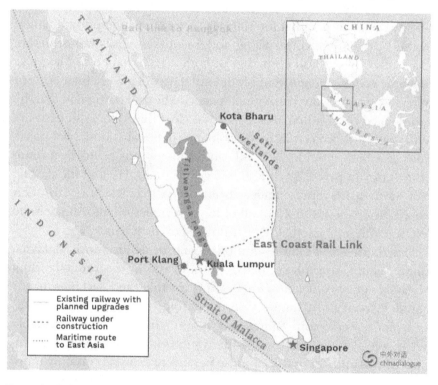

From the link, it states that "Work on the project started in August 2017 but was suspended in 2018 following a general election in Malaysia. The newly-elected prime minister, Mahathir bin Mohamad, accused his predecessor of awarding the project to the China Communications Construction Company (CCCC) without an open tendering process, at high costs and unfair terms for Malaysia."

Source: Retrieved from https://chinadialogue.net/article/show/single/en/11842-Photo-journey-Malaysia-s-new-China-funded-railway-

A photo I took with Mahathir when I was an Academic Advisory Board Member of Universiti Teknologi Petronas. He was the Honorary Chair of the Board.

With the above discussions as preamble, I shall write in this chapter my deep interactions with Malaysia and East Asia. I will try to discuss the ways and means of Malaysia, as best as I can. Much of what I shall present here is based on a keynote speech I delivered to the Malaysia's Science and Technology Congress during October 5–7, 2004, in Kuala Lumpur. The audience included leading members of Malaysia's scientific, technological and entrepreneurial communities. In my speech, I emphasized that to understand Malaysia, one must understand it via its complex history. I have updated much of the information presented in this chapter.

In the past 15 years, for various professional reasons, I visited Malaysia many times. Besides my capacity as a university administrator working closely with the top Malaysian institution — the University of Malaya — I was also a member of the Academic Advisory Council of a semi-private university, the Universiti Teknologi Petronas (UTP). Because of these activities, I had the opportunity to undertake multiple visits each year to Malaysia, and these visits

Class picture of the Academic Advisory Council of Universiti Teknology Petronas.

allowed me to gain deeper appreciation of the complexity, socially and racially, of Malaysia.

A Few Words About Indonesia

Another nation that China must engage with for its BRI activities is Indonesia. With over 18,000 islands and a population of over 200 million, Indonesia is a massive "island nation" in Southeast Asia. It is also one with the largest number of Moslems in the world (the second and third being Pakistan and India.)

From 1962 to 1965, the Indonesian Government led by President Sukarno carried out an aggressive policy of "*konfrontasi*" with the then newly independent nation of Malaysia. I could remember living in Singapore in the early 1960s when the people were deeply concerned about the possibility of an Indonesian military incursion. The fact that on a clear day, one could actually see some of the remote Indonesian islands from the southern beaches of Singapore did not help diminish the concerns!

At the end of the first decade of the 21st century, I became a member of the Advisory Board of one of Indonesia's largest private universities in Jakarta, Binus University. With that connection, I had the opportunity to travel quite often to the country, which, by the way, is the only nation I have visited that lies below the equator. In interacting with Binus' academicians and administrators, I learned that the university is indeed a forward-looking and proactive institution located in one of the most exciting and fast-growing metropolitains of Asia, Jakarta.

Also, through Binus' leadership in an organization known as "Nationwide Universities Network of Indonesia," I met a large number of Indonesian higher education administrators throughout this vast country. From my discussions with them, they were all excited about the rise of China — not as a menace, but as a foundation for peace and tranquility in the Asia-Pacific region.

Finally, with China and Indonesia now working hand-in-hand for the construction of the high-speed rail between Jakarta and Bandung, and the possibility of China or Japan, or a collaboration between China and Japan, to construct the high-speed rail between Bandung and Surabaya, I am confident that Indonesia, within the next decade, will be shining on the global radar screen.

However, I regret to admit that even with such connections, I was only able to scratch the surface — a superficial understanding of the

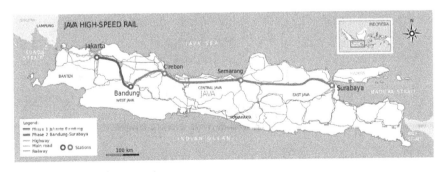

Indonesia's high-speed rail system, from Jakarta to Bandung to Surabaya.

Source: Retrieved from https://en.wikipedia.org/wiki/High-speed_rail_in_Indonesia#/media/File:Java_High-speed_Rail_Indonesia.svg.

depth of this nation. I was quite startled on seeing much of the similarities between Indonesia and Malaysia, such as the official language of both Indonesia and Malaysia, being Bahasa Indonesia and Malay, respectively.

Advisory Board Members of Binus University.

The airport which all foreigners fly into Malaysia is the Kuala Lumpur International Airport (KLIA). In 2004, when I arrived at the airport, I noticed that it was given a nickname "Airport for the next 100 years." Knowing how fast Malaysia was growing, I thought that was at best "wishful thinking." In 2018, when I visited Malaysia last, the airport was no longer recognizable since it had been upgraded significantly! In 2018, I also saw something which caught my attention about the highway going from the airport to the downtown area. I remember in 2004, as we were driving in, I saw on most overpasses the ever-present Samsung advertisements. Now such advertisements have been replaced by Huawei billboards!

The title of my 2004 speech, "Science, Technology and Entrepreneur Spirit in the Pacific Rim in the 21st Century: A

Global Transformation" was chosen because it was my firm belief then, as it is now, that Southeast Asia in general, and Malaysia in particular, is of profound importance to the entire Pacific Rim, from the Asia-Pacific region, to the Oceanic area, to North, Central and South America. For that, the world needs to understand it in a comprehensive manner.

As I have mentioned, I was born in India just before her independence. The travel document I had when I was still a "British subject" had the words *"Bearer has no right to abode in the British Isles"* printed on the cover. These were boiler-plate words on the "passport" for any British "subject" in a British colony. Fortunately, I was too young to comprehend the profound insinuation and deep humiliation of that one particular sentence. After all, the colonial period I was talking about was merely 60 years ago during which many regions of Asia, and indeed many countries in South East Asia, were under the rule by colonial powers. For example, United Kingdom in Myanmar (formerly Burma), Malaya, Sarawak, North Borneo (now these three have together become Malaysia), Singapore and Brunei (technically a British protectorate); France in Cambodia (a French protectorate), Laos and Vietnam; Holland in Indonesia; and last but not least, United States in the Philippines. It should be underscored that colonialism then was not merely a word in the history book, as it is now, but was a stark political reality. As colonial subjects for more than a century, the people in Southeast Asia had developed a "colonial" mindset that took a long time to erase. I must say I am pleased and very gratified to learn that the Southeast Asian youth today probably are as unaware of colonialism as they are about the Beatles!

I remember that during one of my many trips to Asia in the early 1980s, there was an article I read on flight that has since lodged in my memory. In this article, there was a diagram which plotted the number of air passengers between Europe and North America and between Asia and North America as a function of time (year). This diagram had two curves, with the Asian curve tucked below the Europe one in the early 1960s (just when the Boeing 707 came into play) and overtaking it around the end of the 20th century. With this important piece of information, it must mean that in the 21st century, something profound is happening. Today, with China in its current economic prowess, I am confident that more people are crossing the Pacific than the Atlantic. It means that North America, after several centuries of being European-centric, culturally, economically and intellectually, is at least showing a sign of a shift. It also means that the East and West shores of the Pacific — the so-called Pacific Rim — is assuming greater global importance in the 21st century than the Atlantic Rim.

I went to United States in the fall of 1964. My brother went there a year before me. Little did we know that we were on the cusp of two transportation eras. He was probably one of the last batches of Asian students to come to the United States by boat: the so-called American Presidential Lines, and I was the first batch to come by air. It took him 21 days to go from Singapore to Hong Kong, Yokohama, Honolulu, and finally San Francisco! I flew to the States on the Boeing workhorse, the Boeing 707. It took me 24

In 1963, my brother left for the United States on an American Presidential Liner. Notice in 1963, technical students like us were proudly carrying the "slide rule"!

hours to travel from Singapore to New York, with stops in Beirut and Rome!

Asia Pacific Rim in the 1950s, 1960s and 1970s

In the 1950s, 1960s and even the early part of the 1970s, great political instability and backward economies were the norm in the Asia-Pacific nations. Most countries were categorized as third-world, with Japan being the only exception.

In Singapore in the 1960s, the so-called domino mindset was quite palpable. This was exacerbated by the intensification of the Vietnam conflict. Two western powers, France and the United States, were deeply involved in that conflict, and it lasted a quarter of a century, from 1950 to 1975.

First it was the French. The French as Vietnam's colonial ruler, starting from 1884 until 1954, finally departed after a massive military defeat in 1954 in Dien Bien Pho by the so-called Việt Minh led by Ho Chi-Minh. It is interesting that the full name of *Việt Minh* is *Việt Nam độc lập đồng minh*. Anyone with the slightest understanding of Chinese would recognize how similar the Vietnamese language is to Chinese. Indeed, in Chinese, this would be Yue (越) Nan (南) Du (独) Li (立) Tong (同) Meng (盟), or the Independence Alliance of Vietnam. I devote the entirety of Chapter 9 to a discussion about Vietnam.

Although the United States did not establish Vietnam as its colony, it did, at the height of the Vietnam conflict, have more than half a million military personnel there. The Vietnam war was indeed a very bloody conflict, having more than 58,000 American military personnel and more than a million Vietcong military personel and civilians perished. Like the French, the United States also departed the country in 1975 when the Vietcong gained control of the South.

Not all regions of Asia Pacific were devastated by the Vietnam conflict. For example, it was during this period that Taiwan was considered as the "Rest and Recreation" center for the battle-fatigued US soldiers, and this led to its economy benefitting enormously.

Between August 23, 1958 and January 1, 1959, tension in the Taiwan Straits became the center of world's attention, especially the

Quemoy–Matsu (金门–马祖) crisis. During this period, these two islands controlled by Taiwan (officially known as the Republic of China) were under heavy bombardment from the Mainland. That crisis brought the United States 7th fleet into the Taiwan Straits. Recently, I had carefully read the transcript of the televised third presidential debate, which was held on October 13, 1960, between President John F. Kennedy and presidential candidate Richard M. Nixon. The main theme of this debate was how the United States should handle the Quemoy–Matsu crisis. I counted from the transcript of this debate that Kennedy and Nixon mentioned Quemoy–Matsu 16 times.[2] This debate made Quemoy–Matsu the epicenter of global attention during the cold war era.

The tension in the Taiwan Straits lasted for many years after that. In a manner of speaking, it still persists today. In the 21st century, close economic ties exist between Taiwan and the Mainland. During my 7 years in Taiwan, I made many visits to Quemoy and fell in love with this island of exquisite beauty because of its deep ties to Southeast Asia, especially to Singapore and Malaysia. As I have mentioned in Chapter 4, Michael Szonyi, now director of Harvard University's Fairbank Center for Chinese Studies, wrote one of the most important books on Quemoy, titled *Cold War Island*. And, unfortunately, even in 2019, one can still notice the chill, at least in the political realm, between Taiwan and the Mainland.

In Northeast Asia, the "crisis" in the Korean peninsula remains a tinder-box. Even though the Korean armistices were signed in 1953, political instabilities on both sides of the 38th Parallel remain palpable. During my several visits to Seoul in the past three decades, I always had a queasy feeling knowing that what I saw was a technological powerhouse that was only 36 kilometers from the 38th Parallel. Indeed, the region could turn into ashes and dust in the next second. Still, one cannot help but be impressed by the resilience of the South Koreans who, even under such conditions, turned their nation into an economic miracle.

---

[2]Commission on Presidential Debate. (October 13, 1960). *Debate Transcript: The Third Kennedy-Nixon Presidential Debate*. Retrieved from https://www.debates.org/voter-education/debate-transcripts/october-13-1960-debate-transcript/.

A photo I took of the small island next to Quemoy controlled by the Republic of China facing the mainland with the Chinese characters on the side stating "Three People's Principles Unite China!"

Finally, perhaps what was most fascinating and totally unexpected by the world was the rapid economic development of China in the first two decades of the 21st century. There is an interesting Chinese saying "万绿丛中一点红" (among the 10,000 green vegetations, there is one red flower). There were a few signs then that could have given people in the Asia Pacific a glimpse as to what was to come towards the end of the 20th century. These are discussed in the following.

First, I believe there was a very important success story in the 1950's — a very important success story which nowadays receive little attention. That story is the closure of 12 years of bloody insurgencies in the Malay Peninsula. In 1956, my mother took me to visit Kuala Lumpur. We took an all-night train and I noticed that on top of each train carriage, there were British Gurkha soldiers. These were fierce fighters the British hired from Nepal to keep watchful eyes on the insurgents, known as Ma-Gong, or Malayan Communist Party. Needless to say, I was quite frightened. The closure in 1960 gave the Malay Peninsula great breathing space to turn into one of the economic miracles of Asia, where people of different ethnicities, namely Malays, Chinese, Indians and Eurasians, could live harmoniously together. Indeed, I dare say that to understand Malaysia today, one cannot exclusively select one ethnic group only.

A photo taken with Yeoh Tiong-Lay after I delivered a lecture at his alma mater Hing-Wah High School.

A good friend of mine, the late Yeoh Tiong-Lay (杨忠礼) was the 7th richest man in Malaysia and undoubtedly one of the most successful entrepreneurs. I was quite impressed by how he could navigate with great ease among the various ethnic groups in

Malaysia. I am more impressed by the fact that he never hid his profound love of his Chinese heritage. This, he manifested beyond his being a mega-successful entrepreneur by his loyalty to his alma mater Hing Wah High School in Klang. One day, in all seriousness, he told me in one of our many conversations the following words of wisdom:

> Since independence, Malaysia went through a multitude of hardships. One of its greatest successes was how the Malays and the Chinese communities, and to a lesser extend the Indian community (because it is much smaller), which could not be more different in their ways and means, were able to struggle and find their balanced point to live and prosper together. I can tell the world that to understand Malaysia, you absolutely have to understand the various ethnic groups not separately, but in totality!

I saw the "totality" in action when I noticed that in Hing Wah High School there was (and I am sure still is) a concerted effort in recruiting Malay and Indian students. In discussing with one of its Malay students, I was pleased to see that the student was fluent in English, Malay and Chinese! I was especially impressed to note when the student talked to me in Chinese, he was utterly comfortable in using many Chinese idioms (中国成语). This is the best way to measure a student's deep understanding of the Chinese culture. Hence, the words of Yeoh are indeed important words for China and Malaysia in developing their mutual cultural communication!

The second one is among the most important successes of that period — the Tokyo Olympics of 1964. This was the first Olympics to be held on Asian soil. This presented a great opportunity for the Japanese government to showcase to the world that Japan had recovered from the devastation of the global disaster created by Germany and Japan, that is WWII. One of its showcases was the high-speed rail known as Shinkansen (新干线). The Japanese were able to leverage such an international event to send the first salvo of a global ground transportation revolution! This is certainly one of the most important ingredients — ground transportation revolution — that I had mentioned extensively in Chapter 2 as playing a role in developing the BRI concept. In 2008, China also hosted the Olympics. Not surprisingly, China also leveraged its first major international event, just like Japan in 1964, to showcase to the world that China had come of age by introducing the Beijing–Tianjin high-speed rail.

The third aspect was that two exciting developments happened on the Pacific Rim in the 1960s and 1970s, and these were the economic transformations of South Korea and Taiwan. I caught a personal glimpse of the hardworking nature of Koreans when I was visiting my mother in Singapore in 1969. Singapore was then just at the threshold of its miraculous economic transformation, and everywhere on this tiny island, one could see building cranes. I wondered then that having only 2.2 million inhabitants at that time, where on earth did all the workers came from, working 24 × 7 on literally thousands of skyscrapers that were being built. The answer was soon provided for me. They came from South Korea!

In the 1980s, opportunities began to emerge in the region which allowed scientists and technologists with entrepreneurial skillsets to return from North America to Taiwan and South Korea. They brought with them not only their technical skills but also their "capitalistic skills." Some of them are today's economic and industrial backbones, not only for Taiwan and South Korea, but for Asia and maybe even the world!

In the early 1950s and 1960s, the term "brain drain" began to seep into the cognizance of the public. The term was first used to portray how the West, especially United States, sucked away from Asia some of their best minds. That was indeed the case. However, by the 1970s, the trend began to reverse as Asia's economies improved. Indeed, it was the beginning of a reversed brain drain — or "brain gain."

The best example of "brain gain" which resulted in Taiwan becoming a technological powerhouse was embodied by a gentleman named Morris Chang (张忠谋). Born in China and educated at MIT and Stanford University, he was, for many years, a Vice President for Texas Instruments, a semiconductor and integrated circuit giant in the world, with its headquarters and manufacturing plants located on the outskirt of Dallas, Texas. In the early 1980s, with great foresight, Taiwan's government recruited him to become the director of the Industrial Technology Research Institute (ITRI). Eventually, he founded the Taiwan Semiconductor Manufacturing Company Limited (TSMC), which is today one of the most important semiconductor chip manufacturing companies in the world.

A Moment that Changed History

There is no doubt that the most spectacular single event occurred in the 1970's on the cold morning of February 21, 1972 in Beijing. The entire world, at that moment, witnessed President Richard Nixon descending from Air Force One and extending his hand in preparation for his historical handshake with Premier Zhou Enlai of China. In one handshake, Nixon melted away the bitter memories of Zhou and the Chinese people when the US Secretary of State John Foster Dulles refused to shake the hand of Zhou 18 years earlier in Geneva. It also melted away in the minds of the people of Asia-Pacific nations the profound and perceived "red menace" of China. I believe that the new reality, or perception (and perception *is* reality), that China could, and in some sense had, provided an underpinning of stability in Asia Pacific and beyond. It was a major turning point for all nations in Southeast Asia. I cannot help but wonder whether it was merely coincidental that the 1970s was the threshold when Asia-Pacific nations began to grow their robust economies.

Confidence-Building

So, with the gloom and doom that followed WWII, why did the Pacific Rim not collapse into an economic abyss? In particular, how did Asians develop a strong sense of confidence in the past several decades?

There are of course many reasons for the regaining of confidence of the Asians. For me, personally, as a scientist, I could point to Lee Tsung-Dao (李政道), Chen-Ning Yang (杨振宁) and Wu Chien-Shiung (吴剑雄). These three individuals overturned one of the longest held physics dogmas: mirror symmetry must be true for all forces in nature. This discovery won Lee and Yang the highest accolade in science: the

In 2006, I congratulated Professor Lee Tsung-Dao at a physics symposium in Shanghai for his 80th birthday.

I took a photo with Professor Yang Chen-Ning and Mrs. Yang at the banquet of the conference held in Singapore in honor of the 60th year of Yang–Mills Field theory.

1957 Nobel Prize in physics. I recall with great clarity the day in 1956 when the Swedish Nobel Committee made the historical announcement that Lee and Yang had been bestowed with the Nobel prize in physics. I, as a boy of 12, was in a state of uncontrollable excitement. I often wondered whether it was this event that planted the seed in me to eventually becoming a physicist?

I would like to express a heartfelt sense of regret here that in 1957, Madame Wu was not awarded a Nobel Prize along with Lee and Yang! Clearly, without her absolutely brilliant experimental result, it was inconceivable that Lee and Yang would receive this accolade. In my opinion as a physicist, not only was the Nobel Committee absolutely unjust to Madame Wu, but the world truly had missed a glorious opportunity to honor a great female scientist who truly deserved the accolade. There are so few female physicists who have won the Nobel Prize in physics, and it was only in 2018 that the third female was awarded this highest recognition in physics. I cannot help but imagine that if this were to happen, how in that era it could have impacted millions of young women, especially young Asian women.

In the 20th century, one must not underestimate the impact made by this group of Asians composed of such eminent personalities as Lee, Yang and Wu, along with many other Asians such as Hideki Yukawa, C. V. Raman, Subrahmanyan Chandrasekhar and Samuel

A photo with Samual C. C. Ting, Nobel Laureate in physics in 1972.

C. C. Ting, as well as many other great Asian men and women in different areas of human activities. These great individuals were able to instill in the millions and millions of Asians a profound sense of self-confidence. Such self-confidence, I believe, was one of the central ingredients that made a significant difference and contributed to the prosperity seen in Asia Pacific today.

In Chapter 3, I mentioned about a summary talk at an International Conference organized by the Asian Development Bank in Tainan, Taiwan. This happened a year after the financial tsunami hit the world. There, I made a point on the fundamental importance of developing Asian's "inherent self-confidence." This important point I feel is worth repeating here:

> Throughout the 20th century, Asia was psychologically "coupled" to the West, and understandably so. With superior economic and intellectual strengths, it is quite natural that Asia viewed the West as the 'standard of excellence.' However, after such a period as this with the West so palpably exposing its social & economic weaknesses, this may be the first time in the modern global economy that Asia can psychologically "decouple" from the West. This is not to suggest that Asia should decouple economically and intellectually from the West; rather, I am talking about a "psychological decoupling" to undo a sense of reliance on the West, without which it is unlikely that Asia will develop a deep sense of inherent self-confidence, and without which, the 21st century is surely not to be the "Asian Century".

What is the Pacific Rim Like in the 21st Century?

While the Asian Pacific Rim in the 21st century continues to show progress, it also faces significant challenges. First and foremost, North Korea comes to mind. Also, while China is forever struggling with its massive population, it nevertheless shows spectacular economic growth. As I have mentioned earlier in this chapter, Taiwan and Korea are now technological powerhouses. But interestingly, with the rise of technological giants such as Huawei, Tencent and Alibaba, to name a few, so is China rising in the past decade. In the past three decades, despite the country's economic slump, Japanese scientists' creativity showed no sign of slowing down. In fact, in the 21st century, the country's economic slump was ironically accompanied by a large number of Japanese receiving the Nobel Prizes! Indeed, it is now no longer news when another Japanese wins such an accolade.

Of course, how Taiwan and Korea will play out economically in the next several decades in the midst of the massive Chinese economic growth, coupled with intriguing geopolitical ramifications, such as the US–China trade and high-tech warfare, is certainly not for me to prognosticate. One thing is for sure, compared to the 19th and the first half of the 20th century where wars and immeasurable poverty were the norm, Asians in the second half of the 20th century and in the first two decades of the 21st century are now experiencing a spectacular level of economic affluence. Therefore, with optimism abound, despite whatever severe challenges Asia Pacific will be encountering in the coming years or decades, I have confidence that the Asian miracle will continue.

I think that despite the intense popularist efforts pushing the contrary, the world is much "tighter" today than merely a decade ago, certainly compared to 3–4 decades ago. Indeed, the modern form of communication, such as the creation of social media on the Internet platform, has entirely transformed our lives, private or business, and indeed, our existence, even our warfare. In fact, my good friend Jack Pellicci, the former Group Vice President of Oracle made a calculation before the advent of social media that there would be an interesting measurement of time — the "Internet year." Roughly speaking, an Internet year was approximately 5 real years! I dare say that with social media being so omnipresent, Pellicci's calculation could be increased to 10 or even 20 years! In other words, humans do everything more "quickly" now. In this age of agility, we must recalculate and reevaluate how we do things in this new paradigm.

According to InternetWorldStats,[3] it is reported that China, in 2019, has over 800 million Internet users. This is truly astounding because in 1993, when I organized the 2nd International Conference on Computational Physics in Beijing, there were none, and in 2002,

---

[3]Top 20 Countries With the Highest Number of Internet Users (n.d.). *Internetworldstats*. Retrieved from internetworldstats.com/top20.htm.

there were only 46 million users. Such a proliferation is best noticed by how the Chinese utilize the Internet for essentially everything, thus almost making paper money disappearing in China today. In modern China, one can observe how human connectivity has entered a new age of realism. In a sense, in the 21st century, the digital paradigm in China has taken the lead in this direction.

Perhaps the biggest miracle in Asia that is causing anguish in the West in the 21st century, as I have discussed in Chapter 3 in the words of Ms. Skinner of the State Department of the United States, is the transformation of the Chinese economic landscape and the lifting of many hundreds of millions of Chinese out of poverty and into the middle class.

There is no doubt that by any measurement, 1976 was a defining year for modern China, in particular, and Asia Pacific and the World in general. Chairman Mao died on September 9 that year, followed immediately by the spectacular collapse of the so-called "Gang of Four," thus bringing to a close the 10 painful and devastating years of the "Cultural Revolution." A new era was ushered in. Someday, historians will undoubtedly consider the new era as the "miracle of the world in the 20th century." In 1976, China was at the verge of a complete "meltdown," economically, technologically and even intellectually. Possessing quarter of the human population and a land size spanning nearly half of Asia, such a meltdown for China would have alarming global consequences!

Yet, no meltdown occurred.

A fundamental reason why no meltdown occurred, in my opinion, was due to Herculean contributions of tens of millions of Chinese intellectuals. In their darkest hours during that era, enduring the hardest of hardships and suffering the deepest personal humiliations, they maintained palpable hope for themselves, their family, their professions and their nation. Indeed, even without personal liberty, both physically and mentally, they remained important pillars of the nation, holding up its dignity and searching for the dim light at the end of the tunnel. The successes of China of the 21st century are in no small part due to this group of individuals.

The fundamental problem for the entire world was that there was no preparation made to accommodate the surging of an economically powerful nation with 1.4 billion people. In fact, I think it is safe to say that even within China, the growth came so fast that no preparation was made. After all, never before in the history of humanity, was there a nation that possessed such a massive population that could transform with such agility. Indeed, even the United States, which was the only superpower after the disintegration of the Soviet Union, is now scrambling to find a way or ways to deal with China in the 21st century. What will be the outcome of this global scrambling is anybody's guess? In a recent Congressional testimony, the Federal Bureau of Investigation's (FBI) director Chris Wray made the following comment on February 15, 2018 as to how the US government intended, or was scrambling to meet the "Chinese threat"[4]:

> (What) we're trying to do is view the China threat as not just a whole-of-government threat but a whole-of-society threat on their end, and I think it's going to take a whole-of-society response by us. So it's not just the intelligence community, but it's raising awareness within our academic sector, within our private sector, as part of the defense.

These were words that drew a picture of blanket racial animosity and generalization. Once they were uttered by someone so important in the United States leadership, there can be no doubt that humanity should be deeply concerned as to whether, or more importantly, when the US and China would reach ultimately some "impasse." The ultimate issue will surely be one of the critical questions confronting not just these two countries but humanity for global peace in the 21st century.

Malaysia

Basking in the above geopolitical paradigm, Malaysia had benefitted tremendously by its geographical strategic location: From Kuala

---

[4]Joel Gerke. (February 13, 2018). FBI director: Chinese spies 'a whole-of-society' threat to US. *Washington Examiner*. Retrieved from https://www.insidehighered.com/news/2018/02/15/fbi-director-testifies-chinese-students-and-intelligence-threats

Lumpur International Airport, a 3-hour flight will cover an area on earth with 2.5 billion people, which is approximately one-third the population of the globe!

Malaysia is also geologically very stable: unlike California, Japan, Northeast China and Taiwan, it has no volcanoes, does not suffer from earthquakes and is endowed with the perfect soil for agricultural development. In the past six decades, even with much corruption, Malaysia is still one of the most politically stable pillars in Southeast Asia. Through this stability, it has developed a robust economy. Here I would like to single out my friend, the former Dean of the Faculty of Law of the University of Malaya. Her name is Professor Khaw Lake Tee.

Professor Khaw Lake Tee, the former Dean of the Faculty of Law, the University of Malaya.

Source: Retrieved from https://www.thestar.com.my/news/nation/2014/12/06/suhakam-wants-harmony-act-commission-regrets-governments-decision-to-retain-sedition-law/.

I first met Professor Khaw when she was on leave from the University of Malaya and led a delegation from the technologically ambitious Multimedia Super Corridor to visit me in Philadelphia in the late 1990s. I was instantly impressed by her intellectual strength and astuteness. In my many discussions with her, I learned that Malaysia has an efficient and legal infrastructure, having equable and equitable laws. Her successful lifetime career in Malaysia is a clear sign that in Malaysia, "when you are manifestly excellent, almost nothing can stop you"!

Last but not least, in travelling around Malaysia's western peninsular extensively, it is obvious that the transportation system of

Malaysia is of high quality. With the addition of the ECRL I mentioned earlier, and if ever the high-speed rail between Singapore and Kuala Lumpur becomes a reality, in terms of ground transportation, Malaysia will lead the pack of countries in Southeast Asia.

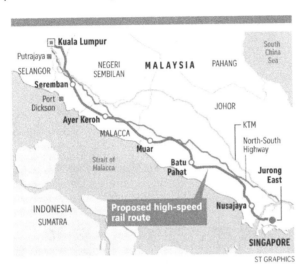

The proposed high-speed rail between Singapore and Kuala Lumpur.

Source: Retrieved from https://www.straitstimes.com/asia/se-asia/kl-spore-high-speed-rail-wont-stop-at-putrajaya.

Linking All Island Nations Japan and Indonesia Together With the Supercontinent

Unlike Africa, North America and South America, nations in the Supercontinent I mentioned in Chapter 2, especially in North Asia and Southeast Asia, are dominated by two important "island nations." They are Japan and Indonesia.

On October 29, 2018, on the website of China Global Television Network (CGTN), I wrote an article with the title "All aboard the Japan, DPRK, ROK and China friendship train."[5] The preamble of

---

[5] Feng, D. H. (October 29, 2018). Opinion: All aboard the Japan, DPRK, ROK and China friendship train? *CGTN*. Retrieved from https://news.cgtn.com/news/3d3d 414f32416a4d30457a6333566d54/share_p.html.

this article was based on the theme that the positive transformation of the geopolitics of these countries can bring about the following "intended" or "unintended" consequence:

> Geographically, Japan is an island nation. So, for any Japanese to go abroad, flying is also the only possible method for now. For a multitude of many painful historical reasons, Japan is subconsciously for all Asians to be "outside" of Asia.
>
> For example, Japan, unlike China and Vietnam, as well as the Chinese communities in Southeast Asia, does not have "Lunar New Year" as its major holiday in Asia.
>
> Japan was the pioneer of highspeed rail. It developed its rail system in the 1960s.
>
> In the 21st century, by developing a comprehensive nation-wide highspeed rail system, China has unquestionably emerged as another powerhouse.

Map of the shortest distance between Japan and South Korea.

Source: Retrieved from https://www.google.com/maps/@34.201184,129.438007,301948m/data=!3m1!1e3

It is worth noting that the closest points between Japan and the Republic of Korea (ROK) are Kyushu of Japan and Pusan of the ROK, which is separated by the Sea of Japan. Although the distance between these two cities is approximately 60 miles (97 kilometers,) there are two Japanese controlled islands in between, Iki and Tsushima.

The distances between Kyushu and Iki, Iki and Tsushima and Tsushima and Pusan are approximately 15 miles, 20 miles and 25 miles, respectively.

On October 24, 2018, China unveiled an engineering marvel, a mega-bridge between Zhuhai in the Chinese mainland and its two special administrative regions — Hong Kong and Macao.

The bridge, which also has an underwater tunnel, is approximately 56 kilometers long. With the completion of this mega bridge, China's engineering prowess has made another quantum jump.

Putting all the above together, one could envision that merging the two powerhouses of highspeed rail, Japan and China, rather than constantly competing globally, and add on the technological and financial powerhouse of Korea, the feasibility of connecting Japan, the ROK, the Democratic People's Republic of Korea and China, creating a China-Japan-Korea rail system, should be without question.

This is true only if the financial and political challenges, which should not be underestimated, can be overcome. As was mentioned, Japan is an island nation. It is physically separated from the Asian continent. If a North Asia mega bridge were build, not only could one embrace Japan into the Asia Pacific, in a "land" manner, it could possibly have a profound impact on the mindset of how Japanese view the Asia Pacific and vice versa!

With the above as preamble, let's now go further and consider another "island nation," namely Indonesia.

Roughly a decade ago, there were serious discussions regarding the construction of a tunnel linking Malaysia and Indonesia. In the Malacca Straits, the shortest distance between the two countries is about 18 kilometers, which is much less than the 51-kilometer "Channel Tunnel," or "Chunnel" as it is commonly known, between England and France.

The shortest distance between England and France.

Source: Retrieved from https://www.google.com/maps/@51.0229209,1.7965904,112772m/data=!3m1!1e3

The shortest distance between Malacca of Malaysia and Rupat Island of Sumatra, Indonesia.

Source: Retrieved from https://www.google.com/maps/@2.101657,101.9276179,185688m/data=!3m1!1e3

At that moment, there was a great deal of expected "pooh-pooh" about the project from the public. Such pushbacks are human nature. For example, before the construction of any large-scale engineering project, like the Chunnel for instance, I am sure an equal amount, if not more, "pooh-poohing" from the public on both sides of the English Channel must have occurred. Once the construction was completed, and public can immediately recognized its collateral benefits, the noise died down.

The benefit of a Malaysia–Indonesia tunnel will not just link the two countries together, it can also be one of the connecting stretches between Northeast Asia with Southeast Asia, and the benefit it could bring to the Asian part of the Supercontinent cannot be more obvious. Furthermore, in that paradigm, Malaysia will be the center of the North Asia and Southeast Asia!

If the Malaysia–Indonesia tunnel and the recently shelved Sunda Strait Bridge (a bridge project to link up Sumatra and Java, the two

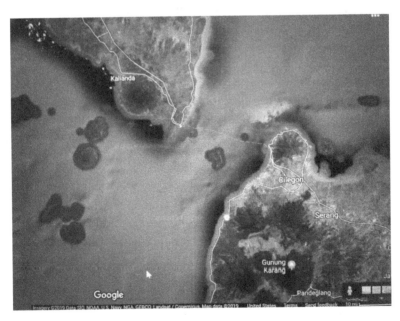

The shortest distance between Sumatra and Java.

Source: Retrieved from https://www.google.com/maps/@-5.8394492,105.8395516,46078m/data=!3m1!1e3

major islands of Indonesia) could become reality, adding on to what I have discussed earlier — the mega bridge between Japan and Korea — then the scenario where one could hop on a high-speed rail in Tokyo and have the final destination of Jakarta, Indonesia would no longer be a pipedream. I am optimistic that linking a vital nation of Indonesia with the continent of Asia could redefine the meaning of "Supercontinent" I mentioned in Chapter 2.

I am, therefore, confident that at some point in time, perhaps soon, there will be a powerful Asian leader who could foresee these benefits for Asians and humanity and bring such massive connectivity to reality.

Finally, with the Chunnel, the Malaysia–Indonesia tunnel and the Sunda Strait Bridge, not only can one take a high-speed train from Tokyo to Jakarta, one can do so from London or Paris to Jakarta!

If that cannot transform the mindset of people in Asia and Europe to think of themselves as people of a Supercontinent, I don't know what can!

Last but not least, in October 2000, the Association of Southeast Asian Nations, of which Malaysia is an important member, had the following statement in its website:

> We considered a study by the ASEAN-China Expert Group, set up in response to the suggestion by Premier Zhu at our meeting in Singapore last year. We endorsed the proposal for a Framework on Economic Cooperation and to establish an ASEAN-China Free Trade Area within 10 years with special and differential treatment and flexibility to the newer ASEAN members. The agreement should also provide for an "early harvest" in which the lists of products and services will be determined by mutual consultation. With a combined market of 1.7 billion people, a free trade area between ASEAN and China would have gross domestic product of $2 trillion and two-way trade of $1.23 trillion. We agreed to instruct our ministers and senior officials to start negotiations with a view to conclude the agreement as soon as possible

This is the genesis of the so-called 10 + 1 plan, whose time has come. Here, "10" denotes the 10 ASEAN countries, and "1" is China. The economic implication of 10 + 1 (or 10 + 3) is so very tantalizing!

Incredibly, even just after two decades, the 21st century is already posing serious economic, intellectual, technological, geopolitical and military challenges for the Pacific Rim. I think the example of how Malaysia made efforts to meet such challenges — one of them being how it culturally communicated with China — could be excellent case studies for all nations in the region.

I believe that the Chinese have the most appropriate phrase to describe the current global situation: embedded with *weiji* (危机) or "dangerous opportunities." Indeed, there are enormous and incredible opportunities in seeking solutions, and business opportunities, to these complex global challenges. To solve these problems on a global dimension, one needs to find people with global thinking and a global outlook. To solve these problems would require bold, creative and innovative solutions never before known to mankind. I hope what I have written in this book seems like the bold BRI is indeed one of the best attempts to meet humanity's challenges.

Chapter 9

Case Study 5 of "Cultural Communication": Reflection on the "Re-Visit" to Millennium Hanoi

The fact that Vietnam sent its leader to the Second Belt and Road Initiative Forum for International Forum in Beijing on April 24–27, 2019 surely imply that while the South China Sea disputes are by no means eliminated, China and Vietnam recognized that something greater could be achieved if both countries could culturally communicate and cooperate within the realm of the BRI.

Throughout the time I spent growing up in Singapore, Vietnam was an enigma. Maybe because I was just too young, I was literally unaware that the French colonial power was defeated by Viet Minh (whose definition I have provided in Chapter 8) in 1954 and was literally driven out of Vietnam. Neither did I realize that before the French left Indochina, it signed an agreement with Viet Minh to withdraw its troops from the southern part of Viet Nam, below a demilitarized zone (DMZ) which was slightly north of the city Da Nang. When I learned about this DMZ, it was the first time I realized that the 38th Parallel DMZ in the Korean Peninsula was not the only one in the world! It was expected that there would be a conference held soon after the agreement was signed so that Vietnam would be

A picture that I took of Ha Long Bay (下龙湾); nature is generous to Vietnam to give it exquisite physical beauty.

unified under the control of Viet Minh. The conference was never held, and South Vietnam essentially became a country with the name "The Republic of Vietnam" or ROV. Thus, this sowed the seed for a long and bitter conflict that lasted for the next 20 years. I also did not know that soon after, the United States was involved and provided significant military assistance to ROV.

Just two and a half weeks before I ever set foot on the US soil, on August 2, 1964, because of some untrustworthy reports by the United States Department of Defense, i.e., the "Gulf of Tonkin Incident",[1] the real Vietnam War began. Little did anyone in the United States know or expect that this bloody US–Vietnam war would last for 11 years, ending only on April 30, 1975, when the

---

[1] Gulf of Tonkin Incident (n.d.). In *Wikipedia*. Retrieved September 1, 2019, from https://en.wikipedia.org/wiki/Gulf_of_Tonkin_incident.

North Vietnamese military forces defeated the Army of the Republic of Vietnam (ARV) and the United States hastily left the country. In fact, I could remember on that day, I was attending the Annual American Physical Society meeting in Washington D.C., and a large group of attendees were watching on TV the retreat of the American personnel via helicopters from the top of the US Embassy in Saigon.

After I arrived in the United States in 1964, nearly every evening, I watched on television the nightly report on the Vietnam War. News reporters such as Walter Cronkite who were made famous by their nightly report of the brutality of the war became embedded in my cognizance. Perhaps the saddest personal moments for me about the Vietnam War were the death of two of my classmates whom I knew reasonably well. One lived in my dormitory and another was the boyfriend of a very nice girl in my class. The former was drafted, and the second joined the US Airforce as a fighter pilot. Both were sent to Vietnam. We learned that the first was literally killed the next week when he stepped into the Vietnam conflict. The pilot, I learned later, was also killed in one of his sorties.

During my graduate school days at the University of Minnesota, there were quite a number of anti-war activities at the height of the conflict. Often, when the anti-war demonstrations got to be too intense, the Minneapolis police and, sometimes, the National Guards would come on campus and use tear-gas to disperse the demonstrators. I remember that even sitting on the sixth floor of the physics building, at times I could hear the noise on the University Mall where the demonstrations were and could even feel the burning sensation the tear gas left in my eyes. That was how my memories were formed and the level of understanding of Vietnam was etched into my memory.

Nowadays, seeing how Vietnam and the United States seem to have a tranquil relationship, thinking about the millions killed in this conflict, I could not help but to ask "why such bloodshed?" Comparing the conflict in Vietnam with that in the Middle East, I noticed that the fundamental difference is that the former, for whatever the reason or reasons, was not a religious conflict while the latter, however one would argue is not, but in perception, and perception is reality, it is! Once religion becomes the reason for the conflict, whether perceived or real, it could reach a far deeper human cognition and as a result, could last *ad infinitum*!

Let me fast forward to August 24–25, 2011. By then, the relationship between the United States and Vietnam were totally different from the days of the conflict. Vietnam, North and South, had long been unified, and I had been in Asia a few years already. As the Senior Executive Vice President of the National Cheng Kung University (NCKU), I had the privilege to represent President Michael Lai (赖明诏) in leading a Chinese Literature Department delegation to participate in the international conference in Hanoi titled "International Conference on Zhu Xi and East Asia Confucianism," or "朱熹与东亚儒学国际研讨会." NCKU was a co-host institution for this conference. In hindsight, I was so pleased and honored to have such an opportunity because it allowed me to gain a wider and deeper understanding of Vietnam as a country, as well as its people and culture. It also allowed me to comprehend how a proud "foreign country" such as Vietnam had some of its cultural foundations so deeply rooted in the Chinese culture. Indeed, it was a precious opportunity for me to carry out a *de facto* field research on Vietnam!

Zhu Xi.

Source: Retrieved from https://www.iep.utm.edu/zhu-xi/

Before I went, I did some homework regarding Vietnam's understanding of Chinese culture. After all, I was unaware of a Confucian maestro (儒学大师) who lived during China's Southern Song Dynasty (南宋, 1127–1279) — Zhu Xi — and whose powerful intellectual legacy not only had a profound impact on Chinese culture but also on the Asia-Pacific region for the subsequent millennium. The research I had undertaken before leaving led me to understand the fact that Vietnam was (and still is) one of the countries with a robust and widespread intellectual activity in Zhu Xi'ism. Therefore, I should not at all be surprised that this was the topic of the conference that was being held in Hanoi. When we arrived at the venue of the conference, I noticed that participants were not only Vietnamese scholars, but Taiwan and Mainland scholars as well.

By leading this delegation, I struck up close friendship with the Zhu Xi Scholars of NCKU. They are Professor Chen Yi-Yuan (陈益源), Chairman of the Department of Chinese Literature and Professor Lin Chao Chen (林朝成), a Professor in the same department. Both Chen and Lin are well-renowned Confucius scholars (儒学学者). It is also worth underscoring that Professor Chen's interactions with the Vietnamese scholars are deep and ubiquitous. They are the consequences of some 40 visits to the country for field research since 1986!

It so happened that this was a particularly exciting time to visit Hanoi. Indeed, as soon as we stepped into the city, we immediately noticed the celebratory aura, what Chinese would refer to as 喜气洋洋, or abounding with happiness. Upon inquiry, I soon discovered that in October 2010, Hanoi will be celebrating its millennium birthday. According to Wikipedia,[2]

> In 1010, Lý Thái Tổ (李太祖) the first ruler of the Lý Dynasty, moved the capital of Đại Việt (大越, the Great Viet, then the name of Vietnam) to the site of the Đại La Citadel. Claiming to have seen a dragon ascending the Red River, he renamed it Thăng Long (昇龙, Ascending dragon.)

With this as preamble, throughout the three days we were in Hanoi, it was not difficult for us to feel the enormous and long history of this country, from ancient to modern!

---

[2]Lý Thái Tổ. (n.d.). In *Wikipedia*. Retrieved September 1, 2019, from https://en.wikipedia.org/wiki/L%C3%BD_Th%C3%A1i_T%E1%BB%95.

Photo of some Conference participants. On my right is Vice President Nguyen. On the extreme right is Professor Nghiem.

The Conference

The Conference was organized by the University of Social Sciences and Humanities, which is under the auspices of the massive Vietnam National University in Hanoi (越南河内国家大学所属人文社会科学大学). There are two national universities in Vietnam: one in Hanoi, and another in Ho Chi Minh City (胡志明市, HCMC), which is approximately 1600 kilometers south of Hanoi. Before the unification of North and South Viet Nam, HCMC was known as Saigon (西贡).

Professor Dr Nguyen Kim Son, Vice Rector (阮金山), and Dr. Nghiem Thuy Hang, Vice Director from the Center for Chinese Studies (严翠恒), were two primary, gracious and meticulous organizers. For their effort, they undoubtedly deserve the lion share of the credit of the success of the conference. At the conference, we also had the pleasure of meeting Professor Dr. Nguyen Van Kim (阮文金), Vice Rector of the National University of Vietnam in Hanoi.

Just as the Russian system, besides universities, Vietnam also has various Academies. One of them is the Vietnam Academy of Social Sciences (越南社会科学院). On this trip, we also visited two Institutes under the auspices of that Academy. They are the Institute of Philosophy (哲学研究院) and the Institute of Hannom Studies (汉喃研究院). In the former, we were hosted by Professor Dr. Pham Van Duc (范文德), the Director, and Professor Dr. Pham Ngoc Ha (范玉何), the Vice Director, and in the latter by Professor Dr. Trinh Khac Manh (郑克孟), Director, and Professor Dr. Dinh Khac Thuan (丁克順), Vice Editor-in-Chief.

I learned from Professor Yi-Yuan Chen that both Institutes have very strong research strengths in Chinese history, literature and philosophy. Therefore, both institutes had actively participated in the Conference, and their representatives made detailed presentations on the subject and were also very much involved during question and answers sessions. One evening, we were also graciously visited by Professor Dr. Tran Thi Hai-Yen (陈氏海燕) from the Department of Medieval-Early Modern Vietnamese Literature of the Institute of Literature, and Professor Dr. Nguyen Hoang Anh, Chairman of the Department of Chinese Language and Culture from the University of Foreign Languages (阮黃英). This university is also under the auspices of VNU-Hanoi.

What Was Discussed at the Conference?

As in any conference on a vast and deep subject, there were no shortage of technical discussions (as it should be) in this one. For an outsider like me, the Conference's intellectual ambiance was particularly noteworthy.

First of all, nearly all the participants were fluent in written and spoken ancient and modern Chinese (Mandarin). This is due partially to the fact that in order to engage in the study of Zhu Xi'ism, it is a necessity to at least be fluent in written Chinese. But the fact that they could converse in day-to-day Chinese effortlessly and flawlessly, and even understand idioms, the opportunity to use Chinese throughout the Conference was abundant. Just as in my field of physics, where I had noticed (see the discussion at the end) that in the past several decades there has been a large number of Vietnamese receiving the most rigorous advanced education abroad. Quite a number of the faculty I met on this trip received their advanced education in Mainland China (e.g. Beijing Normal University (北京師範大学) and Fudan University (复旦大学)) and Taiwan (Soochow University (东吴大学) and Fu Jen University (辅仁大学)). So for us foreigners in Hanoi who could not speak Vietnamese, language was not a barrier, at least not at the conference. In fact, Professors Chen and Lin both delivered their lectures in Chinese. With the number of intense questions following their lectures (and some of the questions were raised in perfect Chinese), I felt that our Vietnamese colleagues completely understood them. Having manpower in a variety of fields, from physics to Zhu Xi'ism, is transparently a Vietnamese strength that will greatly assist the nation to build a powerful intellectual landscape in the 21st century.

Second, I was pleased to learn some of the more intricate details, especially from the lecture by Professor Chen Yi-Yuan, about a great and important Vietnamese diplomat and scholar Ly Van Phuc (李文馥) who lived between 1785 and 1849. His many travels to and lifetime work in China, especially in Min-Nan (闽南), and Southeast Asia (including many visits to Singapore and Malaysia) demonstrated the deep interest Vietnamese had in East Asia and Southeast Asia. It is no wonder that Vietnamese literature and history of today is an admixture of many schools of thought coming from different countries. As a result, it truly has a rich texture. It was emphasized quite a few times in this Conference, by Vietnamese and Taiwanese scholars, that the fundamental importance of bringing together scholars in the Asia-Pacific region, Vietnam, Taiwan, Mainland China, Korea and Japan, is to allow Zhu Xi'ism to assume robust growth and novel understanding. In particular, this would allow Zhu Xi'ism to move forward in importance and relevance in the world of the 21st century. Of course, at that time, BRI was not in my mind. But now, knowing it, this lesson

I learned from Vietnam is truly an important cultural communication between China and Vietnam.

Third, some of the lectures were delivered by up-and-coming young Vietnamese scholars. The vitality of any intellectual effort of a region should and must be measured by the number and quality of their younger generations. Apparently in this aspect, Vietnam is demonstrably well endowed. I should also say that while I could not understand some of the speeches and/or questions put forth by the audience, from the translation, I could tell that some of the Vietnamese had overcome an "Asian disease," which was to remain silent. This is another very good sign about the future development of Vietnam's intellectual communities!

Fourth, an institute known as "Hannom Studies," or "Viện (院) Nghiên (研) cứu (究) Hán (漢) Nôm (喃)" deserves special mention here. This is an institute which was, according to its website,

> ... formally established in 1979. Its principal functions are: to collect and maintain Hán-Nôm documents throughout the country; to organise research, translation and publication of Hán-Nôm documents; and to train researchers in Hán-Nôm studies. The Institute's library holds an important collection of Nguyễn dynasty court documents in chữ Hán (classical Han Chinese, also known as chữ nho), the ideographic script devised for transcribing spoken Vietnamese known as chữ nôm and the romanised script quốc ngữ. ......

The language Hán-Nôm, according to our Vietnamese friends, was the language of Vietnam from the 12th to the 18th centuries. Today it is a "lost" language, and only experts would learn and know how to read and write it. This reminded me of how the Manchurian language was lost in China. It is also how Latin became obsolete in the Western world. However, because it was practiced for many centuries, it is no wonder that there are a massive number of historical documents describing the history, culture and whatever else were written in this language. Hence, even for Vietnamese to understand themselves, they would need to have a comprehensive understanding of what that large body of documents was conveying.

It was truly amazing for me to meet some of the young researchers in the Institute who, according to their mentors, have mastered this "ancient language." To me, that again manifested the deep cultural heritage of Vietnam. *Robust history is generous to Vietnam to give it intellectual depth.* I am especially impressed that the Vietnamese, as a people, are very proud of this history. In developing Vietnam as an important nation in the 21st century, I have every confidence that this pride will come in handy. This is another important aspect for China to have cultural communications with this important neighbor.

A picture that I took with the plaque of the Institute.

I learned something about the Vietnamese language from the above plaque which is placed at the entrance of the Institute. The way one should read it, from left to right, is

Viện (院) Nghiên (研) cứu (究) Hán (漢) Nôm (喃)

This was done in the Vietnamese grammar, as it should. In Chinese grammar, it would be Han (漢) Nan (喃) Yan (研) Jiu (究) Yuan (院).

Thus, one notices that the characters are the same. The difference in grammar would demand a different order of the way they are placed in the phrase. I was informed that nearly 80% of the

Vietnamese language would have identical characters with the Chinese language. Therefore, for a Chinese, if one could master Vietnamese grammar and the pronunciation (for Chinese, the latter would be more difficult than the former), one could learn the Vietnamese language rather easily.

While we were there, we spent a great deal of time trying to absorb as much as we could about the Viện (院) Nghiên (研) cứu (究) Hán (漢) Nôm (喃).

My wife and I spent a great deal of time at this institute. It truly allowed us to have a glimpse of the deep relationship between the Chinese and Vietnamese cultures.

I learned recently that there is now great enthusiasm among Vietnamese students to pursue their education in China. This is perhaps a deep reflection of the profound cultural linkage of both countries.[3]

Hanoi: My Visit in 1994

As in any intellectual effort, and physics is no exception, globalization is the name of the game. Thus, as a physicist, whenever an opportunity arose to open up relations, which for me could be a new country, I never shied away from it. For Vietnam, this opportunity came in 1994.

From March 14 to 18, 1994, I was privileged to work with colleagues from Vietnam, Dr. Nguyen Dinh Dang (阮庭燈) of Vietnam's Atomic Energy Commission; from France, Dr. Nguyen Van Giai of the Institut de Physique Nucleaire or Orsay' and from India, Dr. Yogi Gambhir of Indian Institute of Technology Bombay, to organize one of the first nuclear physics conferences to be held in Vietnam.

As the foreign organizer, I first arrived in Hanoi a few days before. It turned out that at that point in time, the only way to reach Hanoi was to fly from Hong Kong. As I was stepping into the plane which was supposed to belong to Vietnam Airlines, I noticed that the plane was entirely white in color, with no insignia whatsoever. I was concerned about whether I was taking the wrong flight and so asked the air stewardess why the airplane appears to have no insignia. The answer astounded me when she said: "*Most of our airplanes were rented and do not belong to us!*".

The conference was titled "Perspective of Nuclear Physics in the Late Nineties" and was enthusiastically attended by a large number (well over

---

[3]Vietnamese Students Increasingly Interested in Studying in China. (April 28). *Study in China*. Retrieved from https://www.studyinchina.com.my/web/page/vietnamese-students-studying-in-china/.

100) of the world's most highly visible nuclear physicists from Russia, USA, France, Japan, Italy, India, Germany, Mainland China, Taiwan and Malaysia. Perhaps the most notable scientist who attended the conference was Professor Akito Arima, the former President of the University of Tokyo and one of the foremost nuclear scientists in the world.

The conference Proceedings was eventually published by World Scientific Publications, with the cover page depicting a traditional Vietnamese Dragon toying with a "galaxy!" The painting was done by Dr. Dang, who is also a talented artist. Details about how the conference came about can be found on the following website: http://ribf.riken.go.jp/~dang/HNcover.html.

What was most memorable in attending this conference was that after I landed in the then dilapidated airport of Hanoi, I was met by students of Dr. Dang, who was my personal guide throughout the conference. In driving from the airport to downtown Hanoi,

I noticed that the road was a recently constructed highway. Along the way, I saw some large and deep circular holes. So, I asked my guide what these enormous holes were for. I thought they were for some unknown agricultural purpose. To my horror, I was told that such holes were made by the massive bombs dropped by the United States Air Force, probably B52s', during the Vietnam War. As someone who has never experienced war (and hope I never will), a deeply uncomfortable feeling came over me when I imagined how many people were killed in such explosions!

Group photo of all the conference attendees.

As the organizer of many international conferences in many parts of the world, I was quite amazed by how smooth things progressed during the organizing period, from funding to numerous conference logistics. The answer for why this was so, was evident when all the conference attendees were invited to meet with one of Vietnam's top leaders, Madame Nguyễn Thị Bình. Madame Bình became world famous during the Vietnam War when she was the Minister of Foreign Affairs and had played a critical role in the 1973

Agreement on Ending the War and Restoring Peace in Vietnam.

Source: Retrieved from https://en.wikipedia.org/wiki/Paris_Peace_Accords#/media/File:Vietnam_Peace_Treaty_1973.jpg.

Conference participants with the vice-president of Vietnam Madame Nguyễn Thị Bình at the Presidential Palace (Hanoi, Vietnam). Madame Bình is standing in the middle in the front row. I am second on the right in the front row.

Paris Peace Accord. It was when we met her that Dr. Dang quietly mentioned to me that Madame Bình was his mother-in-law! He asked me not to mention this anyone else at the Conference. Since the Conference took place more than a quarter of century ago, I thought this would be a good time to let this information be known!

While the physics discussed was exciting, little did we know that quite by serendipity, this 1994 Conference was sandwiched in time by two profound international events that occurred between the United States and Vietnam. These events are as follows:

February 3, 1994: President William J. Clinton lifted the U.S. trade embargo against Vietnam.

May 1994: Consular Agreement signed by the United States and Vietnam.

These two events between the United States and Vietnam probably marked Vietnam's transformation in opening up to the world.

My impression of Vietnam's physics then, like the country, was that it was recovering from many decades of war. Meeting many Vietnamese physicists then and noticing how well educated they were and how well they organized the Conference, I remember saying to myself, "Vietnam's physics will be an important component in Asia Pacific soon." Indeed, reading all about Vietnam's physics in the recent editions of *AAPPS (Association of Asia Pacific Physical Society) Bulletins, CERN Courier*, etc., and the fact that in the latest 2010 Physics Olympics, Vietnamese students won five medals — one of them gold — my estimation in 1994 was not far off the mark.

Meeting so many elder Vietnamese physicists at the conference, I had numerous occasions to engage them in extensive discussions about the intellectual livelihood since World War II. I was quite impressed to learn that even during the eras of the war with France and the United States, with palpable hardships everywhere in the nation, Ho Chi Minh never stopped or punished the educated elites. Even when the country was facing enormous difficulty, universities were never stopped. Furthermore, the best and the brightest were always sent to Eastern Europe's top universities to be educated.

The Traffic of Hanoi

When we arrived in Hanoi in 2011, we were welcomed by gracious colleagues from the University of Social Science and Humanities. The Airport has a very different ambiance from 1994, which was when I first came to Vietnam. I would say it has assumed a modern touch. Furthermore, on the road from the Airport to Hanoi downtown, we saw none of the battle "leftovers." In fact, on the west side of Hanoi, there is now a massive new development taking place. My understanding is that a significant percentage of Government infrastructures would be moving from downtown to this new area in the next few years.

Hanoi today is a traffic nightmare. In 1994, Hanoi was a relatively quiet city. In fact, Dr. Dang took me on a tour of the city on his

Photo taken when we arrived at Hanoi International Airport.

motorbike then. We went fast around one of the lakes of the city, without encountering any traffic! If we were to do the same on this visit, we would be one of the thousands upon thousands of motorbike riders, mixing with the hundreds of automobiles and bicycles, on the road. It is one thing to be surrounded by automobiles (which is bad enough) at a red-light stop, it is another to be "instantly surrounded" by literally hundreds of motorbikes, which move so closely together that you could almost smell the body odor of the other person(s). It was also quite a spectacular sight to see on a particular motorbike, besides the rider, as many as four passengers, giving the term "family car" a new meaning. All these reminded me what a good friend (and good scientist) once said in a tongue-and-cheek manner: "when the traffic flow is so dense, one could describe it by pure hydrodynamics equations!" Hanoi's motorbikes traffic comes closest to making that statement real!

Perhaps what the traffic is telling the world is that Hanoi in particular, and Vietnam in general, is in an explosive growth phase. In scientific terms, this is known as "non-adiabatic growth." On the one hand, the demand for transportation is so massive because there are great opportunities for Hanoi's inhabitants to move up the economic ladder, and to do so would require them to move from point A to point B quickly. On the other hand, the city's transportation infrastructure improvement simply failed to match the speed of economic change. So, the eight million citizens of Hanoi simply decided on their own to find the quickest and most economical ways to get around. No wonder the motorbike flow in Hanoi is so dense and continuous.

I was truly happy to see that during the Second Belt and Road Forum for International Cooperation held between April 24 and 27, 2019, the leaders of the 10 countries in Southeast Asia were actively participating. The fact that Vietnam sent its leader to this forum surely implies that while the South China Sea disputes are by no means over and done with, China and Vietnam who stand on nearly identical cultural heritages can still recognize that something far greater for the Chinese and the Vietnamese can be achieved if both countries can stand on their long cultural affinity, culturally communicate and cooperate within the realm of the BRI.

Chapter 10

Imminent Challenges of the Belt and Road Initiative*

In the recent G20 Summit visit by President Xi Jinping and his entourage, formal state visits were also made to Spain, Argentina, Panama and Portugal. At every state visit, the Belt and Road Initiative (BRI) was an important, if not dominant theme. It is worth mentioning that while the BRI was proposed merely six years ago, these recent four foreign state visits made it abundantly clear to the world that it has already captured significant global attention. Unquestionably, in going global for the BRI, there are challenges, and we will discuss the means to mitigate them.

First of all, the outside world has the erroneous impression that BRI is entirely a "going out" effort that only intends to promote Chinese enterprises to invest in nations along the BRI route. This, of course, is only half true, because the other half is 'coming in', in which China will aggressively attract foreign investors to come to China to invest. Indeed, from the start, the bi-directional "going

---

*This article was published in Feng D. H., Liang H. M. (2019) Global Realization of the Belt and Road Initiative must be accompanied by a Global Vision. *China and the World: Ancient and Modern Silk Road*, 2(3). Retrieved from https://doi.org/10.1142/S2591729319500172.

out" and "coming in" missions are bestowed with equal importance. In fact, we would say that "coming in" may even assume more importance than "going out." The reason for this is obvious. As China is now the world's second largest economy, it has economic means of "going out." Furthermore, as a massive country with a population of 1.4 billion, it must assume the arduous responsibility of promoting social development and scientific and technological advancements. Indeed, the citizens of China in such a paradigm should and must live and work in peace and enjoy the fruits of the country's economic development.

To achieve such lofty goals, it is absolutely necessary for China to continue to introduce to the nation, advanced and modern experiences, ideas and superior technologies from all countries in the world, especially those from the developed Western countries. There can be no compromise in order for China to meet and serve comprehensive national development.

At the same time, it should also recognize that the Chinese market is significantly more massive than any of the nations along the BRI route. Hence, when a Chinese enterprise is investing overseas, it must not ignore the needs of the nation's domestic market. In fact, in any international business venture, the most important competitive advantage of any enterprise is actually the advantage of its domestic markets. We dare say that without the support of China's domestic markets, Chinese enterprises will have many roadblocks to make progress overseas.

As emphasized by President Xi Jinping from the beginning, the BRI aims to deepen the two-way investment cooperation. Searching for "coming in" and "going out" is a fundamental component of BRI's international effort. To this end, there is a palpable strong encouragement for the nations on the BRI route to invest in China, especially in areas of high-tech industries, advanced manufacturing and modern service industry. Such efforts are aimed at bolstering the Chinese domestic economy development. In addition, establishments of sound platforms of national economic and technological development zones, border economic, as well as cross-border economic cooperation zones are also part of the BRI package!

In the four years between 2015 and June 2018, there were 21, 284 contracts signed with more than 60 countries and regions, with a total worth a of US$410.78 billion. As far as we could ascertain, only a handful of countries (3–5 out of 60) are lamenting (albeit loudly) about being subjected to "debt diplomacy" by China.

However, due to numerous cultural and real conflicts of interest, the public opinions also included negative comments. Of course, as expected, there also were some reports whose real intention was simply to smear. For example, some regarded the BRI as *de facto* a "Chinese version of the Marshall Plan," or a challenge to the "Trans-Pacific Partnership Agreement" (TPP). Some Russian and Japanese scholars even voiced concerns that the BRI would inevitably challenge the existing regional and even global economic system and push out the interests of other countries. Some Southeast Asian developing nations were also worried about being "economically controlled" by China or by the Chinese intention to plunder their resources.

Clearly, if China were not able to reverse such misconceptions or misunderstandings about the BRI, it would be difficult for the Chinese enterprises to be accepted overseas. Under such a condition, when the BRI is resisted by a nation or even a multinational alliance, however excellent the quality of the products and services the Chinese enterprises make or provide, and however advanced their management concept can be, the effort to follow the BRI mission to "go out" would surely be met with strong pushbacks.

Therefore, the official departments within China which are responsible for explaining to the outside world about BRI should and must create a more favorable international public opinion while assisting enterprises to invest in countries along the BRI route. There exists a great demand where the current overseas communications pattern must also be altered. To this end, not only does China need to conduct in-depth and meticulous field research on each country where Chinese investments have or are expected to be made, but attention must also be paid to ensure that the content is accessible to foreign audience as well. Furthermore, what sort of content such audiences are willing to accept, and what languages are most suitable, are equally important.

First, to Promote BRI Externally, One Must Avoid Exclusively Focusing on Politics and Ignoring Financial and Cultural Areas

From the start, the BRI was not at all intended to merely have politics as its primary thrust. In fact, on the contrary, it was to be a major effort to advance economic and cultural interactions with the outside world. Yet, it is quite transparent that in most of the current promotional efforts from China, the theme is still dominated by "current" news and colored by political intonations. Yet, since the BRI intends to capture maximum recognition by countries along the BRI route, to avoid manifesting past "political theory" (excessive display of ideology and political ideals), the promotional effort should and must focus in search of breakthroughs in promoting finance and culture.

It is clear that the modern-day international financial systems have gradually merged, so much so that the financial systems of various nations are increasingly becoming interconnected. In fact, it is not an exaggeration that the financial language has *de facto* emerged as an international "language." To this end, such activities as stock market business, foreign exchange markets, bond markets and heavy metals prices became the comfort zone of all people from every corner of the globe. No longer are people faced with any obstacles when they are confronted with financial market performances, languages, customs, ethnicities and nationalities. With this in mind, as far as the financial sector is concerned, utilization of the universal financial "language" to promote BRI in new regions will undoubtedly enhance its appeal.

When one is introducing BRI to the countries along the route, it is crucial that emphasis be made with regard to China's fundamental role as an economic and financial power in maintaining regional economic stability. For example, during the past Asian financial crisis in the late 1990s or the United States subprime mortgage crisis in the 21st century, China shouldered major responsibilities as a nation in stabilizing the Asian economic fluctuations. With this as background, it is reasonable that China can consider establishing a joint regional financial cooperation network for countries along the BRI route and expand the domestic and overseas markets already realized in the Shanghai–Hong Kong Stock connections for such nations. In this manner, not only can the governments and enterprises of such nations palpably feel the benefits of the cooperation, but the common people can also enjoy the dividends of China's economic prosperity and the new investment opportunities brought on by the BRI.

It must also be recognized that globalization should not be understood simply as the flow of capital within the global economy. Cultural ingredients such as languages, writings, arts and ideologies must not be ignored. It is especially worth noting that unusual cultural recognition prowess can often break geographical boundaries. As it has been proven over and over again, it can even encourage people of different cultural backgrounds to gain a certain degree of cultural identity from countries which may not be their own.

An example of this effect is manifested in the global popularization of American and Japanese cultural products. In the cultural field of BRI, China can leverage its ethnic minorities who have similar ways and means with the population of nations along the BRI route to increase seamless cultural exchanges. To this end, emphasis can be made by promoting the so-called soft stories of China, at the same time displaying the exquisite and profound heritage of the rich Chinese culture.

Another example is the situation in Malaysia. Malaysia is a multinational and multiethnic nation. The population with Chinese heritage accounts for only 23% of the total while the Malays make up nearly 70%. Hence, in interacting with Malaysia, politically and economically or otherwise, China must not place emphasis on and interact with only the 23% because that may and can indeed cause the danger of missing the big picture.

In order for nations along the BRI route to gain confidence regarding such implementations, China can also take into account strengthening the two-way communication in the cultural arenas. Besides promoting it externally, it can and should promote such activities domestically as well and learn from the excellent cultures of other nations. In the end, it will increase the understanding and interest of Chinese of such nations. We are convinced that only through such efforts can the BRI's emphasis of development, tolerance and mutual promotion be realized.

Second, China's Overseas Communication Effort Should Avoid Communicating in Different Countries the Same Content

Along the BRI route, there are about a hundred countries with different languages and cultures. Thus, due to each nation's environment, natural conditions, religion or religions, language or languages, ethnicity or ethnicities and political systems being vastly different, the level of acceptance of external information is likewise highly limited. With this in mind, it is vital that China must take into account the cognitive logic of people of such nations and select the best language and pathway.

Take the example of infrastructure. Clearly, the island and landlock nations' transportation needs are vastly different from other nations. In fact, the geographical conditions will lead to fundamental differences in the populations' ways and means. In this case, the promotional BRI information must focus sharply on such differences and also be ready to psychologically accept different reactions from the local population.

Another important technical issue is the need to utilize different translation languages to overcome the differences in cultures. If China were only to employ Chinese and English as the languages of communication, then in all likelihood those nations whose populations have a different cultural ways and means and speak different languages would have difficulty in being "moved and touched" by the promotion. In fact, it is likely that this will have a negative result on the non-English-speaking population, making them feel neglected at best and rejected at worst.

Furthermore, whenever one encounters geopolitics, the problem usually becomes more complex. We noticed that within Russian, there is a recent crescendo of public opinion showing doubts about the BRI. For example, there is now a discussion about constructing a European–Asian high-speed transportation corridor from Beijing to Moscow. If such a corridor becomes a reality, then within a few days of driving, a far greater number of Chinese people can reach Moscow from China easily when compared with air travel. This will have, in the Russians' mind, the (unintended) consequence of vastly increasing the number of Chinese within Russia. With such a possibility and adding to the fact that Russia has a rapidly aging population and is experiencing a very low birth rate, in the Russians' mind, this will create a population crisis. It is very likely that in the short or long run, an unacceptable outcome of such a corridor is that Russians may become the largest ethnic minority within the country. Having a significant difference in population (some 3 hundred million vs. 1.4 billion) and an incredibly long border between the two nations, the Russian public opinions now seems to be of two minds: welcome, as well as concern about China's BRI of enhancing bilateral economic and trade cooperation, and more personnel exchanges and interconnections.

In fact, at the national level, it is not difficult to appreciate the above dilemma. Russia is increasingly more anxious regarding the Central Asian nations getting closer, politically and otherwise, to China. This was discussed quite extensively in Chapter 5. Many Central Asian nations on the BRI route were originally part of the former Soviet Union and have always been regarded by Russia as its geopolitical, geoeconomic and natural resource partners. Obviously, to strengthen cooperation with such nations leveraging the BRI in areas of energy, economy, trade and infrastructure has made Russia profoundly concerned, if not fearful, of the strength China is gaining in its backyard. Hence, it is natural that in the Russians minds, China may soon replace it as the leading country in Central Asia.

If we conduct a detailed classification study utilizing the above perspective, we will find that the Western developed countries, emerging countries and developing countries along the BRI route are substantially different in multiple dimensions. Western nations led by the United States mainly focus on whether the BRI could alter the current international order; emerging powers, including Russia and India, are concerned about whether China will weaken their sphere of influence; developing nations are looking forward to increasing investments from China, and at the same time, fear that they will be under the Chinese political and military control and that China will also plunder their resources.

With the above understanding in mind, in promoting the BRI, one needs to design different scenarios and themes for the most recent, anxious and specific concerns of such countries. For example, for Europe and the United States, one should emphasize that China is not competing with the United States; for emerging powers, one must strongly emphasize the respect for their existing status.

In addition to the high-level binational considerations, whenever possible, China must take into consideration the interests of all nations and the current international conditions. Of course, even when there are real and unavoidable conflicts, the Chinese position must be steadfast but respectful in maintaining the principle of agree to disagree, and work towards an acceptable solution for all. In this way, direct conflict(s) with other nations can be avoided. Ultimately, any BRI effort should and must strive for a win–win situation.

The aim of BRI should and must be about how China can proactively and successfully coordinate with the interests of countries along the route, reduce their doubts as much as possible, and sincerely welcome more partners to collaborate with it in order to promote the initiative. It is the aim of the BRI to be a shining example of peaceful global cooperation, promote greater win–win implementations and create an ideal investment environment for Chinese enterprises to "go global."

Third, BRI Needs to Laser Focus on Internal and External Differences, Avoid "Preaching to the Choir" as Well as Promote "Two-Way Cultural Communications"

The misunderstandings and speculations caused by the BRI are, more often than not, related to deliberate smearing by some Western media. Of course, it must be recognized that in its promotion, China has also often adopted the "one-way infusion," i.e. a softer way of saying "my way or the highway." Namely, China fails to recognize that there are usually fundamental internal and external differences. The net result is China's inability to create benign mutual interactions.

In the overseas promotion of the BRI, occasional words are found that are commonly used in China but are not used or are obviously inappropriate internationally. For example, the phrase "strategic channel" and "bridgehead" which have military colors or implications, are likely to cause nervousness at best, indignations at worst, in countries along the BRI route. Of course, China is not the only country to be suffering from lack of sensitivity with regard to other cultures. For example, the use of the word "crusade" which should be avoided at all cost by Western countries' leaders in dealing with Middle East nations, is also a common mistake. The use of such words or phrases can only be attributed to disrespect, arrogance or ignorance, or all of the above! No doubt they have often created unnecessary doubts about the intention of the BRI.

In promoting BRI, be it by the government agencies, the media or individuals, high priority must be vigilantly placed with regard to the "internal and external differences", treating domestic and foreign communication targets differently, and more importantly, respectfully. For example, the media should, on the one hand, reduce the tone of "I am the main" in the report, substantially reducing the praise of the Chinese efforts in promoting the BRI, and on the other, strengthen the discussions about the political, economic, social and people's livelihood of the countries along the BRI route. In fact, one must give high praise to their BRI participations. The degree and achievements of such actions will empower the governments, enterprises and people in the BRI route and help them to identify closely with the effort. Ultimately, whenever possible, emphasis must be made regarding the importance of win–win cooperation and convey the goodwill of cooperation with words and deeds.

As was mentioned earlier, the concept of interoperability and mutual benefit are inherently a part of BRI's mission. Yet, it is quite common that when the Chinese current public opinion and the media refer to it, more often than not the emphasis centered only on seeing how it could bring benefits to nations on the BRI route, and less or none about Chinese "self-interests." One can understand that the department responsible for publicity wants to quickly entice the nations along the route to rapidly accept and recognize the BRI developments and promote cooperation between such nations and China under this framework. Unfortunately, from the mutual benefit point of view, such a communication methodology is often counterproductive and may backfire.

The implementation of the BRI cannot and should not be one-sided. It must be mutually beneficial to China and to the nations it is partnering. By not emphasizing it could benefit China as well, it could easily mislead the international community to perceive that China has hidden agendas, which could lead the global public opinions to imagine the worst-case scenario. In fact, this is more likely to, and has led to, Western media with ulterior motives taking the opportunity to speculate, and even worse, to smear this effort. All these would generate a negative impact on China's international image.

The outcome of the abovementioned "one-sided display" is that some Chinese official media tend to concentrate on China's situation. They have deemphasized the mistakes and shortcomings of Chinese enterprises in certain fields and triggered vigilance and fear in nations along the BRI route. What is ironic is that for such nations, the Chinese strength is already well recognized. Therefore, if the media repeatedly emphasized the rapid rise of China's political, economic and military power, the image of a flawless super-powerful nation can only make such nations become increasingly cautious about the so-called "Chinese hidden intentions." It is our opinion that in any overseas communications, one should be impartial and transparent regarding the advantages and the disadvantages, as well as China's real achievements and mistakes. Indeed, it is necessary to underscore that the world, at this point, needs China, and China needs the voice of the world to make BRI more understandable and attractive.

There is another area where China could beef up its activities, and that is it must also be aware of, and in fact incorporate, how the overseas "sinologists" and experts view China from different perspectives. We are confident that by doing so, a more authentic and credible image of China can emerge. Such practices could reveal China's sincere desire for collaboration, reduce or eliminate doubts in the nations along the BRI route and provide additional incentives for such nations to work as partners with China to build a community of future and common interests.

Fourth, It Is Critical to Focus on Improving China's Cultural Tolerance in External Communication

It is obvious that among the nations along the BRI route, there are multiple civilizations as well as hundreds of languages totally different from that seen in China. Facing such enormous differences, it is natural that misunderstandings and frictions can and do occur. To minimize them, not only should Chinese enterprises, the government and promotional efforts undergo a hitherto unprecedented mindset transformation, China should and must also promote a national effort to inform and educate its citizens on the fundamental essence of BRI. Chinese people and enterprises must begin with "self" in the process of "going out." They must earnestly respect and accept different cultures and civilizations, pay extra attention to their own actions and the way they communicate with the outside world, so as to avoid unnecessary foreign doubts and hostilities.

We also want to suggest that at the grassroots level, whenever a Chinese citizen interacts with the outside world, he/she should reflect profoundly on how to take on the attitude to exhibit genuine Chinese graciousness and goodwill to eliminate misunderstandings. It is important that sincerity be the norm in seeking peaceful development. Finally, as an individual, he/she should try his/her utmost to enhance genuine cultural exchanges between China and other countries, both in depth and breadth.

With the above discussion as preamble, we feel that as a matter of principle, the Chinese people should avoid displaying cultural and economic superiority, both with foreign countries and within different parts of China dominated by minorities. After all, it is universally harmful to display a sense of superiority, which usually means arrogance. Take the United States as an example. It is not uncommon that it has leveraged its economic and cultural superiority to belittle other countries' systems, economics and cultures. It is, therefore, not surprising that around the world, United States is often met with resistance.

The German experience is another excellent example to illustrate the important principle of cultural humility. In 1989, after the fall of the Berlin Wall, the former West Germany bestowed massive economic assistance to the former East Germany. As a result, Germans from the West and the associated media displayed a strong sense of superiority towards Germans from the East. At that time, when Germans from the East traveled to Berlin as tourists, for example, they were often confronted with "Berlin doesn't love you" slogans. The Germans from the West even shouted insults and pelted objects at the tourists. To this day, such scars remain deeply embedded in the minds of many Germans who were originally from the Eastern part of the country.

Accompanying the rise of China's all-round national strength is the rise of confidence, even overconfidence, of its citizens. It is noted that when some Chinese travelled to Hong Kong and Macau for touristic purposes, they have a tendency to come with a "savior" attitude. Such an attitude had triggered a "tempest in the teapot" and also can damage the Chinese image, especially after the Western media made exaggerated reports.

It must be recognized by China that many nations along the BRI route lag behind China in terms of science and technology, culture and economy. To this end, for such nations to grow in all dimensions, China's assistance can have a palpable impact. For this, the Chinese people and the media must learn from the lessons of United States, Germany and Hong Kong mentioned earlier, to not adopt a sense of superiority. In communicating with the people in the nations along the BRI route, the stance of equal, friendly, mutually supportive and cooperative should be maintained at all times. Indeed, the attitude of "Cultural Tolerance and Respect" must be manifested at all times to such countries. We are confident that such a practice will not only demonstrate the graciousness of China but also create a more harmonious business environment for the enterprises and citizens in "going out."

To expand on the previous discussion, one should note that countries possessing major emerging global markets would each have their own unique development models. The potential and developmental prospects of some nations are certainly not inferior to those of China. In dealing with such nations, China must maintain an open mind, as well as an appreciative attitude. Perhaps the most glaring example of such a nation would be India, the second most populous nation in the world. India is fundamentally different from China. Unlike China, which developed labor-intensive industries first, India followed the "hail-Mary" approach to develop knowledge-intensive industries and rapidly became the "office of the world" and "extended laboratories of the West." In this manner, India has displaced a large number of its workers with "high added value," and through it gained industrial advantages.

Although it is well known that the decision-making process of the Indian coalition government is tardy, its development model is based on the change of the market through a "bottom-up" effort. Indeed, its free and creative entrepreneurs first made their mark within the country, and then moved aggressively to occupy the world market and became the driving force of India's economic development. The shortcomings of the government will gradually be replaced and solved by the market. The Indian entrepreneurial spirit and strong willpower are clearly sufficient to make up for their many political deficiencies.[1]

At present, China's economy is five times larger than India's. In the past, China relied on investments and export economic growth models. Now, India has started to imitate the Chinese model. Indian Prime Minister Modi has recently publicly pointed out that India needs to adopt an export-oriented, public-based and urban-building-oriented economic growth model, which will shift from its current service-oriented model to one with a large amount of labor and capital to drive economic growth. If India is successful in such an economic transformation, then it is very likely that it can become the new "world factory" and can compete with China.

Fifth, Chinese Must Assume the Attitude That "Global Responsibilities Are Chinese's Responsibilities"

The majority of Chinese believe that since China started the BRI, it will serve the Chinese interest and be utilized to extract resources and energy from other nations. This is understandable because such a mentality and practices have certainly been the *modus operandi* of many powerful nations of the world in the past and the present, such as Spain and the United Kingdom. If the Chinese people were to adopt this mentality, then it would be next to impossible for China to search for a global development model that is fundamentally different from the Western hegemony model, one that is based on harmonious and peaceful principle. If that were the case, then China will certainly disappoint many if not all nations along the BRI route who have expected and hoped that with China's assistance, the current international "rule by force" order can be altered. In fact, it will question the motives of China.

There is an old Chinese saying which goes "以天下为己任," or "taking the world as its responsibility!" In a sense, having the BRI, the Chinese must take on this tall order. In pursuing the BRI effort,

---

[1] Müller, O. (2006) *Wirtschaftsmacht Indien*. Munich: Hanser.

it must on the one hand seek national interest and, on the other, take into account the common interests of the countries along the BRI route. The Chinese should take care of and pay attention to reasonable, legitimate and practical needs and interests of all countries. Only in this manner can China achieve the goal of "winning the world" and ultimately having a win–win situation with all nations. In addition, the Chinese should lead by example, and greatly expand what is known as the "Normative Power," namely spread the China's traditional ethics and value standards, in order to further win the recognition, trust and respect of countries along the BRI route.

The rise of Britain and the United States is reflected by their values of "free trade" and "democratic human rights." One could question what kind of value norms China will bring to the world. Many Chinese believe that the peaceful development, mutual benefit and win–win, openness and tolerance, and mutual learning are the core values that China brings to world peace and development. If so, how to fully reflect the value norms of China facing the world?

In this regard, the EU's experience can be used as a reference.

The core values of the EU can be summarized as follows: peace, freedom, democracy, the rule of law and respect for human rights. The EU member states use the "five diffusions" (unintentional proliferation, information diffusion, procedural proliferation, transfer, and diffusion) through the external activities of their respective official institutions. In this manner, the EU consciously and actively promotes its own values and demonstrates its own normative power in the international arena. Such efforts have not only gained global recognition but also made the world take note that there is another value orientation which is different from the United States. In fact, as such, it also laid the foundation for the EU to exert greater influence in international affairs.

Of course, for China to exhibit to the world the BRI value, not only should individual Chinese demonstrate his/her belief in the peace and security of humanity, equality and unity between nations, freedom and fairness of economy and trade, and the defense of human rights, the China's media, think tanks and university research institutions should also aggressively promote "normative power" through the "five diffusions" to promote the core value of the BRI.

The nations along the BRI route have different nationalities, beliefs, requirements, stages of economic development, event histories and cultures. With that in mind, China must diligently collaborate with such nations in order to achieve mutual benefit, ensure common development and ultimately lead to a win–win situation. Chinese enterprises must invest overseas and in the future, such investments will be full of challenges and variables. As citizens of the founder of the BRI, Chinese should try their utmost to demonstrate the graciousness and elegance of a kind nation, construct a warm business environment for coexistence, and win the recognition, trust, support and cooperation from the nations along the BRI route in order to assist companies investing there to proceed seamlessly and smoothly.

The world-renowned cellist Yo-Yo Ma once said:

> When you learn something from people, or from a culture, you accept it as a gift, and it is your lifelong commitment to preserve it and build on it.

As a nation with rich and robust culture and history, for its vast citizens to accept this fundamental definition of a 21st century powerful nation, with purpose, strength and humility, it can certainly be the turning of a new page in world history and for the betterment of humanity.

Chapter 11

Epilogue

As I have been emphatically stating from the start of this book, not being a Chinese *per se,* i.e. I was not born in China; I have not held any official travel documents from China; and I have never attended a single day of schooling in greater China (the Mainland, Taiwan, Hong Kong and Macau). I was essentially a "Four Unlike (四不像)": I am not a Mainlander, not a Taiwanese, not from Hong Kong, and not from Macau! Couple this with the fact that I was, for more than two decades, a cocoon professor of theoretical physics in the United States, where my life revolved around pursuing, research and collaborating with my students, postdocs and international scientists, writing a book about the Belt and Road Initiative could not have been further from my mind. Yet, what is perhaps quite remarkable is that my combined academic and research careers in the United States and Asia and my corporate position in dealing with interdisciplinary endeavors seem to have bestowed me the necessary skillsets to learn about the BRI! To this end, I have often said that all the positions I had held in my career had prepared me for my interest in the BRI. Putting all these together and writing this book is a natural destiny for me.

Learning about the BRI, in hindsight, is *de facto* learning about China, past and present. It also gave me a window to peek into its future. I guess I am extraordinarily fortunate that I am able to live in an era to see the rise of China, without which, as I have emphasized throughout the book, there could not possibly be a BRI.

Historians often say that centuries ago, China was the most prominent country in the world. According to the article "2000 years of economic history in one chart,[1] during the period from 1 AD to about 1800 AD, the two nations that accounted for much of the world's GDP, were China and India. Remarkably, these two nations that have been geographically standing side-by-side for millennia, never had any hostility towards each other.

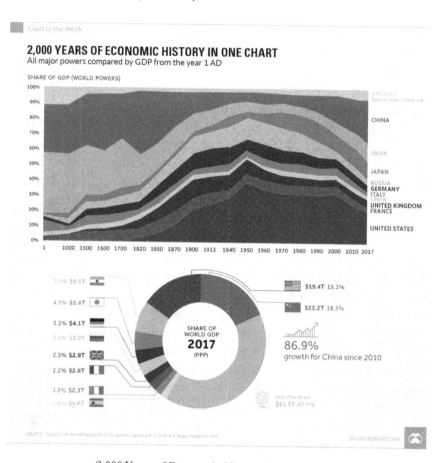

2,000 Years of Economic History in One Chart.

Source: https://www.visualcapitalist.com/2000-years-economic-history-one-chart/

---

[1] Desjardins, J. (September 8, 2017). 2,000 Years of Economic History in One Chart. *Visual Capitalist.* Retrieved from https://www.visualcapitalist.com/2000-years-economic-history-one-chart/

Then in the 20th century, United States and Western Europe (even with the devastation of WWI and WWII) became dominant, and contributions from China and India had shrunk significantly and fallen to the wayside. Yet, starting in the 21st century, China and India, especially China, are growing like gangbusters. I am greatly optimistic that India will soon be catching up as well.

When I looked at this chart, the 12 immortal words that Jawaharlal Nehru said to my father in 1946 suddenly had a new depth of understanding. With the chart as my underpinning, I could now add one more word to the phrase, that is, transform the phrase from

If China and India hold together, the future of Asia is assured

to

If China and India hold together *again*, the future of the *world* is assured.

I can't help but reflect on the fact that during the period when China and India were the dominant nations, they had internal strives, but they were not aggressors. In fact, the only Asian nation to ever have colonies was Japan, in the first half of the 20th century. This happened because Japan learned the lesson from the Western powers.

I have always reminded myself that during Ming dynasty, when the seven massive (and at the time technologically and militarily advanced) naval armadas led by Admiral Zheng He came to Southeast Asia, South Asia, Middle East and East Africa, not an inch of land was taken as colonies for the Ming Emperor. Yet when the British Navy manifested its prowess worldwide, the world became "The Empire on which the Sun Never Sets!"

Graham Allison of Harvard University has, in the past, pushed in his book the so-called Thucydides's Trap, in which if a "rising power" causes fear in an "established power," it will inevitably escalate towards wars.[2] Not surprisingly, as a Western scholar, all the

---

[2]Graham, A. (2017) *Destined For War: Can America and China escape Thucydides's Trap.* Boston: Houghton Mifflin Harcourt.

examples he cited, such as World War 1, The War of the Spanish Succession and the Thirty-Year War and so on, were from the Western civilizations, whose underpinning is winner takes all.

What Allison missed are two important points.

The first is that the rising power of the 21st century is a nation from the Asian civilization that stands on a completely different *modus operandi.*

In fact, with that in mind, I would like to restate the Thucydides' trap in my own words as follows:

> When a "rising power" in the Western Civilization causes fear in an "established power" in the Western Civilization, it will inevitably escalate towards wars!

If either of the two "Western Civilization" phrases in the above redefinition of the Thucydides's Trap are changed into "Eastern Civilization" the result could be totally different. With that as the preamble, while China's BRI is a result (and not the cause) of the country's rise, it is not "rise" in the Western sense of the word. Words and deeds of the BRI are not "winner takes all." Rather it is a "win–win" situation.

The second is even more apocalyptical in that ever since humans have created weapons that can destroy our planet over and over again, wars between major powers are no longer an option for the Thucydides's Trap. Leaders of powerful nations have no choice but to avoid wars as defined by the Trap. To suggest that this is a necessary consequence is the highest form of irresponsibility, if not utter stupidity. To this end, the BRI — whose mission is to enhance the "interactions among people" of the Eastern and Western civilizations — appears thus far to be one of the efforts, if not the only one, aiming to prevent humans from destroying each other completely, through the principles of Supercontinent and Neo-Renaissance.

Finally, I hope that someday there could be another talented film director such as Norman Jewison, who produced the movie *Fiddler on the Roof,* who can produce another movie about a group of ancient Jews living not in the Western society, but in China, in the

Song Dynasty. In this movie, the filmmaker can set an entirely different theme from the one in *Fiddler on the Roof,* wherein unlike the original one where Jews were constantly being harassed, bullied and eventually kicked out of their abodes in Russia, Jews can be depicted as living prosperously, harmoniously and without interference from practicing their ways and means (even religion) within a profoundly Chinese society in Kaifeng! Indeed, the theme would be that the Chinese and the Jews were able to learn about and culturally communicate with each other. Just like *Fiddler of the Roof,* where a young Russian fell in love with a Jewish girl, it would be especially interesting if the new movie could portray the intermarriages occurring between two lovers from the ancient and conservative communities. If nothing else, such a film can project to the world that when there is a meaningful cultural communication between the Eastern civilization (such as the Chinese in Kaifeng during the Song dynasty) and the Western civilization (such as the Jews in the same city), with genuine respect and appreciation for one another, the world can indeed be a wonderful place!

Of course, the theme of this book is that the BRI's mission is to transform the millennium mindset of the Chinese people "to go out" and "open their eyes to the world." It is this that I hope the readers will take away.

Appendix A

Belt and Road Initiative (BRI): China's Mindset Millennium Transformation*

In 2013, President Xi Jinping, in two speeches in Kazakhstan and Indonesia, launched what is now globally known as the Belt and Road Initiative (BRI). In the past five years, the BRI has captured humanity's attention and imagination. As a global effort initiated by China, even in the short five years since its inception, the BRI has made deep impact not just globally, such as the most recently signed Memorandum of Understand (MoU) with Italy, but within China as well.

In the Chinese search engine Baidu, the following words "the first Chinese who opened his eyes to see the world" is used to portray one of China's most famous explorers of the Han Dynasty (206 BC–220 AD), Zhang Qian (张骞). I was stunned by this portrayal of Zhang Qian. After all, by the time the Han Dynasty rolled around, China already had several millennia of rich and deep history under its belt. How is it that Zhang Qian was the first Chinese to open his eyes to see the world? Furthermore, some two millennia

---

*Presented by Da Hsuan Feng at the Thematic forum of the 2nd Belt and Road Forum for International Cooperation (BRF) on April 24th, 2019, Beijing, China.

have passed since Zhang Qian; is China now a nation that is opening its eyes to the world?

With the above as preamble, I would like to discuss in these few minutes the profound impact the BRI has on China: it can and has transformed the Chinese millennium mindset, and with this transformation, it can and will uplift humanity in this very critical period of its existence.

First, BRI can induce a supercontinent mindset. Two of the world's most important and fundamental civilizations, the East and West, evolved and deepened in the two ends of the most massive landmass on earth, which is artificially designated as two continents: "Europe" and "Asia." These two civilizations gave rise to humanity's two distinct and different mindsets and ways and means. This distinction is best delineated by Kipling's famous line: "*OH, East is East, and West is West, and never the twain shall meet.*" Even in as modern a world as today, these two civilizations essentially dictate and govern the two vastly different mindsets of humanity. Furthermore, because of the vast distance between Europe and Asia, to this date, travel by human beings between the two ends are essentially confined to air transportation, which tends to vastly limit people-to-people interactions. It has little impact on merging the two civilizations. The BRI infrastructure construction will be the first time in human history where by constructing surface transportation, there is the possibility that people in "Europe" and "Asia" could construct a new "Supercontinent" mindset, and can and will bring people of vastly different civilizations together.

Second, BRI can create a Neo-Renaissance era. As is well known, from the 14th to 17th centuries, Europe was the birthplace of the Renaissance. Unquestionably, the deepest contribution of the Renaissance to humanity was that it lifted human beings out of the most profound challenges at the time, which was profound ignorance. This was carried out successfully via the "think-out-of-the-box" thinking based on scientific methodology. In the 21st century, humanity is now facing challenges such as global warming, all of which are existential in nature. For example, while there are geopolitical efforts, such as the Paris Accord, which are trying their utmost to seek public policies, and the top research universities in East and West are engaging in research to mitigate this challenge, global warming continues. Therefore, just as the Renaissance of the 14th–17th centuries, along with the enormous growth of Europe in the Post-Renaissance era, I believe that once the Supercontinent mindset is in place, where by overcoming Kipling's dictum where East and West "shall not meet," a new civilization shall emerge, where there will be neo-Copernicus and neo-Galileo, and even neo-Newton and neo-Darwin emerging to mitigate the existential challenges. The BRI, as far as I can see, is the only effort that China has initiated that can lead humanity on this rosy path.

Third, BRI can induce a millennium Chinese mindset transformation. BRI is also termed as the revitalization of the ancient Silk Roads, either maritime- or land-based. However, one must recognize that there is a profound difference between BRI and the ancient Silk Roads. The ancient Silk Roads were organic occurrences. There were no ancient leaders, from China or from the West, who had the concept of creating such a "transportation link." As such, the ancient ones made no demand on China or the Chinese people to understand people from a different civilization. The BRI, on the other hand, is entirely created by China, and as such, it has made an unprecedented and proactive demand on China to become truly "worldly." At the end of the day, a successful BRI will transform the mindset of Chinese from an "outside–in" mentality to an "inside–out" mentality. This will render China a great "power" in the 21st century and beyond, not because of its wealth, not because of its military power, but because of its true respect of other people's civilization and ways and means.

Ultimately, the BRI will render China to truly open its eyes to the world. Its success should and must be judged not merely as the success of China, but the success of humanity!

Appendix B

A Glimpse of Russian Scientific Prowess Through the Late Vitaly Ginzburg, the 2003 Nobel Laureate

When Lee Hong Fah told me about the population of Russia having a high level of scientific awareness, it made me think about my interactions with one of Russia's greatest scientific giants. His name is Vitaly Lazarevich Ginzburg (1916–2009). Judging by his last name Ginzburg, one already knew that he was another great Russian scientist who was Jewish.

When I was the Vice President for Research and Economic Development at the University of Texas at Dallas (UTD), I formed a Research Advisory Board (RAB) which consisted of globally known movers and shakers. One of them was Ginzburg.

According to the Nobel Prize website,[1] the Nobel committee awarded the Nobel Prize to Ginzburg "for pioneering contributions to the theory of superconductors and superfluids."

In the 20th century, Russian scientific geniuses played a pivotal and transformational role in understanding the structure of matter, which eventually led to a technological revolution for the world. Russia is a vast and complex country with profound and deep cultures,

---

[1] https://www.nobelprize.org/prizes/physics/2003/ginzburg/facts/

similar to its highly diverse and talented population. It is the only country which can claim to be as much Asian as it is European. However, one thing which no one can or will dispute is that ever since modern science unveiled itself to the world, the scientific and technological prowess of Russia, well before the Soviet Union days, became an inalienable part of human existence. So, to find a strong partner for alliance for UTD — whose primary strengths are in science and technology — approaching Russia for this is what an American youngster would say a "no-brainer!" The only surprising fact is that we did not do it earlier!

I can, of course, go on and on about the scientific achievements of Russia in the past century, and the great work they are doing today. However, let me be more personal and discuss my own deep feelings about Russian science. I am confident in saying that my experiences are not special but very typical, which can easily be extrapolated on a much grander scale.

Russian science became a part of my scientific soul ever since I embarked on my career as a physicist. I also dare say that this feeling is not mine only — it is shared by physicists all over the world. I could not forget as a student my many late-night struggles, some would call it joy, in enriching my knowledge and preparing me for exams to solve problems embedded in the series of books written by two great Russian physicists: Nobel laureate Lev Landau and his coauthor Evgeny Lifshitz. Also, what a joy it was for me later on as a research physicist to read beautiful papers on phase transition by Vitaly Ginzburg and Landau and the magnificent treaties on a branch of mathematics known as group representations by the great Russian group theorist Israel Moiseevich Gelfand. All my colleagues (and I was one for a brief period of my career) studied one of the toughest quantum systems called the three-body-problem that basically revolved around the Faddeev equations, named after the great Russian mathematical physicist Ludwig Faddeev of St Petersburg.

It is worth noting that many top-notch Russian scientists, such as Landau, Gelfand and Ginzburg, were Jewish.

Anyone working on nonlinear dynamics should and must be aware of the profound contributions of Vladimir Igorevich Ar'nold, another

In 2014, I attended a conference in Singapore in honor of the 60th year of Yang–Mills field theory. There, I met Professor Faddeev up close for the first time and was proud to take a photo with him. It is with great sorrow that three years later, Professor Faddeev passed away.

great Russian mathematician. There is, of course, Igor Tamm, a Nobel Laureate in 1958. Again, Tamm–Dancoff Approximation, or TDA, is a standard procedure in theoretical physics. I also simply lost count of how many times I discussed with my collaborators about quasi-particles Bogoliubov transformations at or near the Fermi surface for nuclear pairing in my nuclear physics research. Many of you know well that this concept of pairing found its genesis in the theory of superconductivity, and one of the great Russian scientists Kapitza was unquestionably a towering figure in that field.

Among many fundamental contributions, which included his in-depth contributions to physics at low temperature (near absolute zero Kelvin), one that is known by nearly all physicists, and now even other scientists such as chemists and biologists, is the theory Ginzburg developed with the late and legendary Lev Landau on how physical systems make the transition from one phase, such as liquid, to another, such as gaseous. The work is so well known as the Ginzburg–Landau phase transition, that when other scientists mentioned it in their scientific publications, a reference is no longer a necessity (just as no one would refer to the original paper of Sir Isaac Newton when one talks about classical mechanics).

Thus, to be able to tap into the wealth of wisdom and broad knowledge of someone as eminent as Ginzburg, who was a leader in Russia in the science arena, I felt it could only be considered as another major milestone for RAB.

The opportunity for me to meet with Professor Ginzburg came when UTD hired an outstanding Russian scientist (who grew up in Uzbekistan), Anvar Zakhidov, to be the deputy director of the NanoTech Institute. Anvar's teacher in Russia, Vladimir Agranovich, a world-renowned scientist and director of the theoretical physics group of the Institute of Spectroscopy of the Russian Academy of Science, and who is now a member of UTD's prestigious "Pioneers in Nanotechnology," is a lifetime friend of Ginzburg. When Vladimir learned of my desire to meet with Ginzburg and to invite him to be a member of UTD's Research Advisory Board, he was enthusiastic and gracious enough to arrange for me to meet with Ginzburg!

There was only *one* catch: Unless there was an absolute necessity, such as going to Sweden to receive the Nobel Prize, Ginzburg did not travel much. So, if I wanted to meet and extend the invitation to him, I needed to go to Moscow. Moscow is, of course, some 9000 kilometers from Dallas!

Well, considering what UTD could leverage from the profound wisdom of one of the greatest scientists of the 20th century, I decided to go to Moscow for a week from August 15, 2004, to meet with Ginzburg and also sign a Memorandum of Understanding (MOU) for collaboration with one of Russia's most prestigious universities: Moscow State University. Mind you, just less than a year before, Professor Ginzburg received the Nobel Prize in physics.

Me, Anvar, Ginzburg and Agranovich outside of Ginzburg's summer apartment in the suburb of Moscow

A relaxed moment with Ginzburg in Ginzburg's apartment balcony

So, on the sunny afternoon of August 17, 2004, accompanied by Anvar Zakhidov and Vladimir Agranovich, I met Vitaly Ginzburg and his charming wife, Nina, who was also a physicist. The venue was their rented apartment in a beautiful resort, some 76 kilometers outside of Moscow. At around 2:30 pm, I told Ginzburg that one of the reasons I came to Moscow was to invite him to be a member of UTD's RAB.

During my graduate school days, I had spent countless hours trying to understand the deep meaning of the Ginzburg–Landau theory of phase transition. I never realized that one day I would come face to face with Ginzburg himself to engage in an exhilarating discussion about this issue. It was truly an experience I shall treasure for the rest of my life.

Having already been told by Agranovich about my proposal weeks before, and having understood that all communications from him and the RAB will be in Russian (and therefore, Zakhidov will play a tremendous role as a translator), Dr. Ginzburg, without any hesitation, accepted my invitation!

Finally, I cannot resist my temptation to mention about the situation of the theoretical physics institute of my alma mater, the Willian I. Fine Institute of Theoretical Physics of the University of Minnesota. This institute is one of the best in the world. Currently, it has seven world-class scientists as permanent staff, of which 6 originated from Russia:

(1) Andrey Chubukov (Ph.D. from Moscow State University),
(2) Alex Kamenev (M.Sc. from Moscow State University and Ph.D. from Israel's Weizmann Institute),
(3) Mikhail Shifman (Ph.D. from Institute for Theoretical and Experimental Physics in Moscow and a member of the US National Academy of Sciences),
(4) Boris Shklovskii (Ph.D. from St. Petersburg's Ioffe Institute and a Landau Prize laureate),
(5) Arkady Vainshtein (Ph.D. from Budker Institute of Nuclear Physics in Novosibirsk, Russia), and
(6) Mikhail Voloshin (Ph.D. from Institute for Theoretical and Experimental Physics).

Both Vainshtein and Voloshin are recipients of the prestigious J. J. Sakurai Prize of Theoretical Physics of the American Physical Society.

If one wanted to find a true talent to assist his/her institution to reach the next level of excellence, lay down all your pride and go the extra 9000 kilometers to convince him/her to do so!

As my Jewish friends would say, MAZEL TOV!

CPSIA information can be obtained
at www.ICGtesting.com
Printed in the USA
FSHW011740230620
71470FS